D1765688

WITHDRAWN
FROM STOCK
QMUL LIBRARY

Politics of Urbanism

To see like a city, rather than seeing like a state, is the key to understanding modern politics. In this book, Magnusson draws from theorists such as Weber, Wirth, Hayek, Jacobs, Sennett, and Foucault to articulate some of the ideas that we need to make sense of the city as a form of political order.

Locally and globally, the city exists by virtue of complicated patterns of government and self-government, prompted by proximate diversity. A multiplicity of authorities in different registers is typical. Sovereignty, although often claimed, is infinitely deferred. What emerges by virtue of self-organization is not susceptible to control by any central authority, and so we are impelled to engage politically in a world that does not match our expectations of sovereignty. How then are we to engage realistically and creatively? We have to begin from where we are if we are to understand the possibilities.

Building on traditions of political and urban theory in order to advance a new interpretation of the role of cities/urbanism in contemporary political life, this work will be of great interest to scholars of political theory and urban theory, international relations theory and international relations.

Warren Magnusson is Professor in the Department of Political Science, University of Victoria, Canada.

Interventions

Edited by:
Jenny Edkins, *Aberystwyth University*, and Nick Vaughan-Williams, *University of Warwick*

> "As Michel Foucault has famously stated, 'knowledge is not made for understanding; it is made for cutting.' In this spirit The Edkins–Vaughan-Williams Interventions series solicits cutting edge, critical works that challenge mainstream understandings in international relations. It is the best place to contribute post disciplinary works that think rather than merely recognize and affirm the world recycled in IR's traditional geopolitical imaginary."
>
> Michael J. Shapiro, University of Hawai'i at Mānoa, USA

The series aims to advance understanding of the key areas in which scholars working within broad critical post-structural and post-colonial traditions have chosen to make their interventions, and to present innovative analyses of important topics.

Titles in the series engage with critical thinkers in philosophy, sociology, politics and other disciplines and provide situated historical, empirical and textual studies in international politics.

Politics of Urbanism

Seeing like a city

Warren Magnusson

 Routledge
Taylor & Francis Group

LONDON AND NEW YORK

First published 2011
by Routledge
2 Park Square, Milton Park, Abingdon, Oxon, OX14 4RN

Simultaneously published in the USA and Canada
by Routledge
711 Third Avenue, New York, NY 10017

Routledge is an imprint of the Taylor & Francis Group, an informa business

First issued in paperback 2012

© 2011 Warren Magnusson

The right of Warren Magnusson to be identified as author of this work has been asserted by him in accordance with the Copyright, Designs and Patent Act 1988.

All rights reserved. No part of this book may be reprinted or reproduced or utilized in any form or by any electronic, mechanical, or other means, now known or hereafter invented, including photocopying and recording, or in any information storage or retrieval system, without permission in writing from the publishers.

British Library Cataloguing in Publication Data
A catalogue record for this book is available from the British Library

Library of Congress Cataloging in Publication Data
Magnusson, Warren, 1947–
  Politics of urbanism : seeing like a city / Warren Magnusson.
    p. cm. – (Interventions)
  Includes bibliographical references and index.
  ISBN 978-0-415-78241-8 – ISBN 978-0-203-80889-4 1. Municipal government.
2. City-states.   3. Communities–Political aspects.   I. Title.
  JS78.M237 2011
  320.8′5–dc22
                                                              2011001037

ISBN 13: 978-0-415-78241-8 (hbk)
ISBN 13: 978-0-203-80889-4 (ebk)
ISBN 13: 978-0-415-83126-0 (pbk)

Typeset in Times New Roman
by Graphicraft Limited, Hong Kong

QM LIBRARY
(MILE END)

Contents

Acknowledgements

I began this book in the context of a joint project with Rob Walker on "Ontologies of the Political". The project was financed by a Standard Research Grant from the Social Sciences and Humanities Research Council of Canada (SSHRC), which enabled us to host two productive workshops, at the University of Victoria and Keele University respectively. I am grateful both to SSHRC and to the participants in the workshops, whose contributions stimulated my own thinking: Richard Ashley, Andrew Barry, Didier Bigo, Michael Brown, Mitchell Dean, Michael Dillon, Sakari Hänninen, Christine Helliwell, Barry Hindess, Engin Isin, Timothy Luke, Karena Shaw, Hidemi Suganami, Mariana Valverde, and Reg Whitaker. As usual, Rob's and my conversations were of immense assistance, and he provided helpful comments on various parts of the book manuscript as it progressed. Arthur Kroker also commented on the first draft of the book, as did a number of my present and former students, especially Jen Bagelman, Ilan Baron, Andrea B. Gill, Simon Glezos, Maria Koblanck, Sébastien Malette, James Rowe, and Delacey Tedesco. Serena Kataoka, Nick Montgomery, and Mark Willson helped me directly or indirectly with my local investigations, and stimulated me through their own work. I also profited from comments on papers I delivered at the Urban Affairs Association, Conference for the Study of Political Thought, Canadian Political Science Association, Western Political Science Association, Pacific Northwest Political Science Association, BC Political Studies Association, and American Association of Geographers. Routledge's anonymous reviewers made many helpful suggestions that guided me in my final round of revisions. The University of Victoria's Department of Political Science has provided a supportive environment for this research, and its Interdisciplinary Programme in Cultural, Social and Political Thought (CSPT) has enabled me to make connections with faculty and students in many different departments. I owe a great deal to my students, both graduate and undergraduate, and I hope that this book will be of some help to them in their ongoing reflections on the puzzle of politics.

Introduction
Re-imagining the political

Are we stuck with the conception of politics that emerged within the Western tradition, or can we think the political differently? This question has been at the heart of radical political thought since the *soixant-huitards* were young. The New Left, participatory democrats, feminists, the Greens, and the later advocates of "civil society" and the World Social Forum: all in their different ways have raised the possibility of a new politics, no longer centred on the state but instead on everyday life.[1] The body, the bedroom, the kitchen, the workplace, the street, the neighbourhood, the mall, and even the camp, the border zone, the slum, and the dump have figured as venues for an imagined politics no longer shaped by the requirements of a state that governs us and political parties that contest for state power.[2] This idea of a politics become otherwise, with different characters, venues, objects, and purposes, has shadowed mainstream political thought – and practice – for a long time. Many of the key theorists of it are French,[3] but the most renowned practitioners are from various countries: India, South America, South Africa, Eastern Europe, and (not least) the United States.[4] It is fair to say that anyone who recoils from the poverty, injustice, waste, and violence of our contemporary world, and who sees that these ills are effects of the present order of things – capitalist, patriarchal, racist, anthropocentric, and (I would say) *statist* – is likely to be attracted to the idea that politics *might* be completely different if only people could be persuaded to approach it differently.

Life in the real world is not so simple, however, as we all know. Institutions, practices, and ways of thought are sedimented, and cannot be wished away. What seems practical at a particular moment is likely to be something that fits with established ways of doing things. Moreover, these established ways are entrenched in our own thinking as "common sense". We resort to the familiar patterns without even knowing it. I do not imagine that I am any more able to escape than the next person, and in fact I think that the effort to escape is part of the problem (Walker 2010). Escapees just leave things as they are: the point is to effect some change. As Hegel (1965) suggested almost two centuries ago, change does not come about just because we wish it to happen, or declare it has happened, or put forward schemes for it to occur. In his phrase, we cannot give instructions to the world. Change is not just a matter of exercising our sovereign will, because we are not in fact the sovereigns of our own domain. Nor, as I try to make clear here, can we become sovereigns: we should not even try. Unfortunately, the dream of sovereignty – the belief that we can somehow become masters of our own world, and change it into what we think it should be – lies behind both radical and mainstream conceptions of politics. Changing the venue of politics from the state to everyday life and giving the aims of politics an environmentalist, feminist, socialist, or some other twist, will not in itself produce the difference that takes us past dreams of sovereignty. Those dreams are too much a part of our heritage, too much a part of the political ontology that we assume without thinking.

When I speak of "political ontology" I mean two things. First, there is an ontology of "politics" or "the political":[5] an account of the sorts of things that count as political, such as governments and elections, power and authority, ideologies and social movements, interests and identities. My claim is that the dominant political ontology is statist, and that radical alternatives are parasitic upon this statist understanding. This is most obviously the case with respect to ideas about democratization or the extension of human rights, which refer back to the ideals of modern republicanism and hence to ideas about the well-ordered polity or sovereign state.[6] Thus – and this is the second sense in which I talk about political ontology – the dominant ontology of politics is in fact a *political* ontology in that it conceals within itself a certain orientation towards the things that it designates as political. In a way, we are called to act within this domain if we are to be properly human or civilized. To disavow citizenship is apparently to back away from the responsibilities that we have as people who share in a common world. As Margaret Thatcher put it, "there is no alternative" – in this case, no alternative but to think the political in the ways that "we moderns" have come to do.

I am not with Thatcher in this (or any other) respect, but I am acutely conscious of the hold that the statist ontology of the political has upon me and those around me, and I am more than a little sceptical about claims to have put it aside and found a new way of thinking. Even so, I want to suggest that a different ontology of the political already exists, and that it has been implicit from the beginning in the thought we have inherited from the Greeks: the thought that gives us the terms we use to identify the political, whether we are thinking of politics in the conventional way or are exploring radical alternatives. The key to seeing this is to recognize that the *polis* – the ancestor of the modern republic or liberal democracy or the state – is also a city, and hence a node for what Louis Wirth (1938) called "urbanism as a way of life". If – to borrow a term from James C. Scott (1998) – our current tendency is to "see like a state" when we think about politics and hence to imagine things from the viewpoint of a sovereign government or a sovereign people (or sovereign individuals or a sovereign "world order": these are all similar ways of thinking), then an alternative already implicit in our own way of thinking is to see like a city.

When I *see like a state*, I see three things immediately:

(1) The world is divided into states, each of which has its own territory and claims sovereignty in relation to it.
(2) Within each state, there is a hierarchy of authority, so that there is always a final authority with respects to issues in dispute.
(3) Within each state, everything and everyone is ultimately subject to the state's authority: in that sense, the state is sovereign.[7]

What follows is a certain conception of politics, one that is centred on the state as the ultimate authority. Politics is partly a matter of who gets to decide: in other words, who will occupy the high offices of state and under what conditions. But, more broadly it is about *policy* (what the state does and how) and *diplomacy* (what remains to be negotiated between states, so as to determine the conditions under which they operate). It seems quite clear that the politically oriented must focus on the state or on relations between states as their objects of attention. Any other orientation would be misguided.

Of course, I may question this image of a state-oriented politics even while keeping it front and centre. What happens within states and between them seems to be largely determined by economic interests, cultural or national loyalties, religious commitments, and the usual array of human concerns that are beneath the level of statesmanship. So, the idea that we can change things by acting in and through the state or the state system seems problematic, despite the state's claim to sovereignty. In fact, it is arguable that there are venues outside the state – the economy, culture, religion, or even science – that offer better opportunities to effect change. Perhaps the state and the state system are both paper tigers. Many people have thought so.

Nevertheless, the world is organized as a system of sovereign states, which claim ultimate authority individually and collectively. It is hard to ignore that fact, or to imagine a politics that would not work through the state or the state system. The nineteenth-century anarchists and socialists came up against this problem, even though they imagined a future in which states had disappeared. In the end, they thought of politics as something that would break up the state or transform it. The state might be an obstacle to change, but it was nonetheless at the centre of things, structuring the space for political action and offering a focus for political campaigns. The twentieth- and twenty-first-century heirs of the anarchists and socialists – calling themselves pacifists, feminists, environmentalists, or whatever – have tended to situate themselves in civil society, at one remove from the state. But, the state haunts them nonetheless, as it did the anarchists and socialists, for the state still appears as the sovereign authority. Mustn't politics ultimately lead to the state, and hence to the great problems of policy and diplomacy that weigh on our leaders and their advisors?

I began writing this in the aftermath of Barack Obama's victory in the 2008 Presidential election in the USA, and am now finishing it in the midst of commentary on his party's defeat in the 2010 "mid-terms". Meanwhile, many of the same commentators are still fussing over the failure of the Copenhagen Climate Summit in 2009, and worrying about the apparent inability of the great powers to agree on a common economic policy. All these things have been presented in the media as matters of world-historic (as opposed to national or local) importance. Why should they be so conceived? The question almost answers itself. We believe that it matters who occupies the US Presidency and how the powers of that office are deployed. It matters even more whether sovereign states can agree on policies to deal with global warming, public finance, nuclear proliferation, international trade, and so on. To say that such things are of no importance is absurd. The more difficult question is whether it follows that politics in general must be centred on the state. Although such a conclusion may make many of us uneasy – not least because most of us live in minor states like my own, which obviously cannot determine the course of world events – there is nonetheless a certain enchantment to the state, because it seems to have the gift of sovereignty. Who could not be moved by the emergence of a new figure or figures who might use that gift of sovereignty differently, and so act the part of good Tsars and deliver us from the ills that beset us? And, who might not fear the latest demagogues who might lead us to disaster?

On the other hand, when I *see like a city* I am neither so dazzled nor so panicked. Other things strike me:

(1) The world is characterized not only by its division into sovereign states, but also by the presence within it of a multiplicity of political authorities in different registers, ones that are there for different purposes and heed the call of different drummers. Many of these authorities claim that they are not political – only cultural, economic, religious, communal, or whatever – and such a move often enhances their autonomy, not least in relation to authorities that claim sovereignty.[8]

(2) Only some of the political authorities are arranged in a neat hierarchy: most are not. The space of the state is only one of many. Other histories are enacted in spaces that are qualitatively different, and cannot be assimilated to the space of the state. In fact, what we call social movements are ones that generate new spaces of action and new histories, in relation to which new identities, interests, and forms of authority are established.[9]

(3) The result is a pattern of interaction that defies easy modelling. If there is an order to the whole, it is not one that can be controlled by a sovereign authority or even by a network of sovereigns acting in concert. The privileged points of intervention can only be discovered in practice: they cannot be anticipated in advance. So, politics, in the sense of an activity whereby we attempt to gain some control over our own future, has no obvious centre.

It follows that whoever or whatever seeks to be sovereign is bound to be disappointed – and our dreams of a good Tsar will not help us. A more realistic politics would not ignore the state or the state system, but would place them in a different context. We would have a better understanding of things if we recognized that the world is more like a city than a state or system of states.[10]

The city in this sense is both localized and globalized: that is, it takes form in particular places, but also generates an order of sorts on a global scale. How that order is to be understood is a difficult problem, but when I see like a city I notice a few things immediately. First, the proximate diversity of urban life poses problems that can only be solved when people govern themselves and those around them in appropriate ways. Thus, what I call (following Foucault[11]) governmentalities, or "proliferating practices of government and self-government", tend to generate an order of sorts that tends to persist in and against sovereign authority. Second, I see that political authorities of different sorts arise or assert themselves in this context. Some of them claim sovereignty, others make no such claims. Some are this-worldly, others are other-worldly. Some assert themselves violently, and others do not. Their spatialities and temporalities differ and are sometimes completely incommensurate. As a result, they are as likely to go past one another as conflict. Third, the effort of any authority like the state to put everything onto the same register and manage things accordingly is likely to be futile. This means, among other things, that a uni-focal politics will be deeply disappointing to all concerned. Fourth, the larger order that is generated will not have an easily comprehensible form. It will always be in the process of refiguration, for reasons that are as diverse as the city itself. If we were to model it, it would be with reference to ideas about self-organizing systems, non-linearities, and emergent properties. It is not an order susceptible to sovereign authority.

To see both one's own locale and the world as a whole *as a city* is to envision it quite differently. What follow are a different politics, political theory, and political science from what we have been used to. That is what I try to explain in this book.

The argument I want to make is at once complex and simple: complex in that it has many dimensions and simple in that it always returns to the same theme. Any sophisticated reader will find parts of the argument familiar, although the implications I draw from well-known facts may be unusual. I am attempting to say something about the way people in general practise politics and think about what they are doing, but my point of entry is through the academic literature in political theory, urban studies, political economy, international relations, geography, constitutional law, and the social sciences more generally. I refer explicitly to some of the literature I am thinking about, but I am also responding to the *zeitgeist* of the universities, the intelligentsia, and the mass media. My students are a point of reference, as are my academic colleagues within my own discipline and outside it. Readers should test what

I have to say against what they see and hear around them, and not just against the leading academic sources. I am not interested in establishing my own originality or criticizing other people for the work they do academically or politically.[12] Such criticisms as I offer are incidental to my main purpose, which is to excavate and explicate a political ontology of urbanism as a way of life and to make some suggestions about the issues and problems that we might explore further on this basis. I cannot *prove* that this is a distinct way of thinking or that it has the possibilities I suggest. I can only gesture at things that I think that we already know, but don't fully recognize. It is for the reader to work out whether the argument could be sustained against objections that I do not consider here.

In the student world, which I deal with as a professor, there are both politicos who get involved in party politics and activists who try to challenge the system from without. A similar division appears in the wider world. For many students, the activists seem like the heroes, because they are prepared to take the risks involved in challenging things radically. On the other hand, the activists themselves are caught between two visions, one that orients them toward the state, the sovereign authority to be challenged, and another that orients them toward a broader field of action in which distinctions between state and civil society begin to break down. It is a commonplace now to suggest that politics is everywhere and anywhere, but if it is everywhere and anywhere, it seems to be nowhere. What can one say about a practice that has no definite locus, no aims that can be specified in advance, and no set forms? What is it about? Who or what is involved and to what ends? If there are friends or enemies to be dealt with, who are they? How would one decide? What mode of action is entailed by being political? If politics is a particular aspect of life, which aspect is that? A wider conception of politics, one that overcomes the divisions implicit in the dominant ontology of the political, seems to leave everyone at a loss. Many fall silent in these circumstances. Certainly, most of my students do. Although they are fascinated by critiques of the existing order of things, they have embarrassingly little to say about politics, since the critiques lead everywhere and nowhere.[13]

I think this a problem with political theory, not a problem with my students. The students are caught between two types of theory, one that takes the existing order largely for granted and pursues detailed questions with regard to it and another that re-poses all the key questions in philosophical terms. The first type of theory offers a nice, stable ground on which to think about political questions. Those questions can be posed in fairly general terms, but the assumed relevance is to the field constituted by the liberal-democratic nation-state and the liberal order more generally. The second type of theory offers no stable ground and no obvious point of reference. There are concepts, to be sure – rhizomes and lines of flight, singularities and emergent properties, cyborgs and networks, übermenschen and dasein – but it is hard to know what to do with any of them in the absence of an alternative ontology of the political. That is why I think it is so important to think the political through the city. The city is difficult to understand, but we can see how it works all around us. It offers us a place to begin, both as analysts and as activists. Urban life is as familiar as it is strange and complex. If we look at it carefully, many of the standard political and analytic categories begin to melt before our eyes, and other ones more adequate to the purpose begin to take shape.

We would see several important things if we were sufficiently attentive to the dynamics of urban order:[14]

(1) Both particular cities and the "global city" are self-organizing.
(2) A multiplicity of political authorities in different registers and at different scales is characteristic of urban life.
(3) Practices of self-government enable civilized order and produce public benefits both in the presence of sovereign authority and in its absence.
(4) Order is always temporary and local.
(5) Transformations are non-linear and hence inherently unpredictable.

If this is what appears when we "see like a city" the implications are far-reaching. One implication is that sovereignty is infinitely deferred. It may be claimed or posited, but it is never realized – not in the sense that gives the idea of sovereignty such force as an attractor for everyone who would like to change the world, or just preserve it as it is supposed to be. So, the problem of politics is not one of working out what one would do if one were sovereign – a favourite conceit of political theorists, as well as political activists – but of positioning oneself in relation to a political order that subverts pretensions to sovereignty and forces everyone to deal with life in more measured terms.

To describe a particular city or the global city as "self-organizing" is not to say that what emerges from this process of self-organization will be good. There is no particular reason to suppose that it will be good or bad. It is simply to say that some form of overall order will emerge whether or not anyone is trying to produce such an order and whether or not there is any "sovereign" authority in place. In fact, the presence or absence of a sovereign authority will be only one factor in the complex equation that determines the results. Before we rush to judgement, we need to understand the dynamics of a system of great complexity. Economists – and rational choice theorists more generally – seem to believe that they can model things realistically, despite the simplifying assumptions they have to make to get their models to work. I remain sceptical in this regard: our understanding of the dynamics of urban life is still very shallow, and it is obviously a mistake to model all human interactions on the logic of commercial transactions. The city exceeds the economy in complexity, and overdetermines it. One aspect of this is that religious, ethnic, and class differences are generated within the city and refracted through it, sometimes violently and sometimes not. The resultant conflicts are as much a part of urban life as commercial exchanges

or sophisticated cultural productions. How those conflicts play out in relation to more cooperative activities will determine the form or order that the
city takes. To speak of "self-organization" in relation to these complex
processes of adjustment is to draw attention to the fact that shocks and
changes are internalized and that the overall order will take shape from the
adjustments that various actors make.

A key factor in any situation is the multiplicity of political authorities.
Political authorities tend to proliferate: they command the loyalty of different groups of people on different bases. Few of them make any pretence to
sovereignty in the normal sense, although some of them expect their adher-
ents to offer them ultimate loyalty. Many of these authorities claim to be
apolitical: this is a common political tactic, which may enable an authority
to secure itself in face of a rival (perhaps sovereign) authority that purports
to have a monopoly over political decisions. So, what is described as political
in any given context will itself be the effect of uneven struggles between
authorities that often have an interest in concealing their political character.
This means that we cannot take the labels assigned to various authorities
for granted if we want to produce a realistic analysis of the politics that produces, sustains, and disrupts the city. In the current context, that means that
we have to treat businesses, churches, and non-governmental organizations
(NGOs) – to say nothing of social movements and covert networks – as
political organizations that command different forms of loyalty and different resources. This applies as much globally as it does regionally or locally.
Although the tendency recently has been to assess the overall effects of
political organization in terms of good governance, it is clear that much
more is at stake. The proliferation of forms of political authority reflects
the diversity of human purposes, only one of which is to achieve good
government.

This is not to say that cities are ungoverned: quite the contrary. A key
to understanding how cities work is to recognize that practices of *self-*
government are ubiquitous. These practices are so much a part of everyday
urban life that we often take them for granted: to a remarkable extent
people line up, take turns, let one another pass on the street, respect one
another's privacy, dispose of their wastes appropriately, and generally go about
their business without interfering with other people. We notice the exceptions
and the cultural variations in these practices, but are less cognizant of the
fact that they constitute the infrastructure of self-government that makes
life in cities possible. Social life anywhere would be impossible without it,
but urbanization intensifies and broadens the requirements. These micro-
practices of self-government, which enforce responsibility on the individual,
are collectivized through initiatives to deal with particular problems:
initiatives that bring people together under an authority for definite purposes.
Late nineteenth-century analysts were particularly aware of the way organs
of local self-government emerged, sometimes under state patronage and sometimes not.[15] For a city to work at all as a city, it must develop a political

infrastructure to manage violence, deal with external threats, and provide the public facilities, services, and regulations necessary for people to live in relative safety and go about their daily business. The incentive to do such things is strong, since people will try to go elsewhere if they find a particular city inadequate. To understand how urbanism works, we need to pay close attention to its political infrastructure. This infrastructure develops from practices of government and self-government that arise from the necessities of urban life and that are at one remove from the state.

The order of a city – however civilized it may seem – is always temporary and localized. If we know anything about cities, it is that they are always changing. To see like a city is to recognize that the static order we so often associate with the state is an illusion. Things are in flux. What seems benign now will not seem so benign in a decade or two. Problems that vex us now will be transformed into something different. So, what appears in any place at any moment will be a pattern that is about to disappear, that differs from what went before or what will come after, and that departs from the pattern elsewhere. The scale at which patterns emerge will itself be highly variable: sometimes global, sometimes regional, and sometimes highly localized. Moreover, the direction of causation will also vary. It is a mistake to suppose that what happens on a wider scale will always determine what happens locally. Often as not the direction of change is just the opposite: from Silicon Valley or the valleys of Afghanistan to the wider world. So, the principles of transformation implicit in urbanism as a way of life are of particular interest. It may seem like the transformations occur behind our backs, but we are always already implicated in them because they result, in the main, from human activities: activities that are always mediated politically.

Although we would like to think that we could gain control of things – at least to the extent of predicting what is likely to happen – it seems clear that we are caught up in recursive processes that generate transformations whose timing and impact cannot be anticipated. That it is impossible to make accurate predictions in these circumstances is a mathematical certainty. We have scarcely begun to come to terms with the implications of this for public policy or institutional design. The more profound existential issues get even less attention, especially from political scientists. It is comforting to assume that the form of the political is constant, for that enables us to make comparisons across time and space and tease out definite meanings. Nevertheless, a more realistic analysis – one that comes out of seeing like a city – requires us to recognize that the form of the political (and hence its meaning) is always in transformation. We cannot be certain about what the politics of the moment is or what it means. We can only trace its patterns, note its instabilities, and keep watch for signs of change. This involves a different way of relating to what we study. To imagine ourselves as rulers – which is what the state-centric social sciences encourage us to do – is not appropriate to the task. If anything, we need to be more attentive to the ungovernable and the unpredictable than to the governable and the predictable. Moreover, we have to be aware that the relevant political actors are not necessarily the ones we have in mind. The pattern of transformation will never be exactly what we imagine. We have to attune ourselves to deep uncertainty just as we do in a strange city whose ways are unknown to us.

I live in a small "provincial" city that is actually part of a loosely articulated trans-national metropolis anchored by Seattle and Vancouver but tied to Chicago, Toronto, Washington, and New York, as well as Shanghai, Delhi, and many other places. My milieu is as much a part of the wider world as is anyone else's, but I am not as likely as people in Manhattan or LA to delude myself into thinking that I am at the centre of things. Ideas about the centre or the apex, which inform people's obsessions about top performers, top business executives, top scientists, top universities, and top everything else, are tied to the ideas that inform the statist ontology of the political. Learning to see like a city is not a matter of beginning from the places that are supposed to be the centres of power, although there is nothing *wrong* with starting from there. Nor is it a matter of focusing on the latest "shock city" – the one that changes our thinking about what cities are like or can be: is it Shanghai now, or Mumbai or Lagos, or is it still Sao Paulo or Mexico City? – although again there is nothing *wrong* with starting from there.[16] The point rather is that we can start anywhere. In a previous book (Magnusson and Shaw 2003), Kara Shaw and I started from Tofino, a village on the West Coast of Vancouver Island. That enabled us to see the "global city" in a different way. There is no privileged point of access, and I refuse the temptation to suggest that this or that place reveals the world as it really is now.

The result, perhaps, is that this book is more abstract that many people would like. Where are the examples and illustrations? Where are the stories and pictures that reveal the complexity at which I am gesturing? I offer a few, but generally I take it for granted that people are already in the world I am talking about, and that they are as capable as I am of filling in the details. My argument does not turn on any particular example, although I begin from where I am. I have never been to Shanghai, Mumbai, Lagos, Sao Paulo, or Mexico City. I make no claim to understanding "the Global South" – least of all from the perspective of those who live in what Mike Davis (2006) calls "The Planet of Slums".[17] I make no suggestions about what people in those places should do, or what people elsewhere should do for them. I have some experience of the big cities of the Global North – New York, London, Tokyo, Paris, Los Angeles, and so on – and in fact have lived in London (as well as Toronto) for extended periods of time. So, I have some sense of what it is like to be in a big, crowded place, although the ones I know are generally rather prosperous. I have read about, thought about, and watched my share of movies and television programmes about the underside of the great cities, as well as the horrors of life for people trying to get into "the West" or just trying to make a go of it in some city in the

Global South. I have nothing to add to what others have said about such matters or – to go in another direction – about the virtual worlds in which many people now live. I take it that my readers know as much about these things as I do, perhaps more. My purpose is not to *represent* the urban world as it has become or to make predictions about how it is likely to be a generation from now. Rather, I am inviting readers to stand back from what they think they already know and consider it differently.

I must emphasize that my argument does not depend on claims about the *transition* that is now going on between a predominantly rural world and a predominantly urban one. To my mind, the world has been predominantly urban for centuries, even though most people in most parts of the world lived in so-called "rural" areas until recently. Predominance is not simply a matter of numbers: if it were, the wretched of the earth would long ago have triumphed over their oppressors. The so-called "modern" world – the world that people have been living in for the last five centuries – is urban. So, the remarkable changes that are occurring now in Asia, Africa, and parts of Latin America are the latest iterations of something that has been going on for a very long time, something that urbanists in Europe and North America have been writing about at least since the mid-nineteenth century (Parker 2004). It is not that what happened in Manchester in the 1840s or Chicago in the 1890s will tell us what will happen in Shanghai, Mumbai, or Lagos in the 2030s. In fact, it is not clear that what has happened recently in Shanghai, Mumbai, or Lagos will tell us much about what will happen there two decades from now. Future forms of the urban are unpredictable, and it is a mistake to suppose that we can go from something that we can observe in the present or find in the past, and expect to see it duplicated in the future. Too much of the literature on the urban depends on some story of inevitable movement – the *progress* of universal history – and reads its political lessons off that, as if what we can be is always already determined by the unfolding of the World Spirit, the succession of modes of production, the development of human understanding, or the violence of our own nature. Perhaps the clue to everything is in this or that centre of power, urban slum, flow of people, practice of government, mode of violence, social movement, simulacrum of life, or whatever. I doubt it, though. There are many things we have to understand, and we are ill advised to begin with the assumption that we have already grasped what is most important.

So, although I invoke many of the standard stories of the urban, I am not making the claim that those stories are true as told. I am trying to tease out some ideas that I think are helpful for understanding politics in a way that is not so immersed in dreams of sovereignty – and fears of anarchy – that we cannot see what is staring us in the face. Although I take it that we already are urban and are likely to remain so in the future, I offer no account of why this is so, and try to distance myself from arguments about whether it is good or bad. I am trying to understand the world we live in, and work out how we might respond to it politically. I do *not* think that we are passing from a world of states into a world of cities. I think we already live in a world of states *and* a world of cities, and that the world is *both* a system of states and a global city. This complex situation poses many difficulties for us. The difficulty that most concerns me here is the constant pressure to *see like a state* and to repress what we know or can know from *seeing like a city*. Much of the contemporary literature on the city actually prompts dreams of sovereignty, because it focuses on the injustices, violence, degradation, and depredation attendant on the urban *in extremis*. My focus is different, in that I am trying to understand the *other* of sovereignty, the political practices that enable forms of order whether or not standard sovereignty-practices are effective. I go to what I know, rather than to the sites that induce panic or despair, because it is easier to see the practices we need to understand when we approach them as old familiars. We are constantly told that the practices that enable civilized life – and that could in principle give us a just world – are the ones bound up with sovereignty, but that is not what I see in the city where I live, or in the places I have visited or have lived before. Nor is it what I see in reports from the latest sites of panic or disorder: people are coping as best they can, and the authorities that pretend to sovereignty or are trying to establish or re-establish sovereignty seem to be making things worse, as often as not. Since the West projects itself as the model of civilized order, it is worth thinking about the practices that actually enable order in the West. Close analysis seems to suggest that plays of sovereignty have relatively little to do with it.

As I argue in Chapter 1, and throughout the book, urbanism is in itself a security system, but that does not mean that it is always or even usually benign. Urbanism seems to generate its own distinctive forms of violence. Violence is not just a matter of killing people or destroying things. It is also a matter of intimidation, degradation, exclusion, deprivation, and depredation, and it is not just *people* who are the victims. We may cooperate with one another, but do great violence to the world around us. And, if we restrain violence, we do not necessarily achieve justice: in fact, we may perpetuate it. So, what's at issue in the question of benign order – a question that is bound to plague us if we engage politically – is exceptionally complicated. I keep drawing attention to the way that problems are solved without recourse to sovereign authority, because I think we need to consider things calmly, without panic. To think about how cities *work* is to bring to light the practices we need to nourish, and on which we already rely to live as well as we do. So, a relatively peaceful place at the edge of the world, like the one where I live, is not necessarily a bad place to begin this inquiry. (Although that beginning is implicit in the argument of the book as a whole, I come back to it more explicitly in Chapter 7 and the Conclusion.) Nor is it a mistake to look at those authors – like the ones I consider in Chapters 3 and 4 – who are more interested in what works than in what doesn't.

One must ask, of course, "What works for whom?" A slum dominated by gangs or a city overrun by rival militias still has a discernible order to it.

Although there may be little or nothing that is "good" about that order, it is still an order of sorts, and the question for anyone who might want to act or intervene there is always, "What would my action achieve? How would it change things, if at all?" The important thing to recognize – and the thing that is at odds with a statist or sovereigntist imaginary – is that it is never a matter of going from disorder to order, but rather of moving from one form of order to another. In encouraging people to "see like a city" I am – among other things – suggesting that it always makes sense to figure out the form of order we are dealing with before we engage, rather than posing abstract alternatives that have little to do with the possibilities inherent in the situation we are dealing with. We have had too much political theory, too much social science, and too much political activism that turn on abstract ideas, and not enough engagement with concrete situations. If what I say here remains abstract, in the sense that there is no obvious way of applying it, that is a good thing: it will deter anyone who thinks that I am offering concrete solutions to concrete problems. At most, I am suggesting that we can approach problems more productively if we learn to see things differently.

I have been developing these ideas for a number of years, and have drawn from papers I originally presented to international relations scholars[18] (Chapter 1), urbanists[19] (Chapter 2), political scientists[20] (Chapter 4), political theorists[21] (Chapter 5), ecologists[22] (Chapter 6), political economists,[23] and political philosophers.[24] In the last case, I also had constitutional lawyers in mind. Readers may sense the original emphases in what appears here. Although I am following on from previously published work of mine,[25] what appears in this book (except for certain passages in Chapter 2 and this Introduction) is new in published form. It has taken a long time for these ideas to take shape: Chapter 1 is mainly from a 2002 paper; Chapters 2 and 3 are mainly from manuscripts I developed in 2004; Chapter 5 is from a 2008 paper; Chapters 4 and 6 are from ones delivered in 2009; Chapter 7 was written in 2010, but draws on papers I wrote in 2003 and 2005. I hope that the seams are more apparent to me than to readers of this book. Some shifts of mood, style, emphasis, and approach remain, however, as befits the fact that I have been struggling with these ideas for some time, and have been trying to express myself to different audiences. My own internal struggle is with my desire to offer political prescriptions, rather than stick to my analytic tasks.

Chapter 1 is entitled, "Urbanism as Governmentality". It sets out, in a general way, the conception I am advocating. I focus first on the relationship between urbanism and what Michel Foucault called "governmentality". I argue that urbanism *is* governmentality, and that this has profound implications for the way we understand politics. I try to show that a city-based political imaginary is implicit in the way that we are coming to think of regionalism and globalism, and go on to suggest that urbanism is in itself a security regime, different in principle from the one centred on the state system. Chapter 2 is entitled, "Ontologies of the Political". There, I explain in greater detail what I mean by the dominant ontology of the political, and the alternative that I think is implicit in conceptions of urbanism as a way of life. My argument is especially oriented to urbanists – people who study urban affairs or the city from various disciplinary perspectives – because I want to suggest to them that they have so far failed to challenge the dominant ontology effectively and so have relegated urban studies to a minor position within the academy. In both these chapters, I am struggling with the principle of sovereignty: trying to imagine the political otherwise, through the urban, while insisting on the ways in which we are haunted by dreams of sovereignty. If I privilege any experience, it is the American rather than the European, because it is more suggestive of what emerges through urbanism as such.

In Chapters 3 and 4, I deal more directly with some of the literature on which we might draw in developing a political ontology of urbanism as a way of life. Followers of theoretical fashions will notice that I pass over many recent debates in favour of earlier discussions. Those earlier discussions interest me because they deal with familiar ideas and practices, ones that already have some currency outside the academy. I am looking for points of entry that do not depend on attunement to particular intellectual fashions, or on the embrace of particular commitments. I draw on ideas from across the political spectrum, in order to develop an assemblage that might be useful in more than one context. In Chapter 3 ("Politics of Urbanism as a Way of Life"), I follow a line that takes me from Max Weber to the Chicago school urban sociologists (especially Louis Wirth) and thence to Friedrich von Hayek (guru of Chicago school economics) on the one hand and Jane Jacobs and Richard Sennett on the other. My aim is to tease out a set of ideas that I think are important: ones about non-sovereign authority (Weber), urbanism (Wirth), unplanned order (Hayek), and proximate diversity (Jacobs and Sennett). My argument is that we can politicize the analyses offered – all of which have been immensely influential – without resorting to the crude binaries of the dominant ontology. In Chapter 4 ("The Art of Government"), I turn my attention to Michel Foucault's influential lectures on the art of government, in which he explores the relationship between liberalism and neo-liberalism on the one hand and governmentality on the other. I argue that these lectures enable us to see the problem of government differently: not as an effect of the "growth of the state" but instead as a problem intrinsic to the city, typically resolved through some form of liberal governmentality.

This leads me to Chapter 5 ("Seeing Like a State, Seeing Like a City"), where I address myself more directly to political theorists. I argue, not surprisingly, that they have typically seen like a state, when in fact they need to see like a city. The particular claim I make is that the axiological or normative emphasis in Anglo-American political theory depends on an implicitly sovereigntist political imaginary which puts the theorist at a distance from the world, issuing instructions to it like a would-be king or president. I suggest that realistic political theory must instead be developed *in situ*, attuned to the complexities of a world that we cannot control as sovereigns. That world is urban, whatever else it is.

In Chapter 6 ("*Oikos, Nomos, Logos*"), I explore the twin logics of economy and ecology, in which the world is re-conceived as a home for humans, and we are urged to attune ourselves to its requirements. I argue that the proposed attunement intensifies the governmentalization of politics, and that the tensions that this exposes are best understood through a political ontology of urbanism as a way of life. In Chapter 7 ("From Local Self-Government to Politics"), I focus on local self-government, which I take to be a hidden principle of modern republicanism, and hence an appropriate focus for our attention. I use my own neighbourhood and my own city to illustrate some of what I can see when I approach things from my own place. What seems clear is that things are out of scale with a statist ontology of the political.

In my Conclusion, I suggest that a matter as trivial as the bunnies on the lawn outside my office connects with the larger realities I am trying to understand, because in seeing like a city – seeing the world *as* a city in which I live, and seeing the world *through* the city in which I live – I discover connections to war and peace, justice and injustice, environmental degradation and restoration, government and self-government, emancipation and oppression. In fact, new political possibilities occur to me. I can think realistically but calmly, rather than in the mode of panic induced by the sovereigntist imaginary. The city calls to me and to you, and offers us a place to act politically, but it also dispels our fears and illusions about mastery. We actually can live there without becoming kings or summoning kings to our rescue.

1   Urbanism as governmentality

So, where to begin? With the *polis*, of course, because the *polis* is at the centre of Western political thought. Not only do most of our key analytic terms derive from the ancient Greeks – democracy, oligarchy, and tyranny; politics, politicians, and policy; practice, theory, technique, and logic – but ancient Greek thought – particularly Plato's (1991) and Aristotle's (1996) – provides the point of departure for most thinking about political possibilities.[1] The ancient Roman idea of the republic (Cicero 1991) is connected to the Greek idea of the *polis*, and both are in turn connected with the modern ideal of the liberal-democratic state. In light of this, it is curious that so little attention has been given to *the city* in Western political thought, since Greek (and Roman) thinking was so obviously city-centred. Whatever else the *polis* was, it was certainly a city. In Greek thinking, citydom and polity were not two different possibilities, but the same one. Who founded a city, founded a polity. Moreover, the modern idea of *civilization* invokes the Roman word for the same process, whereby tribesmen and peasant farmers were gathered together in places of an entirely different sort, where at least some of them could be transformed into *citizens* of an urban polity: a city. So, this ancient idea is apparently preserved in our thinking: the idea that people have to be citified, organized into cities, to become capable of politics in the proper sense. We also retain the ancient Greek idea that an order sustained only by tradition or violence is not political (which is not to say that either tradition or violence is absent, or ever could be absent).[2] A political order is generated somehow by discussion, deliberation, negotiation, and compromise, by the exchange of reasons, and by adherence to a logic sensitive to our nature as human beings. A political order is somehow both rational and consensual. It is not merely tribal or familial, nor is it an order imposed by naked violence. It is an order that emerges from our nature as civilized beings, one that comes from the best, most progressive, most rational, most humane part of ourselves.

But, if all these good things are somehow bound up with the creation of a *city* as a new form of human order, why are political theorists and political scientists so reluctant to think about cities when they sketch the possibilities for that form of order? The short answer is that they have been obsessed with the state, which they have come to understand as the necessary and sufficient condition for overcoming the disorder of the city and establishing the ground for politics. If one has a theory of the state, why bother with a theory of the city? The latter subject can be left to sociologists, geographers, economists, and cultural theorists. That in fact has been the general division of labour for the last century or more. Urban analysts *other* than political scientists have developed elaborate and interesting accounts of the way cities come to be, how they generate the forms of order peculiar to them, what their characteristic problems are, and so on.[3] To the extent that there has been a political science of cities, it has mostly been an account of local government. Local government has in turn been conceived as government in and through local agencies of the state. Local political authorities that appear to have other origins are re-conceptualized as agencies of the state. Since this re-conceptualization has already been effected in state law, no cognitive dissonance occurs (Frug 1980, 1999). Whatever exists in the way of governmental/political authority at the local level can easily be conceived as an emanation of the state. So, in a way, cities simply disappear within a state-centric analysis, only to re-emerge as minor entities of local administration. Serious political science is about states and the relations between states. It is not about cities. The study of urban politics or local government is subordinate to the more important study of state politics and policy.

Even so, the city returns to haunt political scientists, just as it haunts politicians. As Max Weber (1978) argued a century ago, the city is a domain of "non-legitimate" domination.[4] That is, a city is a form of social organization characterized by market relations, and hence by the form of order implicit in "free exchange" (Smith, A. 1993). Relations of domination may be implicit in the market, but they are not the explicit objective of the market, which has other purposes. In fact, according to most accounts, the market is supposed to be a sphere of freedom, in which relations of domination have no place. So, to the extent that the market entails domination – as clearly it does – that domination is non-legitimate. Most theorists believe that such non-legitimate domination is insufficient practically as well as morally: the market/city will not be sustained (and certainly not thrive as it should) if there is no external authority, with its own source of legitimacy, which can maintain order. In the Weberian account, that external authority is most properly the state, under modern conditions. The state can mobilize loyalty and deploy violence as necessary. The state plays a vital role in legitimizing and enforcing the rules of the market; moreover, it can and should modify the rules of the market so that they do not work against other objectives, like military security, environmental preservation, and social peace. On this conception, the state is the guardian of the market and hence of the city. In so far as people come to rely on the market for their means of livelihood – that is, in so far as people become dependent upon and engaged with a market economy – the state is drawn into a regulatory/protective role that is determined in large degree by market rationality. To put it otherwise, the state must adapt to the rationality of the city, rather than the other way around.[5]

The city, nevertheless, transcends the market. The market may be the condition of possibility for the city's founding and the city's flourishing, but the "gathering together" entailed by the market involves human relations that are not and cannot be regulated by market rationality. People make friends, form families, establish neighbourly relations, engage in religious rituals, plant trees, create gardens, form choirs and do all manner of things involved in human social life. These various activities have their own rationalities, and, although those rationalities are sometimes mediated by the market, often they are not (or only incompletely). A city will not work as a civilized order unless these other rationalities come into play. Almost every serious student of cities has noticed that these rationalities proliferate in quite unexpected ways, and that tolerable social orders emerge even in the absence of overarching state authority. This is not to say that the state is useless or that the orders concerned are in any way ideal: only that orders do emerge in some fashion and there are always aspects of those orders that are more-or-less satisfactory for the people involved. So much, almost everyone recognizes. On the other hand, there is an aspect of the implicit order of the city that modern sociologists and political scientists prefer not to see: namely, that a functioning city generates *political authorities*, which may or may not be recognized by the state. To say that a city exists is to say that political authorities have already been created.

It is at this point that the Graeco-Roman image of the "founding" of a city becomes misleading. The Greeks and the Romans had much experience of such foundings, as did the European colonists of the modern era. However, cities develop as they do for reasons that states – to say nothing of long-dead "founders" – have difficulty controlling. It was not the government of the United States that decided that New York would be the greatest city in the country.[6] States do influence urban development (which is why capital cities are often major urban centres), but there are multiple *rationalities* at work in the development of cities. The rationality of the market is the most obviously influential, but there are other rationalities, like the rationalities of culture or religious worship, that may also be important. In this context, we can also see that there are various political agendas at work, some of which are present from the time of "founding," others of which emerge much later. These agendas do not necessarily or even usually relate to the development of the city as a whole. They tend to be much more specific than that, and to refer back to particular communities, networks, gangs, sects, clans, enterprises, and so on. *Political* authorities, in the sense of authorities that have the capacity to regulate and deploy violence, as well as articulate and enforce rules of conduct, emerge for many different reasons. These authorities may or may not attract the notice of the state. On the other hand, any state (or other authority) that wishes to govern a city as a whole must deal with these existing political authorities in some fashion. This is partly a matter of dealing with pre-existing authorities. It is also a matter of negotiating with, controlling, or suppressing *new* political authorities as they are created. A city is not static. It is an ensemble of movements, and those movements give rise to new authorities. Those new authorities are more-or-less political, and some of them, like the so-called terrorist networks that have developed in recent years, can be quite violent.

So, wherever there is a city, there are pre-existing and newly emerging *political authorities*, the exact configuration and disposition of which is always changing. This makes urban government particularly challenging. Either the state adapts itself to the multiple rationalities and political authorities of the city, or it attempts to control those rationalities and authorities – or both. Historical experience suggests that the state's capacity for control is severely limited. Hence, the idea of governing *through* freedom: which is to say, through the rationalities and authorities that the city generates (Rose 1999). This strategy is not necessarily consistent with the one implicit in the modern state. The modern state is supposed to be a monopolistic institution: the only institution that can confer legal authority and, in particular, the only one that can authorize the use of violence. As authorizer of authority and monopolist of legitimate violence, the state is supposed to be at the centre of the system of government, and as such it is the main subject, perhaps the only *proper* subject, of political attention. Politics, government, law, and legitimate violence are all located imaginatively in the same place, the state, and the state is presumed to enjoy a certain autonomy in relation to "society": the form of life that the state is to govern. "Society" is conceptually bounded, so that it is in a one-to-one relation with the state. State and society are ultimately one, but the former is to govern the latter. On this conception, the rationality of politics is dependent on the presence of a sovereign centre (the state) from which the people concerned (society) can be governed (Hegel 1965). In the modern view, democracy is about making a society self-governing by enabling people in that society to control the state that governs them. Democracy is a sort of benign feedback system, which ensures that the entity concerned – call it a state or a society: it makes no difference – develops in accordance with the needs and aspirations of the people who form it. Obviously, this is a nice idea, which has endeared itself to the leading intellectuals of our time, but it begs the question of the relation between state/society on the one hand and the city on the other (to say nothing of the question of how the ideal of the liberal-democratic state is to be imposed).

The standard view is that each state/society contains a number of cities and towns, all of which are subordinate to the state/society of which they are part.[7] In so far as this is true, urban governments can be understood as local governments, subordinate to the higher authorities. However, the truth is that urban systems tend to break the bounds of their own containers, not only in the sense that cities spill over their administrative boundaries and occupy the surrounding countryside (often linking up with other towns and cities in the process), but also in the sense that the urban system ultimately transcends particular countries. Since the 1980s, urban analysts have been giving more and more attention to the phenomenon of "global cities": that is, cities whose economic, social, and cultural reach is truly global (Sassen 1991, Knox and Taylor 1995, Scott, A. 2001). At first, attention was directed mainly at the primate cities, like Tokyo, London, and New York. Gradually, analysts began to recognize that there were many other cities that operated on a global scale, in that (at least to a significant degree) they oriented themselves (culturally, socially, and economically) to the world as a whole. Moreover, the political leaders of many cities began to recognize that a global orientation was an advantage, if not a necessity. This rise of global consciousness was connected with a sense that the "global village" Marshall McLuhan (1964) had foreshadowed was starting to become a practical reality, the sort of practical reality that businesspeople had to deal with every day. Given that, urban life – what Louis Wirth (1938) described as *urbanism as a way of life* – could no longer be conceived as something that could be governed by individual states. It was a way of life that had already burst the boundaries of states, and established itself as a global system.

Globalized urbanism is not the same thing as a globalized economy. Just as the city exceeds the market (which may be the original rationale for its "founding"), the urban global exceeds the global market economy. Implicit in a globalized urbanism are the emergence of new forms of political authority and the transformation of others. States do not disappear, but they are refigured within a more complex political field. To get a sense of that field, we need to have a better understanding of urbanism, particularly of the way it has become globalized. We also have to understand how urbanism works as governmentality[8] or (if you prefer) as a system of government. As I note in this chapter, there are intriguing and influential arguments to the effect that good governance depends less on state authority than on relationships among authorities that retain their autonomy. Although such arguments are most familiar with respect to the economy, there is a social dimension to them as well. Moreover, as I shall suggest in this chapter and again in the next, a certain security regime is implicit in urbanism as a way of life. If so, our obsession with the state may be misplaced.

From urbanism to governmentality

The common-sense conception of a city is deceptively simple. A city is a gathering together of many people, who live in close proximity to one another. It is like a village or a town, but on a larger scale. Historically, it is characterized by relatively dense settlement, and hence by a clustering of many buildings in a small space. But, in many ways, this characterization is anachronistic. Modern means of transportation and communication make it possible for people to live further apart, while nonetheless participating in the life of the same city. People can live in an outlying village, and still work in a big city. Or, they can live in one city and work in another. Or, they can divide their time between two different cities, or between a city place and a country place. More remarkably, they can live and work in very remote places – for example, cottages in "the bush" in British Columbia or Vermont – and nonetheless be more-or-less full participants in an urban life that stretches between New York, Toronto, and San Francisco, and indeed across the world. At one time, a person had to be unusually wealthy and otherwise favoured to live such a life, but this option is becoming more and more available to middle-class people in the more prosperous parts of the world.[9] Perhaps the more extreme forms of such a life are still unusual, but the number of people who live in country villages in southern England and work in London is by no means small, nor is the number of dual-income families whose partners commute in different directions from "rural" New Jersey or "rural" Connecticut. Moreover, what once so dramatically distinguished rural from urban life – its relative isolation, its dependency on agriculture or other primary industries, its long-term stability – is no longer as apparent. Rural life is becoming more and more like urban life, especially in those parts of the world where urbanism is most advanced.[10] In this context, classic distinctions between the city and the country or the urban and the rural come to seem much less useful, except for historical analysis.

It is a well-known fact that the great majority of people in the so-called industrialized countries live in urban areas, as they are commonly defined. It is also a well-known fact that a (slight) majority of people in the world as a whole now live in urban areas. These statistics probably underestimate the degree to which the world has been urbanized, since they obscure the fact that rural areas have become so much more urban as a result of modern transportation and communication. A farmer in Europe or California who checks the markets every morning on the computer, negotiates with product brokers in distant cities, buys food at a supermarket, watches television every night, and takes vacations half a continent away is not exactly living a traditional rural life. In most respects, such a farmer is an urbanite living in the countryside, albeit an urbanite who has many good reasons for perceiving of himself or herself as a rural person. Perhaps the key thing to recognize is that cities are no longer like islands within a rural sea. Instead, the islands have formed continents, continents on which the majority of people now live. Rural life, in any form, has become very much the exception in the more prosperous parts of the world, and there is every indication that a similar pattern is emerging elsewhere. Modern life is urban, but the modern city spreads out and links up with other cities and the countryside in a way that gradually obliterates the urban–rural distinction. As urbanism as a way of life becomes predominant other forms of life are marginalized or incorporated within it.[11]

So, what exactly is involved in urbanism as a way of life? Clearly, it is not characterized simply by the massing of people together in cities, for cities soon spread, connect with one another, and colonize the countryside. Urbanism is characterized less by a particular physical form than by a particular relation to the environment. A city is an environment created by human beings. We know now that people have been shaping their environments for a very long time: that, for instance, the meadows and open woodlands of New England, which the Europeans imagined to be "natural", were deliberately produced as such by native farmers and hunters (Cronon 1983, Knobloch 1996). *Pace* the Greeks, people who live in pastoral, shifting agricultural, or hunter/gatherer societies take control of their own environments, civilize them, and make them hospitable for human life. Nonetheless, city-building, forest-clearing, fence-raising, and so on take this effort to bring the natural environment under control to a new level: at some point, a quantitative increase in human efforts to control the environment involves a qualitative change in the character of human life (Brody 2001). The change is not necessarily for the better, but it does alter the conditions of possibility for human life. Gradually, humans come to live in an environment that they have produced for themselves: an environment of constructed buildings, artificial light, telecommunications, automotive transport, and so on. Almost everything that I can see as I write this consists of manufactured materials. Even when I look out the window and admire the greenery, I am conscious of the fact that everything there was planted by city people like me. Only the sky seems as it was in ancient days, and even that is filling with greenhouse gases from the passing cars, trucks, and helijets, and is in any case always illuminated at night by city lights. To live an urban life is to live at several removes from a nature undisturbed by human activity: it is to live within a humanly produced environment that constitutes a second nature.

But, to see urban life only in this way (as a life alienated from first nature) is to obscure its positivity. Urban life entails reflexive activity. The forms of such activity are not fixed for long. They tend to proliferate and change shape. It is just this fecundity and changefulness that has caught the attention of every close observer of urban life. Openness and expansiveness are implicit in urbanism as a way of life. What was once the exception – a meeting with the Other: strangers from another tribe, clan, or village – becomes increasingly the norm (Simmel 1971). If enclosed communities are formed or preserved, the enclosures have to be sustained under new conditions, in which people from different communities rub up against one another on a day-to-day basis, see one another on the streets and in the markets, and are offered an endless stream of telemediated images of other forms of life. In an urban setting, it is relatively easy for an individual or a group to escape a previous enclosure and establish a new way of life. The density of human interaction – cultural, social, economic, and political – is such that possibilities for earning a living, finding a place, making a name tend to proliferate. Thus, the city is widely perceived as a locus of freedom: a place where the enclosures of family and tribe and tradition can be escaped and where new modes of life – perhaps ones that refigure family, tribe, and tradition in new ways – can be created. In short, urbanism as a way of life is a form of human freedom: for many people, the ultimate form of human freedom.[12]

Nevertheless, urbanism homogenizes as much as it liberates. Urbanism requires a certain way of being: a way of relating to strangers, dwelling together, employing oneself, expressing oneself, disposing of one's wastes. Urbanism may be more expansive, differentiated, open, and changeful than other ways of life, like farming, goat-herding, or buffalo-hunting, but that does not mean that it makes anything and everything possible. Other ways of life can be accommodated within urbanism – goat-herding can be offered as a kind of career option, or preserved as a sort of historical relic in special places – but the terms of accommodation are necessarily such that the other way of life is transformed into something different. An urbanized farmer or goat-herder or buffalo-hunter must have a sense of self and a way of being in the world that are compatible with urbanism as a way of life. For the vast majority of people who are drawn into the urban global, the conditions of possibility for everyday life become much the same: shops and apartments, streets filled with other people, schools and health clinics, and enticing possibilities of employment which offer the chance of access to the goods and services of modern urban life. Urbanism may be a form of freedom, but it is nonetheless totalitarian. It tends to extinguish forms of life that are incompatible with it.[13]

Another aspect of urbanism is self-government. No doubt, every way of life entails self-government, but the need for self-government is especially apparent in an urban setting. People need to show restraint in this world of strangers, and to a remarkable extent they do. What the city exposes is that many of the rules observed in smaller human groups are not actually necessary for wider social order. A minimalist regime of peaceable interaction and non-interference is sufficient to produce a form of order that enables large numbers of people to live together. Within that regime, smaller groups can adhere to their own rules, without necessarily disturbing others. Although this minimalist regime is often described as "liberalism", the root of it is actually in urbanism as a way of life. In a way, liberalism is just a doctrine that articulates principles implicit in urban life: a certain tolerance for others, a willingness to live and let live, and ultimately a kind of enthusiasm for what urbanism has to offer, namely, a wide range of personal choice. It is no accident that a liberal thinker like John Stuart Mill (1991) interpreted freedom as a matter of *self-government*, for it is self-government not "anarchy" that the city has to offer. Urban life has its rules, its conditions of possibility, and those rules have to be well observed if a city is to work. But, the rules have to be understood, accepted, and observed by a myriad of individuals who cannot be effectively watched and regulated by external authorities. Each individual has to assume responsibility for him- or herself, and become self-regulating or self-governing. Otherwise, the order of the city breaks down – or, more accurately, is displaced by an order of a different type. What one has to do as a self-governing urbanite is implicit in urbanism as a way of life. The most important laws are simply elaborations of what everyone knows is necessary.

So, what Foucault (2003) called "governmentality", and what others have described as "government at a distance" or "governing through freedom" (Rose 1999, Dean 1999), is implicit in urbanism as a way of life. It is a condition of possibility for urbanism and also a name for many of the practices implicit in urbanism. Urban analysts from Max Weber (1978) to Richard Sennett (1970) have emphasized again and again that an urban order tends to arise, regardless of whether the state or the imperial authorities try to create such an order. Urban life has a logic of its own, a logic that tends to impose itself on the authorities. Nonetheless, there is another aspect of this: namely, the proliferation of autonomous or semi-autonomous political authorities, whose authorizations are from many different sources. One of Foucault's insights was that sovereign centres tend to be effaced by the proliferation of governmentalities, each of which has its own specific logic.[14] This proliferation of governmentalities is the logical complement to individual self-government. Self-governing individuals who work out their conduct in isolation from one another will soon confront a lack: an absence of thoroughfares, drainage systems, garbage disposal, fire protection, open space, and so on. Left to their own devices, self-governing individuals will soon generate political authorities of one sort or another, authorities that will fill or exploit such lacks. Gangs that regulate crime are one example, but there are many more positive ones. A vacuum of authority will not exist for long, and so the people concerned will have a great incentive to form an effective authority, if only to keep the gangs at bay. In this context, the authorization of authority by a state can be quite functional. Local authorities can turn to the state (or the king or emperor) to help secure their own authority. That was the pattern in medieval and early modern European cities. Nevertheless, it is a mistake to suppose that the state is the condition of possibility for local authorities: such authorities will arise regardless, as is happening now in many cities of the Global South.

The problem of urbanism is not that it fails to generate political authorities. It generates political authorities as it generates governmentalities: every governmentality is a form of authority, and every form of authority is (in some degree) politically contested. The anxiety attendant upon urbanism is related to the fact that it is a system without a centre, and hence a system that defies regulation *from* a centre. It keeps proliferating in accordance with its own logic, and new authorities are constantly emerging in that context. Keeping all those authorities in line is an extraordinarily difficult task – as American presidents soon discover. Urbanism is ultimately uncontainable, and that means that its politics always exceeds the regulatory efforts of the highest authorities. That means that urbanism and statism are always at odds, since statism (which is not necessarily incompatible with liberalism or neo-liberalism, and indeed has developed in concert with the latter in the modern era) is inspired by the idea that everything can be contained or controlled by a higher authority that is properly constituted and empowered.

Regionalism and globalism

The recent weakening of the United States has revived speculation about global political institutions. The most prominent of the existing institutions are inter-state agencies or forums, like the World Trade Organization (WTO) or the G-20. Many of them, like the ones mentioned, have essentially economic purposes. They raise the question of what political institutions are necessary for global prosperity. Although there has been much attention to the peak inter-state institutions in the context of the economic downturn that began in 2008, another discourse, one of global cities or global city-regions, per-sists. The presumption of that discourse is that prosperity, social cohesion, and the alleviation of poverty all depend on appropriate political organiza-tion at the level of the global city-region and that what works at that level may also work globally. The analytical focus of the global-city discourse has been on the most powerful and prosperous regions of the world, and in this respect it mimics the more conventional idea that the liberal democracies of the West provide a model for everyone. This should give us pause, but the ideas advanced are worth exploring carefully.

At an earlier stage of urbanization, the larger cities spread out, so that their suburbs extended far beyond the administrative boundaries of the cities concerned. Then, on the outskirts of these cities, new centres began to develop as part of a network extended across the urban region. In some places, most notoriously in California, these networks became polycentric. In Western Europe and in the north-eastern and midwestern United States, greater and lesser cities began to grow toward one another, incorporate smaller towns as shared suburbs and secondary centres, and so form regional networks of cities that stretched over hundreds of kilometres (sometimes crossing national boundaries).[15] Once globalization emerged as a theme of business development, these nascent urban regions or city-regions were faced with a new challenge: how to organize themselves to take advantage of the new opportunities. More and more analysts noted that business was burgeoning in some regions rather than others, and that the successful regions seemed to be ones that organized themselves to take advantage of the "new economy": an economy organized for global production, distribution, and finance; one characterized by outsourcing of production and franchis-ing of distribution; an economy in which services were more important than physical goods and in which sales depended on effective branding; an economy that catered toward a variety of urban "lifestyles". It seemed that some regions were locked in the past, still trying to produce by old industrial methods. Other regions, by contrast, seemed to be fully oriented toward the new economy and were surging ahead. Was there some underlying reason for the failures of the first group and the successes of the second? Could the reason be connected to political organization?

If there is a consensus among analysts on this issue, it is this: successful urban regions are characterized by effective cooperation between all the relevant actors; the relevant authorities (economic, social, cultural, and political) are networked in a way that facilitates communication and collaboration; and there are political leaders in the region who know how to bring people together and help them to work toward common goals (Gertler and Wolfe 2002). One way of describing this is that there is an effective urban regime (Stone 1989, 2005), a mode of governance that works. Crucially, that mode of governance is not on a sovereigntist model. On the contrary, the assumption is that authority is necessarily and properly dispersed, that there are different types of authority and sources of legitimacy, and that the point is not to make one authority (or form of authority) predominant in relation to the others, but rather to get all the authorities working toward some common goals. In the literature, those goals are sometimes expressed in narrowly economic terms: to increase the region's prosperity, to make it a global centre of business enterprise, and so on. On the other hand, those economic goals are often connected with social and political objectives. It is said that the greatest asset of an urban region is a well-educated, well-motivated workforce. Natural resources are useful and a good location is important, but a city-region may grow vigorously even if it lacks these advantages. The key is "human capital". Human capital is partly a matter of the talents, education, and experience of the individuals concerned, but it is also a matter of the way those individuals are related to one another. People have to be able to work together despite their differences. They have to have a sense of common purpose. They have to feel part of a community of some sort. Such a community is unlikely to emerge if political leaders fail to work at it.

As one high-tech, corporate recruiter put it: it is not just a matter of persuading someone that our own company offers good opportunities; people want to know where their *next* job is going to come from; they want to be in a community where there are many different companies competing for the available talent.[16] A dynamic regional economy, in which there are dozens and dozens of companies competing and contracting with one another for various purposes, is an economy with many outlets for ambitious and talented people. Such an economy does not exist on its own. It must be in a conducive natural and social environment. High-flying entrepreneurs and technicians want to have access to parks and recreational facilities, to be able to get back and forth to work conveniently, to breathe clean air and drink clean water, to go to interesting clubs and restaurants and enjoy the urban "scene", to have good daycare and schools for their children, to get proper health care, to be protected from potential plagues, and to be able to live their lives in reasonable personal security. So, there must be mechanisms that not only preserve some of the natural environment, but make the urban environment more habitable. A common view is that the children of the poor should be assisted, so that they can enter the pool of human capital in the region. That means providing good schools, recreational facilities, health care, and so on throughout the region. It also means doing something to overcome the divides of class and culture, divides that make the "truly disadvantaged" a threat to social peace and public safety. So, a liberal (or at least a "compassionately conservative") relation to the less fortunate is a necessity for making a regional economy work properly. Business leaders have to be encouraged to accept their social responsibilities and to work with other leaders in a way that improves the quality of life and enhances social harmony within the region.

The presumption is that there is a benign circle: investments in the natural and social environment will pay off economically, and vice versa. Obviously, there is much room for debate about the sorts of investments that ought to have priority, and there is no doubt that most of the literature on this subject has an economic emphasis that betrays its business bias. That said, what is interesting for my purpose here is that a different model of the polity seems to emerge from thinking about the prospects of urban regions. It is a model that de-emphasizes sovereignty in favour of networked authority, largely ignores the boundary between state and society in articulating models for political leadership, and recognizes the inevitability of multiple forms and sources of authority (Castells 1996). In the urban region, the connected problems of governance and political organization are differentiated from questions about the organization of the state. In fact, the organization of the state is thought to be a relatively minor issue, one liable to distract attention from the *real* political problems. The *real* problems are ones like these: how to get people thinking about the opportunities implicit in the new economy rather than worrying about things that are about to pass away; how to broaden the concerns of people who have been focused on just one aspect of life (be it making money or finding God); how to get people who previously thought of themselves as enemies or aliens collaborating on joint projects; how to identify common objectives and mobilize resources for pursuing those objectives; how to stimulate enterprise and creativity in areas of life where those qualities have not been apparent locally; how to generate understanding across divides of culture and religion; how to make the underclass a part of mainstream society. The presumption is that the answers to problems like these depend on creating appropriate networks of authority and generating new authorities where ones did not exist before. The sovereigntist model of an authority that commands all authorities is irrelevant to the tasks at hand.

An immediate implication of this is that effective governance for a dynamic "global city-region" will be on an entirely different model from the model of "the state". Indeed, the Hegelian distinction between state and society becomes profoundly misleading in this context, for the question of "ultimate authority" is always deferred. There never *is* a moment of final resolution, and so, in a sense, the state never appears. There is only the restless activity that generates authorities, establishes links between them, facilitates some activities, forestalls others, and renders everything obsolescent in a Schumpeterian process of "creative destruction". Schumpeter himself focused on the economy when he analysed these things, but current debates about urban regions enable us to see that much more than the economy is at stake. Urbanism as a way of life produces a politics – governmentalities and authorities – in continuous transformation.

It is not news that there is a sharp divide between "the citadel" – the glitzy shopping precincts, office towers, hotels, entertainment districts, and highrise condominiums – and "the ghetto" – where the people who serve the rich live, often in derelict buildings or shanty towns (Friedmann and Wolff 1982). Engels wrote about this in Manchester in the 1840s, and urbanists have continued to track the patterns of inequality ever since. Forms of the urban may change, but this issue remains. The role of the state is complex, because it works to produce and sustain inequalities even as it pretends to alleviate them – for reasons that Marx and Engels explained a long time ago. The patterns of inequality and response in the metropolises of the North and the megacities of the Global South are various, but even where the state is theoretically strong, as in contemporary China, it consists of an ensemble of authorities with differing constituencies and purposes. This is nowhere more evident than in a place like the Pearl River Delta. There, as elsewhere, what appears under the sign of the state bleeds into other forms of authority – of cliques, gangs, families, factions, and businesses – that are asserted and contested in ways that bewilder even those with local knowledge. How things might be mobilized for the better is an open question, just as it is in New York or London. It is clearly not just a matter of strengthening the state on the one hand or civil society on the other. The problem is how to act from within the city to establish new solidarities, and that requires a sophisticated understanding of the particularities of urban order.

Throughout the neo-liberal era, speculation about the organization of the state has centred on the lessons learned from urban politics and local public administration (although this fact is rarely acknowledged).[17] The experience of American cities has been crucial in this respect. It is an old idea – dating back at least to the 1880s (Bryce 1893) – that American cities are ill-administered and that the politics of American cities is especially venal. In the common view, the inner core of most American cities is a disaster, and the more prosperous suburbs spread out chaotically, without any effective regional planning. Whatever the truth of this view, it governs the perceptions of many reformers inside and outside the United States. Partly because of this, American cities have been regarded as an especially intractable problem. The European or European-influenced "solution" has been sovereignty: the creation of a powerful, overarching regional authority, closely integrated with the state as a whole. However, this solution has been impossible in the American context. No such authorities have been created, nor is it likely that such authorities ever will be created. What to do, then? The answer that has emerged (from the bottom up, as it were) has been networked authority. This is not just a matter of linking distinct public authorities (central cities and suburban municipalities, school boards and police forces), but also of connecting with entities that are not part of the state. Links with business are crucial, it is said, both through a chamber of commerce and through less formal organizations. Business has to be mobilized not only for economic purposes (how do we revive the downtown core? how do we create incubators for new businesses?), but for charitable ones as well (how can we provide opportunities for unemployed youth? how can we raise money for cultural organizations?). Moreover, the networks have to extend into the poorest and most alienated communities; otherwise, resources directed towards those communities will be wasted and the alienation and poverty of the people concerned will be expressed in acts of hostility against others. So, good governance, it is said, is less about implementing preconceived plans from a sovereign centre than about creating effective networks of authority that generate resources and focus them appropriately. The obstacle to good governance is political, not administrative. The hostilities that prevent people from working together have to be overcome. Once they are overcome, much can be done, even if the administrative arrangements seem cumbersome. In any case, there is no other alternative, because sovereign authority cannot be established over the people concerned.

In ways often not noticed, American public administration is the model for government more generally, and American public administration is keyed to the reality of multiple authorities and multiple rationalities. Moreover, the model *within* the model of American public administration is civic government. It is at that level that the *multiplicity* of authorities and rationalities is most apparent. Administrators confront the people whom they are supposed to administer, and those people insist on their right to behave freely. There is no option but to negotiate this politically. The legitimation of multiple authorities, which is implicit in American ideas about democracy, federalism, and individual liberty, means that the resistance local administrators face is particularly stubborn. To be an effective local administrator means to be an effective urban politician: the line between the two roles is blurry. So, the model of "government", which is keyed to European notions of centralized state, has to be re-framed. To say "governance" is to speak of the problem in a way that links politics and administration, state and society, the rule of law and personal freedom. It is to work against ideas bound up with state sovereignty and in favour of conceptions of politics and government that are keyed to notions of "self-government". If self-government is not a matter of having a state with leaders chosen by and accountable to the people, but is instead a matter of civic administration on the model of networked authority, then the implications for thinking about democracy are quite profound. Such thinking has always been more advanced in the USA than elsewhere, and the idea is now being exported under the rubric of thinking about "regimes" and "governance".

If we consider how questions of continental and global governance are now being posed, we can see that the model of the American city – and, more generally, of the global city-region – is at the heart of much recent thinking. European notions about subsidiarity are a re-framing of American ideas about federalism and pluralism. The re-framing is intended to bring these ideas into line with more traditional statist thinking, but it nonetheless enables a conception of the European Union that allows for multiple levels of authority. In turn, this encourages a re-conceptualization of local authority as a network that stretches across the state–society divide. American pluralism is re-valued in this context as a more sophisticated form of networked authority than European corporatism. The European Union appears as a mechanism for the deconstruction of tightly centralized nation-states, in favour of more complex relations of authority. On a global scale, attention is focused on the development of new regulatory regimes to open markets, facilitate the movement of capital, free the flows of goods and services, control threats to the environment, establish standards for the protection of human rights, inhibit the spread of diseases, limit the spread of dangerous weapons, and so on. In each of these instances, the model of governance is networked authority. The presumption is that common standards can only be established by agreement among the various authorities that have the capacity to regulate the matters at issue. The problem that a regime is supposed to solve is not just that there are many different states. There are also other forms of authority wielded by business corporations, religious groups, environmental lobbyists, village elders, gang leaders, and others. The regime will only be effective if a sufficiently wide range of authorities in all parts of the world accept it. In this respect, the problem of governance on a global scale is akin to the problem of governance in an American inner city – or in the remote villages of Amazonia or Central Asia.

Urbanism as a security regime

The implication of this line of analysis is that the only possible form of global governance is one based on networked authority. World order would be the order of the city writ large, rather than the order of the state. Many people find this frightening because they think that we need a strong state (or state system) to secure economic and social justice, protect the environment, or even to provide us with a modicum of personal security. That states have been highly deficient in these terms should give us pause for reflection, but most people would say that we cannot have the least security without the state to protect us. On the other hand, if urbanism does stimulate proliferating practices of government and self-government, it is in itself a security regime.

Urbanism as a way of life actually depends on an optimistic but not unrealistic assessment of the human capacity for living together. The premise is that people will find enough advantage in living closely with others, to begin modifying their behaviour and making it more consistent with the needs of strangers. Commonalities will stimulate collective action. Political authorities with different constituencies and different sources of legitimacy will emerge, but these authorities will be open to cooperation with one another. Urbanism as a way of life is too changeful, too multifarious to be described by any simple model. It cannot be tamed to fit a particular model of author-ity relations. The question of who will have the decisive authority or what regime will actually work will always remain open. The model of the state will sometimes fit, but more often it will be inappropriate to the problems at hand. Political solutions, such as they are, will always be extremely messy. But, that does not mean that those solutions will necessarily be ineffective. (American cities do work after a fashion – often much better than their counter-parts elsewhere.)

Since Hobbes's time, theories of the state have been keyed to the claim that the state alone can provide effective security. The state is to deal with what Mitchell Dean (2007) calls "the dark side". This means controlling marauding armies and reinforcing local police forces. The claim is that civilized life is impossible, unless there is a monopoly of the means of legit-imate violence within the territory concerned. Matching state to society is important within this context, because the activities at issue are more easily policed if they are contained within the borders of the state. Thus, to the extent that a way of life transcends state boundaries, it makes the security apparatus of the state ineffective. This is one of the incentives for imperial-ism, as we can see today. If the activities at issue are complex and varied, and if, moreover, new activities are spinning off from the old in unpredictable ways, then the state will be tempted to make its control more *intensive* as well as more *extensive*. Intensive control involves close surveillance and minute regulation. Extensive control means stretching out the security apparatus and policing territories far from the home state at least as intensely, if not more intensely, than the home territory. It seems to be part of the logic of security that the further the force goes from its home territory, the rougher its methods become. The dangers are less understood, and thus more men-acing. The people appear alien, hence scarcely human. The immediate costs of rough methods are not borne by those to whom the security apparatus is accountable. Thus, the logic of violent policing plays itself out in "remote" territories: Afghanistan, Colombia, inner-city Los Angeles, and the grey *banlieues* of Paris. The remoteness that generates violent policing is not just geographic, it is also social and cultural.

The fact that a minority within the state may be the object of violent policing is a reminder that states rarely succeed in unifying the societies they are to govern. The outside is always inside. Moreover, urbanism as a way of life means that the inside is always outside, always articulated on a scale that transcends the state.[18] In fact, globalism is implicit in urbanism, in that the urban system tends to become global and draw people into it from the surrounding "countryside". So, the continent of the urban – what we call "civilization" or urbanism as a way of life – cannot be secured by an apparatus of security confined to a particular territory. That apparatus of security must be stretched, by imperialist means or otherwise. On the other hand, this stretching is inevitably a thinning, unless resources are available for simultaneous intensification. The greatest resources imaginable may be insufficient, since urbanism as a way of life is inherently proliferative. Each measure of security generates a new activity, which must in turn be "secured". The fecundity and expansiveness of urbanism – the very qualities that prompt extension and intensification of the security apparatus – tend to defeat the security apparatus laid over it. Only if security practices are internalized, only if they become part of urbanism as a way of life, do they become really effective. To put it more positively: urbanism is itself a security regime, in so far as it involves people in practices of self-regulation, mutual tolerance, and collective action for public benefit. Such practices are implicit in urbanism as a way of life, and they are surprisingly effective in securing people against threats involved in massing millions of strangers together.

The premise of the liberal-democratic nation-state is that sovereign identities can be established all the way up and all the way down: that individuals can be constituted as sovereign-subjects, with rationally ordered desires; that the desires of these subjects can be rationally mediated by the market, the state, and the voluntary sector; that the nation-state can establish itself as the focus of ultimate loyalty, not only by being serviceable, but also by embodying a supreme collective identity. Sovereignty is supposed to resolve identity conflicts at both levels, individual and collective. To the extent that it does so, it simplifies the field of action, by making the actors into coherent (and thus in principle predictable) agents. Clearly, this conception of human order is wildly utopian. If one were to map the field of action realistically, one would have to recognize that people were not coherent individuals in the relevant sense: that people moved uneasily and unpredictably from one identity to another; that the desires related to these different identities were sometimes radically at odds; that to live in accord with some sovereign identity for the whole of one's life was not necessarily desirable (and for many people, in any case, impossible). One would also have to recognize that the collective identities that people treasured and that moved them to act were quite various, rather unstable, and by no means easily reconciled with one another. One would have to recognize that the multiple rationalities and multiple authorities implicit in urbanism as a way of life mirrored the complexity and instability that went all the way up and all the way down.

If there is any promise in contemporary speculations about global governance, it is in the growing recognition that the most effective authorities are ones premised on the principle of self-government. Were we to adhere more strictly to that principle, we would see that it cannot be implemented from a sovereign centre: instead, it must develop from the ground up. Moreover, we would see that self-government entails networked authority, in a great variety of forms. There is no doubt that the current superpower is attempting to secure control over existing networks of authority for its own purposes. Nor is there doubt that the networks dominated by businesses and investors are exceptionally powerful. It is also true that Westerners dominate many of the key networks of other kinds. But, to concentrate only on such familiar features of the current configuration is to miss something important about the imaginative shift implicit in speculations that move away from standard assumptions about the relation between sovereignty and political order. There is a still poorly articulated political imaginary, keyed to the realities of urbanism as a way of life, that encourages us to think of political possibilities in a different way. It points us away from the false securities of states and empires, towards the securities that emerge from the everyday politics of urban life. Whether securities of the latter sort will be sufficient to deal with the dark side of life is anyone's guess. What is clear, however, is that efforts to deal with such problems by applying external force are rarely effective. The effective forces of civilization are the ones implicit in urbanism as a way of life.

2 Ontologies of the political

The implication of my analysis so far is that the fundamental political question is the question of the city, not the state. In a way, urbanists have always believed this, but they are in a distinct minority. Moreover, as I will try to show in this chapter, the city is *inevitably* devalued as an object of political analysis, because the dominant ontology of the political suggests that attention *must* be focused on the sovereign authority, which is not the city. That ontology also suggests that there is a necessary distinction between the state on the one hand and culture, economy, environment, and society on the other hand. In so far as the city is a unit of the state, it is subordinate to a national or provincial government: it is normally a "third tier" authority. In so far as the city is a cultural, economic, environmental, or social unit it is in a domain apart from the one that is always already constituted as "political". Although it is always possible to think of the political in broader terms, by drawing attention to configurations of power and authority that are outside the state or that somehow transcend or overdetermine it, there is always a reference back to sovereign authority by way of analogy. Sovereign authority inaugurates the political by establishing a domain within which people are ruled and in which rule is contested, from within or from outside. Some theorists have tried to draw a distinction between "politics" – what happens within that domain – and "the political" – whatever involves a challenge from without. Others construe the domain of politics very broadly, so that it encompasses much that is outside the state, normally understood. But, the effect is still to maintain the line that establishes the political as something distinct and connects it with the practices by which we are ruled.

To construe the political otherwise is to focus on the practices by which we govern ourselves, individually and collectively, and to problematize familiar distinctions between rulers and ruled, public and private, law and custom, economic and political, social and cultural, and so on. To see like a city is to focus on what happens between people, what enables urban life, what questions arise within it, what solutions are developed, what conduct develops, and to what effects. To see the political in these terms is to refer back to these practices rather than to the ones by which people are ostensibly "ruled". The question of rule is secondary, because it only arises – as a threat or a possible solution – in a context in which people are always already engaged in making their lives work, under conditions in which they are thrown together by their own aspirations or by the immediate necessities of life. When we speak of "the city" or "urbanism as a way of life", we address ourselves to this context. When we insist that what happens is fundamentally political – rather than social, cultural, or economic – we refer back to an idea that is implicit in Greek thought but that has been pushed aside in favour of the one that suggests that politics is about the way we are ruled. On the latter conception, politics is under the shadow of kingship. In the former conception, it is ultimately about how people organize themselves in order to live.

The modern social sciences, which began to develop in the late eighteenth century and took their present shape at the beginning of the twentieth, are all keyed to different notions of what determines us. It is said that we are determined by social norms, or the requisites of the economy, or by culture, the environment, or human psychology. The aspiration of the social sciences is to explain politics away: to show that we are such and so because we must be. In this context, the state is just another institution to be explained, and politics a particular type of human activity. The reaction to this way of thinking has been to suggest that everything is political, to imply that the political character of things is to be found in the often hidden practices of ruling and the overt or inchoate challenges to those practices. To politicize something is simply to identify its political character in this sense, and to call people to think of the matter politically. Such an approach inevitably confirms what it is meant to challenge, in that it suggests again and again that we are being *ruled* even if it seems that things are determined by processes that are oriented otherwise (in other words that seem to be about raising children or making money or building bridges or doing something that has little to do with ruling as such). Uncovering the secretly political character of things has become something of an obsession among radical critics over the last half-century. They certainly have succeeded in convincing many people that rule is ubiquitous, that the king or the father is always present in our lives, that we are always already trying to liberate ourselves, and that this perpetual struggle is politics.

I want to say: *not so*. This way of thinking about things just replicates the dominant ontology of the political and distracts us from the more difficult problem of understanding our way of life – urbanism or the city – politically. To understand things politically is to focus on what we do, how we think, and interact with one another without assuming *either* that how we are ruled is the central issue *or* that how we act is predetermined by processes that unfold behind our backs. The focus is on human agency and hence on purposive activity. The presumption is that people could do things differently, and that they might do so if circumstances change, new ideas emerge, or opinions altered. Things are not fixed, and people engage

with one another in the hope of changing things. This activity is political
by virtue of the fact that it brings our way of life into being, sustains it, extends
it, develops it, and of course challenges it. To what extent *ruling* is involved
is variable. Authorities emerge within this context, but few of them pretend
to sovereignty. The ones that have such sovereign pretensions are not
alone, and – as I shall argue – are never really effective in establishing their
sovereignty. So, questions about sovereign authority and about ruling more
generally actually occur within a broader field of political action, most of
which has little to do with ruling per se.

Why should we not conceive of this broader field as "social" or "cultural"?
The reason is simply that terms like "cultural" and "social" – as well as
"economic" and "environmental" – were meant to depoliticize the object of
analysis. If we adopt such terms, we imply that there is another domain, the
political, to be distinguished from the cultural or social, a domain that may
be understood as the domain of the state, or of ruling, or of contests for
power and authority, or of the perpetual "war" that is always with us. I would
like to reverse this move and suggest that the cultural, the social, the
economic, and the environmental are all domains of the political, ways
that we think and act politically, but that do not exhaust what we do.
I cannot name the remainder because the remainder is amorphous, yet to
be shaped into a determinate form by political action. The political, as that
which brings our way of life into being, sustains it, and challenges it,
cannot be defined in advance, contained, or delimited. In identifying it with
the urban, I make the dangerous move of suggesting that it has a form that
I can readily perceive. But, my suggestion is that in thinking the political
through the urban we can start to loosen the hold of old assumptions and
challenge the dominant political ontology. My argument in this chapter
is directed especially towards self-described urbanists, who have done much
to illuminate the city but generally have fought shy of challenging the
dominant ontology – and in the process have marginalized themselves as
political analysts.

Questioning the dominant ontology

So, what is the dominant ontology of the political?[1] Put simply, it is that
humans are faced with an ongoing security dilemma as a result of what
Kant called their unsocial sociability. In Hobbes's analysis, the only way out
of the dilemma is for people to transfer the sovereignty that naturally
belongs to them to an artificial being: namely, the state. The sovereign state
will then have the authority to lay down the law and enforce it effectively,
thanks to what Weber called a monopoly of legitimate violence. Even if we
allow (as Locke supposed) that people might be able to establish a rudimentary
form of civil society prior to the formation of the state, the order they could
create would be deeply flawed, because there would be no sure and effective
mechanism for enforcing the law equally. Moreover, there would be no

good procedures for ongoing amendment of the law to take account of new problems and accommodate new understandings. The activity of law-making or public policy-making is supposed be at the heart of politics proper, as liberal-democrats and civic-republicans have understood it. The modern state is thus the surrogate for the ancient republic or *polis*, and hence the home for activities that, since Aristotle, we have understood to be political. Other activities may be political by analogy, in that they are concerned with ruling. Nevertheless, rules that arise in other domains of life or within the subordinate territories of a state must ultimately be integrated with one another, if the society is to function properly. This is a normative necessity. As Hegel suggested, the state's high responsibility is to ground and complete the order of civil society. Thus, the high politics of any society is concerned with the form and disposition of the state. This high politics is concerned with questions of overall order, including the disposition of the state in relation to other states. It is of high seriousness, because the greatest questions about social justice, individual rights, economic organization, and communal identity have to be resolved at this level. Everything is at stake at this point, and only here can the ultimate questions of moral and legal order be resolved in a way that allows for effective enforcement. But for the state, there would be anarchy, and anarchy means the loss of all that we hold dear in a war of each against all.

To put things so starkly is to pass over many complications and equally many debates. My point is that a shared ontology of the political lies behind the debates, and actually enables them. The shared assumption is that there will always be an ultimate or sovereign political authority. If there is no ultimate authority in a particular place, there will be a contest or war, which will only end when such an authority is established. Moreover, the establishment of such an authority, which is inevitable anyway, is a necessary condition for creating and enforcing a legal order that protects the weak and enables the pursuit of other humane values. High politics is concerned with the creation, maintenance, or seizure of sovereign authority, as well as with the organization and disposition of such authority. Political theory is centred on the question of sovereign authority. What form should such authority take? How should such authority be used? By what means should such authority be established? How can such authority be legitimated? For a political theorist, questions of power are always secondary to questions of authority, because the problem to be addressed in politics is one of action, not explanation. The question is what we should do, but that raises the questions of who "we" are and by what authority "we" are to act. The ultimate political questions are not about who has the power, but rather who has the rightful authority or how rightful authority can be created. The presumption that sovereignty is both inevitable and necessary enables a theoretical discourse that presumes ethics as a source and lawful order as a product of a high politics that makes the best of the human condition.

In this context, urban politics is necessarily inferior to the high politics of the state. In geography, the urban is contrasted with the rural. That contrast is carried over into political analysis, to make a distinction between one part of the state's territory and the rest. The urban is conceptualized as a particular field, within which particular problems of government and forms of politics arise. The question is how that field relates to the whole. In the standard view, urban politics is highly localized (Judge *et al.* 1995, Beauregard and Body-Gendrot 1999). Local authorities of the state deal with a variety of issues related to the management of urban development, and so confront a variety of social and economic forces. Certain movements may arise, and authorities of a sort may be established from below. Normally, this is all a matter of low politics, however. It is low because it is beneath the vision of the high authorities of state (and the politicians and commentators who contest their policies). It is low also because it mainly involves authorities at the bottom of the state hierarchy. It is low, moreover, because it is confined to particular territories within the state, and fails to spread in a way that would make it of high concern. Of course, what emerges from urban politics may become a matter of high politics, but this is contingent on many things. There are other dimensions of politics in general, and at any particular time those dimensions may loom much larger in the high politics of the state. Urban politics is thus akin to the politics of the environment, human rights, or public health. It is not even a permanent part of the main agenda at the highest levels of the state. It goes in and out of fashion depending on the issues of the day, whereas questions about national security or the overall level of public spending or taxation (for instance) are always central to the high politics of the state. Not surprisingly, political theorists think that urban politics is a specialist concern, of no more interest than any number of other such concerns.

There is a further difficulty. Conventional political understandings entail distinctions between the state and society and one's own state and other states. One's own state is the locus for the politics in which one can engage, with one's own fellow citizens. The politics of other states is foreign. The immediate question is always how one's own state is to be constituted, and what policies it is to follow. Thus, the society, culture, or economy immediately at issue is the one bounded by one's own state and governed by its laws. It follows that one must know one's own society, culture, and economy, and understand how they are placed in the wider world. Urban analysis may be helpful in this regard, but it is in the service of understanding the country, nation, or society which is to be governed (and from which relevant political forces might be mobilized). In the conventional view, urban is a geographical category, and not necessarily the most important of its kind for analytical purposes. Regional differences may seem much more pertinent. On the other hand, non-geographical categories like economy, society, culture, ethnicity, and religion may be more helpful for analysing different dimensions of human life. Urban analysis benefits from its interdisciplinary character, but it is tied to the specificities of particular places and bound up with concerns associated with tasks of local authorities. In the conventional view, it can only be one element in an overall analysis of the society at issue. That society is constituted as such by sovereign authority. It is the task of political analysis to bring the findings of the various social sciences to bear in a way that clarifies what the high politics of the society is and could be. Urban analysis is valued mainly as a contribution to social scientific understanding.

The thrust of the modern social sciences has been towards a naturalistic understanding of the human condition, and hence towards explanations of politics and political choices in naturalistic terms. In this sense, the social sciences attempt to explain politics away. More importantly, perhaps, the social sciences are situated within a discursive field in which politics is an object like any other: something to be explained and understood, at whatever distance enables objectivity. The political actor as such is not and cannot be a social scientist, for the actor's task is to conjure new things into existence. This is not a matter of letting things happen that would inevitably happen, but of exercising and encouraging the human capacity to change course, be different, or make things anew. The presumption of politics is that humans have a creative capacity: they are free and they can be different from what they are now. This presumption is at odds with the presumption that enables the modern social sciences: namely, that the patterns of human life are susceptible to a naturalistic explanation. Of course, being human, we often shift between the one presumption and the other, not always conscious of what we are doing. One effect of our lack of consciousness is that we often slide from social scientific explanation to political prescription without noticing that our prescriptions are quite arbitrary in relation to our explanations. Another effect is that social scientists often adopt a very conventional political theory, without even noticing that they are doing so. In particular, they adopt what I have described here as the dominant ontology of the political, and offer their political prescriptions with that ontology in mind. This saves them from having to think very hard about the nature of politics (or the relation of the social sciences to it), for the prescriptions will at least seem relevant, even if they appear arbitrary. On the other hand, urbanists' prescriptions will always be regarded as specialist views that bear only indirectly on the great questions of state.

Things could be otherwise if we took urban analysis more seriously as the ground for a different political ontology. That ground is to be found in the practices of self-government that enable cities to exist. Jane Jacobs's (1961) analysis of these practices is particularly interesting, because she builds it up without much reference to the standard categories of the social sciences. Famously, she talks about the "eyes on the street" that provide for human security. These eyes do not belong to the authorities. They are the eyes of ordinary people going about their ordinary business. Jacobs noticed that in a dense urban neighbourhood used by many different people for different purposes at all times of the day, a sense of security developed because people were rarely isolated with potential wrong-doers. Little that was not noticed could happen on the streets; when bad things did happen, there was a good chance that someone would intervene. Because people felt more secure, they used the streets more, and this added to their security in a benign circle. Jacobs deals with many other aspects of neighbourhood order, but one of her constant themes is that a relatively benign order can arise out of the everyday practices of free people, provided that the state or some other dominant institution does not impose itself in a way that disables these practices. She applies a similar analysis to the processes whereby a productive economic order emerges. She suggests that the effort to squeeze productive city-based economies into the framework of nation-states is likely to be perverse. In some ways, her analysis is reminiscent of Hayek's account of catallactics: how a market-based order can work as a self-organizing system (Hayek 1960, 1973–79). Like Hayek, she recognizes that market order is insufficient of itself. Hayek finds the necessary support for the market in a gradually evolving system of common law. Jacobs looks to what she calls "guardianship" as a complementary "system of survival" (Jacobs 1992).

I will have more to say about Jacobs (and Hayek) in Chapter 3, but for the moment the details of her analysis are less interesting than the ground that she has adopted for that analysis. Considered one way, that ground is simply everyday life, in its urban form. She focuses her attention on a particular aspect of that everyday life: namely, self-government. There are two aspects to self-government. On the one hand, it is a matter of taking control of oneself and organizing oneself for one's own purposes. We might regard this as part of the exercise of freedom. On the other hand, self-government is also a matter of self-restraint: controlling oneself to avoid conflict with others or to confer benefits upon them. This is the aspect of self-government that addresses the problem of unsocial sociability. In so far as we exercise self-government, we contribute to social harmony. In so far as people succeed in governing themselves for their mutual benefit, they have less need to resort to sovereign authority to solve their problems. As Machiavelli noticed a long time ago, a people practised in self-government was not easily subordinated; moreover, such a people was likely to be more prosperous and virtuous (Machiavelli 1995). On his account and others, there is a benign circle to practices of self-government, so that what is done in this regard at one level or in one domain tends to reinforce similar practices at other levels and in other domains. Jacobs taps into a long and distinguished line of political analysis from the Greeks and the Renaissance humanists to the nineteenth-century exponents of local self-government and the twentieth-century advocates of various forms of participatory democracy. Again, the particularities of her view may be less important than the fact that it is grounded in an alternative political ontology.

How might we characterize that other ontology? The key idea is that the security dilemma can be resolved through practices of self-government, which build upon one another over time. Whether an attempt to assert sovereign authority facilitates or retards these practices is an empirical question. Politics is involved in the practices of self-government, as well as in the relations between those practices. It also is involved in the relationship between self-government and sovereign authority. It is not evident that we can resolve normative issues by referring back to an overarching ethic, because an ethic of this sort would itself be a type of sovereign authority. The value of such an authority is at issue. Nor is it evident that the rules and procedures for mutual accommodation can be formulated as law. Law even more than ethics is bound up with expectations about sovereign authority. Machiavelli, especially, is suggestive about the need for thinking the political on its own terms, rather than resorting to legalistic, religious, or ethical categories. He stresses that sovereignty is not a solution but a problem that is constantly posed and re-posed. Moreover, he sees that the space and time for political action is always shifting. For political actors, the field of engagement is always shifting, thanks in large measure to the fact that others in the field are always responding to their problems and opportunities. In a sense, the fact that we are all self-governing in some degree makes the field of the political especially mutable and unpredictable. So, we mistake the political when we fix it in a definite form in our imaginations. Politics shifts and changes because people are free to act non-normatively. Violence is always in and against politics, because it can be an effective means to various ends. So, politics must always deal with violence, even if violence does not give politics its form.

This alternative political ontology, which arises from seeing like a city, has never been as fully explained or explored as the dominant ontology. Nonetheless, it suggests a different way of thinking about the political, which can be rooted in an understanding of urbanism as a way of life. If urbanism is distinguished by ubiquitous and proliferating practices of self-government – as many analyses other than Jacobs's seem to imply – then it is (among other things) a particular way of being political (Isin 2002). The city is not just an effect of certain natural processes. It is also a political artefact. The same is true of the urban region or urbanism in general. We can think of both the city and the urban as political productions or performances that have effects we need to explore.

City, state, empire

At the end of the nineteenth century, states actually were not the norm: empires were.[2] Nor was liberal-democracy the norm. Nevertheless, the disciplinary structure of the academy – especially the American academy – anticipated the form of world order that would be produced by the political struggles of the twentieth century. In fact, there was always a close connection between this way of seeing the world for academic purposes and the policy-makers who brought such a world into being. Since 1945, the aim in the West has been to produce a world of sovereign states, organized on liberal-democratic principles and buttressed by nationalism, but integrated with one another through international institutions, a global economy, and a shared culture of human rights. In this context, it has seemed logical to study the economy, society, culture, and environment separately from the state, because the former clearly affect the latter and the state's organization is obviously crucial to world order. Political scientists have put themselves forward as the experts on how states are formed, how they become effective, and what they actually do. The presumption is that politics proper is focused on the state, because the state is supposedly the supreme authority. For those who are not grasping for political power themselves, the key concern is policy: What policies are being pursued and why? How can those policies be changed for the better? The state is at the centre of the policy question. Thus, it is the silent centre of the social sciences in so far as they strive to have "policy relevance". To be relevant, it seems that the social sciences must learn to see like a state: in particular, to produce knowledge that is intelligible to those who seek to govern the societies for which they are responsible. The state authorities must understand their own populations, come to grips with their own national societies, manage their national economies, secure their own territories, and negotiate with other states. As Scott (1998) and others (Dean 1999, Rose 1999) have argued, this means imposing uniform analytic categories – such as land ownership, inflation, unemployment, drug addiction, commutersheds, and urban development – and using them to create a governable field. As states become more effective, the populations they govern come to understand themselves to an ever-increasing extent within these state-given categories. Thus, the process is self-reinforcing: a certain reality is brought into being by insisting that it was always latent and expecting people to behave accordingly.

Such practices ought to be troubling to us all, but especially to urbanists, who carry with them the recognition that cities are not states and that the form of political order that arises from urbanism is different from the one implicit in the project of state-building. Unfortunately, urbanists – herded as they are into separate disciplines – have been too deferential to the project of state-building and hence to the concepts of policy and politics associated with it. One move has been to retreat from the state and focus on urban society, the urban economy, urban culture, or simply "geography" as ways of conceptualizing the field independently (Parker 2004). This just leaves the state where it was, however: in its familiar position as the locus of both politics and policy, properly conceived. A real change of vision involves a challenge to political science: an attempt to detach it from the state by changing into an urban discipline. This involves much more than promoting the study of politics in cities or local communities. It means challenging the idea that cities are subordinate to states. At stake is the very idea of sovereignty, the principle that has been invoked to justify the division of the world into autonomous states. Although this principle is a norm, it is often presented as a simple fact about the world. Urbanists are especially well positioned to challenge this fact or factoid, because they have learned, however haltingly and incompletely, to see like a city rather than a state. As I have already suggested, to see like a city is to envision the world in terms of what results from distinctively urban practices: ones that enable cities to be as they are. These practices are not well understood when we attach the labels of the state-centric social sciences to them. We can bring forward the ancient idea of politics – traditionally associated with the city – to help us understand our problem. If modern urbanism transcends the city – as Wirth (1938), McLuhan (1964), and Lefebvre (2003) all suggested, in their different ways – what sort of political order do we now inhabit? Clearly, the world is not just a *polis* writ large. Is it nonetheless a global *city* (Knox and Taylor 1995, Magnusson 2006)? If so, what does that mean? What are the practices that enable it to be like a city? How do the sovereignty-claims associated with the state system affect it? How do particular cities come to be within the larger order of the global city (that is, the world *as* a city)? How are they sustained as such, and when and how are they overwhelmed? What political practices overdetermine the particularities of cities and the generalities of the wider urban order? In answering such questions, I want to insist on the primacy of the political, because the more modern terms – social, economic, cultural – obscure fundamental questions of power and authority, as well as the political character of our everyday practices. We need to recognize that the world is always produced, sustained, and ultimately transformed by exercises of power and authority that may or may not involve ruling, but are nonetheless political.

Famously, Weber analysed the occidental city as an order that emerged at one remove from the rulers or sovereign authorities of the time (Weber 1978). According to him, this order was not an effect of ties of clan and sect: in fact such ties could inhibit the development of an autonomous urban order. Such an order could only develop out of everyday transactions and the needs associated with those transactions, which included freedom for the individuals involved and for the city they produced through their activities. Weber's interest was in explaining why occidental cities took a distinctive form. There is no doubt that he exaggerated the differences between occidental and other cities (Isin 2002). In any case, his explanatory emphasis led him to give less attention to the character of the city as a political production. Weber came at the end of a long tradition of civic republican speculation (Skinner 1998, Viroli 2002, Honohan 2002, Pocock 2003), in which analysts had tried to imagine the optimal form of the city as a political order. A number of his contemporaries and immediate predecessors had been fascinated by the form of political order that seemed to have developed in the medieval cities of Europe (Gierke 1900, Pirenne 1925, Mumford 1938,

Skinner and Stråth 2003). On many accounts, practices of local self-government were ubiquitous in early medieval Europe, only gradually to be suppressed by powerful lords and kings (Reynolds 1997). The cities managed to retain their freedoms longer than most, and (again, on many accounts) it was the free activity that burst forth from the cities that ultimately gave Europe its peculiar vitality and ushered in the modern era. If we read more recent figures like Fernand Braudel (1981–84) or Immanuel Wallerstein (1974–89) in light of these earlier accounts, we can see that this understanding of how the West became predominant has not disappeared. Analysts still point to the way that cities have developed at one remove from the sovereign authorities, and have flourished because of their relative freedom. Analysts have also noted how networks of cities have developed, and so made the urban global. There is a hazy, but intriguing sense that the urban global is itself a relatively autonomous political production, which cannot be well understood as a simple effect of states and empires.

There is a standard story about global order in political science, which focuses on the production of the modern state system through the understandings that brought an end to the Thirty Years War in Europe in 1648 (Holsti 1995, 2004; compare Teschke 2003, Sassen 2006). On this account, the principle of state sovereignty was accepted as an ordering norm at that time, and thereafter structured international relations. It is a norm that enables both war and peace, and gives structure to both. The dominant ontology of the political suggests that the only real alternative to a state system is empire. There can be a balance of power between contending sovereigns, or one sovereign can overwhelm the others. In any case, sub-sovereign political entities will inevitably be subordinated to sovereign authorities. Cities are among these sub-sovereign entities, and so they are doomed to subordination. On this account, the lost autonomy of medieval cities is irrecoverable. That same account raises questions about the fate of contemporary states, however. Will states themselves lose out to an advancing empire, either one dominated by a particular country like the United States or one organized through the United Nations and other multilateral institutions? The dominant ontology of the political suggests that the key issue for the future of the world is the locus of sovereignty. Will states retain their sovereignty? Should those of us who are *not* American be fighting for the sovereignty of our own states? Or, should we be working for the formation of a universal order that contains American power appropriately, and enables a kind of global-scale democracy? (Archibugi and Held 1995, Held 1995). A few moments thought reveals that these questions are misleading. Both American hegemony and multilateral cooperation are dependent on the continued existence of the state system. The state system is a key element in a complex order characterized by various forms of local autonomy, including national sovereignty (Sassen 1996, Hardt and Negri 2000, Shaw, M. 2000). Such sovereignty is far from absolute: ordinary states can enjoy it only in so far as they submit to rules that are not of their own making. Both sovereignty-endowed states and sub-sovereign municipalities must struggle for autonomy in a system that offers few guarantees to either.

If this is so, the choice we face is not between the existing state system and some form of empire. We are likely to have both, and much else besides. The alternative political ontology implicit in Jacobs's work (and urbanist thought more generally) leads us to take the city seriously as a form of political order that develops in and against states and empires, both locally and globally. Since individual cities rarely make a claim to sovereignty, they have to be understood through the ubiquitous and proliferating practices of government and self-government that give them political presence. These same practices link cities to one another, through the mode of life that Wirth called "urbanism" (Wirth 1964). To the extent that the sovereign state or universal empire is present in the cities concerned, it tends to be colonized by these practices of self-government. The paradigmatic political form of the self-governing city is not the city-state, but the municipality: an autonomous, self-governing, but non-sovereign political entity. Although the dominant ontology of the political suggests that such entities are doomed to subordination, the alternative ontology suggests that there is no necessity to this doom and that in any case global order will be more like the order of the city than anything else. Practices of self-government may eat away at sovereignty, and create space for a politics that makes the exercise of sovereign authority more difficult and less necessary. As the analysis in the last chapter suggested, the authority necessary to a good politics is likely to take different forms and to be networked in complicated ways. Ostensible sovereigns may be there, but their presence or absence is not the be-all or end-all of benign political order. Practices of self-government, rooted in every-day life, are most crucial, and it is through urban analysis that we can see most clearly what those practices are or could be.

The current political analysts who make most of the possibilities of self-government are the contemporary civic republicans (Pettit 1997, Honohan 2002). Unfortunately, their work is abstracted from urban analysis. Often, they invoke the ancient Greek conception of cosmopolis – literally, world-city or global city – to make sense of the global order they would like to bring into being (Archibugi and Held 1995, Zolo 1997, Beck 1999). The city-ness or urbanity of this order is not made apparent, however; nor is there any use of urban analysis to make sense of the emergent or desired cosmopolis.[3] Instead, the appeal is to two concepts: global civil society, imagined as a transnational form of nationally bounded civil society (Keane 2003, Kaldor 2003); and governance, conceived as modes of government that involve civil society actors (Commission on Global Governance 1995, Hewson and Sinclair 1999, Pierre 2000, Sinclair 2004). In effect, categories derived from the dominant political ontology are stretched to cover a situation in which actors link up regionally and globally across state boundaries. The utopianism of such visions is covered by a patina of realism, thanks to the way that the state is invoked to provide anchoring for governance and the familiar practices of civil society are extended to cover the world. There are appealing features to these analyses, but one is struck by the fact that cities appear, if at all, as beneficiaries of a devolutionary strategy, based upon European principles of subsidiarity (Nicolaidis and Howse 2001). No word could better describe the assumption that cities or urban regions are necessarily subsidiary and hence inferior to larger political entities. These analyses simply fail to take seriously the idea implicit in cosmopolis: namely, that the world could become (or perhaps already is) a single city or network of cities that generate political order primarily through the practices of self-government revealed by urban analysis.

Of course, there is a literature within urban analysis, which I discussed in a different way in Chapter 1, that posits the global city (in the sense of an individual city that is globally oriented) as a key node in the organization of global power (Knox and Taylor 1995, Scott, A. 2001, Sassen 2002). This literature is generally limited in its ambitions, however. It tends to be sociological, geographic, or economic in approach, and hence to push to the margins the question of how the city works as a political production. There is much interest in mapping the hierarchy of cities, understanding how cities mediate global flows, and establishing whether (and how) dense cities may be necessary to the ongoing development of the global economy. All this is interesting, but there is little in it that would persuade anyone that urban analysis is essential to understanding the political organization of the world. State-centric accounts of the global political order are extremely robust, and they will not be much disturbed by information about the importance of Wall Street or the City of London. Such accounts are rooted in an ontology that explains that cities are inevitably subordinate politically if they lack sovereignty, and that no amount of economic or cultural clout can possibly make up for that lack. Thus, the analysis of so-called global cities tends to be folded into an analysis of economy, culture, or society. State-centric or sovereignty-centred political theory has already taken the latter analysis into account. Whatever form economy, culture, or society as such might take, the problem of sovereignty remains, and that (according to the conventional view) is the problem that must be analysed to make a political theory of the global work. In so far as cities are just subordinate political entities, they seem largely irrelevant to analyses grounded in the conventional ontology of the political. As a result, theories about global cities and global city networks are simply noted and set aside.

More interesting in a way are new theories about the "ecology of fear" (Davis 2000). They allow us to look at the security dilemma at the heart of conventional political theory in a different way. Jacobs was acutely conscious of the way that security concerns shaped urban life. She tried to understand how people were able to achieve security through their everyday activities. I have characterized the relevant practices in terms of self-government. We might also say that these are practices that build upon freedom and diversity to produce the mutual understandings that enable people to live in security despite their differences. The hopefulness of Jacobs's vision is important, because it stands opposed to the panic that leads to walls, gates, surveillance cameras, identity checks, bag and body searches, police raids, detentions, demolitions, beatings, and occasional torture. The conventional ontology of the political leads us to think in terms of a sharp distinction between the land (and people) under sovereign authority and the savage world beyond. It works with the panic to produce a distinction between us, the civilized and law-abiding people, and them, the ones who cannot be trusted. The presumption is that the uncivilized are like dangerous animals who have no rights as such. Our sovereign is authorized to use any means necessary to protect us. It is important to recognize that the panic that produces gated communities in the United States or South Africa is of the same character as the panic that produces the fences along America's southern border or the patrols that try to keep illegal migrants out of Italy or Spain. The various security practices of the current era – up to and including punitive military expeditions against rogue states, guerrilla strongholds, and terrorist training camps – are of a piece with one another. They flow from related fears, and are routinely justified in terms of a Hobbesian vision of reality. The ontology invoked is the one that enables conventional political theory and marginalizes urban analysis as an approach to political understanding.

Debates among urban analysts following the destruction of the World Trade Center (Sorkin and Zukin 2002, Clarke *et al.* 2002, Swanstrom 2002, Molotch 2003, Savitch 2003, 2008) are indicative in at least three respects. First, there is a widespread recognition that one cannot do urban analysis in abstraction from the security dilemma, however conceived. The supposed terrorist threat has led to an intensification of security practices, which have a profound effect on everyday urban life everywhere. It is hard to deny that some sort of problem exists, and that various things have to be done about it. In any case, things are happening, and urban analysis has to explain those things and help us to understand how we might do things differently. Unfortunately, there is a second feature of the debates that undermines one's confidence about possible analytic progress. The high politics of international security is still routinely separated from the low politics of urban planning and day-to-day policing. This enables urbanists to maintain their privileged position as analysts of the low politics of cities, but at the expense of shutting themselves off from serious engagement with high political issues. A false distinction is maintained, and urbanists fight shy of developing a global analysis that would put the activities of George W. Bush as President of the United States, Osama bin Laden as leader/founder of Al Qaeda, and Rudi Giuliani as Mayor of New York City within the same analytical framework. Urbanists will not be taken seriously until such an analysis is properly elaborated. The third feature of the debates is also troubling, for a different reason. The common assumption is that a distinction can be made between them (the terrorists and their supporters) and us (good law-abiding folk, despite all our other differences). This distinction is at the heart of the conventional ontology of the political: we are OK, but we need the sovereign to restrain *them*. In the common version of this, we the civilized are identified with the West or (in another version of the same thing) America and its close allies. The arrogance and self-satisfaction of the West are thus subsumed in an analysis that is supposed to deal with the security dilemmas that have been generated by that same arrogance and self-satisfaction. This creates problems, to say the least.

Much of the most influential urban analysis focuses on American cities. There is a tendency inside and outside the United States to take the American city as a harbinger of the world's future, and indeed to pick out one particular city as paradigmatic. In the early years of the twentieth century, the Chicago school sociologists focused attention on Chicago as the paradigm for the future. More recently, Los Angeles has received such attention: hence, we have the Los Angeles school of urban analysis (Scott and Soja 1996, Beauregard and Body-Gendrot 1999). The implicit assumption is that we can read backward and outward from these cities and come to see the urban world as it is likely to be in the foreseeable future. This form of analysis fits with the popular assumption that America is the world's most advanced country, and hence the path-breaker to the future. One thinks of Alexis de Tocqueville's (1945) analysis of *Democracy in America* as a respectably academic version of this idea. One also thinks of the long tradition dating back to the seventeenth-century Puritan settlements in New England, in which the new world is presented as a beacon to the old, and America is conceived as the promised land or the city on the hill (Bercovitch 1980). The eschatology of this tradition is such that America has to be conceived as a blessed land apart, which may (although this is not certain) have the capacity to redeem the world. Traces of this eschatology appear in almost all American writing, both popular and academic, regardless of the writer's political positioning. One can also see how people outside the United States respond to this eschatology, sometimes embracing it themselves, sometimes responding angrily to it, and sometimes developing their own alternatives to it. The idea of a united Europe as an alternative to America is one example; ideas of the Middle Kingdom, Hindutva, or the Islamic caliphate are others. If urbanists are to develop good political analyses, they will have to become much more conscious and self-critical about the eschatological assumptions that they bring to bear in their work. It would be good to get away from the assumption that there is one particular country or civilization that represents the future. If we did so, it would be easier to see that there are no paradigmatic cities, and that the cities that shock us are not necessarily the ones that reveal our future.

That said, there are features of American urbanism that deserve close attention. Local authorities in many countries operate under tight state control. The United States is an extremely strong, prosperous, and dynamic country. To what extent are its virtues a consequence of the relative freedom of its local authorities? What can we learn from its experiences about the advantages and disadvantages of various regimes of local freedom? These questions are especially pertinent in relation to a European and European-influenced literature that makes the assumption that local authorities have to be controlled, disciplined, and (as necessary) reorganized to serve the wider purposes of the state. In contrast to the standard European view, American public choice theorists have celebrated the fragmentation of public authority at the local level as a beneficial effect of free enterprise (Bish and Ostrom 1973, Ostrom *et al.* 1988). As they see it, the state can and should be colonized by enterprise culture. This means opening up the possibilities for creating new local authorities to serve the purposes of particular communities or to provide for particular public goods. A public economy in which there are many different enterprises of different kinds, all competing for public favour, is (on this view) more likely to be responsive to public needs and desires. Since coercive authorities are likely to be corrupt, oppressive, and inefficient, it is important that they be subject to competitive pressures: in particular, people should be able to escape the local jurisdiction they inhabit and put themselves under the control of authorities more favourable to their own needs and interests. Whenever possible, it is said, public goods should be provided by private, for-profit enterprises, which operate under the normal competitive pressures of the market. Non-profit enterprises are the next best providers, especially if they have to raise their money by public subscription. Public authorities with coercive powers are the worst, although they are certainly necessary for some purposes. They should be kept small, and put into a position in which they have to compete for favour. On this theory, what appears like a chaotic system of local self-government is actually more dynamic, responsive, and efficient than its counterpart in more statist regimes. We may well doubt this, but it is not an argument that can simply be set aside without examination, especially since it has had such influence on neo-liberal thinking more generally.

The standard objection to the American-style public choice model is that it favours the rich and the powerful and enables business (and wealthy people generally) to escape just and necessary taxation and regulation. The criticism – well developed within the United States itself[4] – is apt as far as it goes, but it tends to neglect the rather obvious fact that states themselves are akin to gated communities which dump environmental problems outside their bounds and exclude the poorest people in the world from the benefits that they offer. One cannot think seriously about the boundary question, or about the appropriate relationships between different sorts of public authority, unless one opens the black box called the state and puts it at issue along with the rest. If there is an advantage in beginning from the American experience – as Jacobs did – it is that one is immediately confronted with a confusing array of authorities with various mandates and differing missions. Most of these authorities are regarded as emanations of a free people, who organize themselves and govern themselves in and through these bodies.

Distinctions between state and civil society are not very meaningful in this context. Words like public and private are wielded as ideological weapons, but shed little light on what is going on. To do a good analysis, we have to be prepared to invent new categories, and to bracket the ones implicit in the dominant ontology of the political. We need to ask ourselves what forms the practices of self-government take in an urban context. If we do, we will begin to see that some of these practices extend far beyond the immediate local community. They extend through urban networks. In fact, they produce those networks, and so enable a globalizing urbanism. If we then drop our analytical brackets, we will be able to pose the question of how the state relates to these ubiquitous and proliferating practices of self-government and to the globalizing urbanism that flows from these practices.

The idea that urbanism transcends particular states is especially important, because it enables us to see that states are entities within the urban global. The conventional ontology of the political puts cities in a position subordinate to states. A focus on urbanism enables us to invert that hierarchy. The inversion is unsustainable, however, if we remain at the level of social, economic, cultural, or geographic analysis. The political has trumps, because it is the domain for action on matters of the highest concern. The conventional ontology of the political is not affected by analyses that show that the world has become one socially, economically, or otherwise. Indeed, as the events of 9/11 illustrated, the very oneness of the world is at the heart of the case for having states: the bad guys can get in, and we need powerful states to keep them out. We can think differently about our political possibilities only if we put the conventional ontology at issue. That means taking urbanism more seriously as a political phenomenon, and thinking about it as a global phenomenon. It also means taking the municipality more seriously as a political venue.

Urbanism as a political production

Efforts to create, maintain, or use sovereign authority occur within a wider field of practices, many of which can be conceived as efforts at self-government. A bid for sovereignty takes the quest for autonomy to its logical extreme. There may be a number of sovereignty-aspirants within the same field. Mutual recognition is one way of stabilizing relations among them. It is also a way of effecting the subordination of lesser authorities, who are shut out by a lack of recognition. On the other hand, "sovereignty-free" authorities (business corporations, religious bodies, charities, political movements) may be able to create their own spaces, in which they can operate with relative freedom (Rosenau 1990). One of the strategies for securing sovereignty is to license liberty (as Hobbes certainly knew). Thus, we have the symbiosis of state and civil society in modern theories of political order. By freeing society, culture, economy, and religion, one is supposed to strengthen the state. Everyone will recognize that the state is still necessary to secure the freedoms that have been provided, and so the state's ultimate authority will be more secure. The more secure the state is, the more freedom it can allow (just as Hobbes told us, more than three hundred and fifty years ago). Nikolas Rose (1999), Mitchell Dean (1999), and others have offered acute analyses of the way the modern state governs through people's freedom, working at a distance to encourage people to take responsibility for themselves and others and to govern themselves accordingly. On this view, the current regime in the most prosperous Western countries is best understood in terms of an advanced liberalism, which builds on the key liberal idea that people are best governed when they govern themselves. The state's role is not to govern directly, but to orchestrate practices of self-government in a way that secures a certain order.

When we consider self-government in this way, we can see that it does not occur in a vacuum. People aspire to self-government for their own reasons, but that aspiration may be encouraged by outsiders who wish to relieve themselves of responsibilities or gain indirect control through the rules and conditions they establish. Even sovereign authority has a limiting context: of other sovereignties, the society or territory to be ruled, and the non-sovereign authorities that proliferate within it and transect it from without. Practices of self-government are generally more limited in aspiration, and so they are likely to be hedged, penetrated, colonized, displaced, or governed in a variety of ways. Moreover, the individual or collective self empowered by such practices is not necessarily (or even usually) the idealized self of liberal democratic theory. Many sorts of peoples, communities, tribes, clans, sects, gangs, corporations, associations, religions, and movements seek to become self-governing (and sometimes to exercise sovereignty over others). Neither the goodness nor the democratic purity of any of these entities can be guaranteed in advance. What we have, rather, is a complex field in which various individuals and collectivities claim the right to govern themselves and/or others. The exercise of sovereignty is only one way of influencing the field as a whole, and not necessarily the most effective. So, the political problems that we confront are much more complicated than the ones that the "just so" stories of conventional political theory put before us. Very little is solved by creating states or empires, and efforts to articulate the just form of the state or empire are largely a diversion from the hard work of identifying and evaluating political options.

The municipality is the paradigmatic form of civic political organization. If it is conceived simply as the local apparatus of the state, then it is has limited political significance. On the other hand, the municipality may be conceived as a political organization apart from the state: one that operates in a different register, politically. This difference may be expressed in the way groups and parties that compete for control over the municipality detach themselves from the party apparatuses that contest for state power. It may also be expressed in constitutional law, such as when a distinction is made between local administrative districts of the state (counties, prefectures) and organizations for local self-government (municipalities, communes). Most important is the attitude of local electors and leaders. If they think that the municipality is apart from the state or the government, they are likely to make it into a political organization of a qualitatively different type. Of course, this qualitatively different political organization is not necessarily of the type we would like. Municipalities have often been dominated by burgher elites who seek to pool resources for mutual advancement. The interests of the poor get short shrift, and public activities are judged in terms of their contribution to the city's economic advance. When more broadly based political leadership has emerged, it has often been unimaginative. States with wider jurisdiction, greater resources, and the patina of sovereignty have been more attractive to reformers who want to regulate the economy for the public benefit and organize high quality public services for everyone. Thus, there has been particular pressure from the left to integrate municipalities into states. On the other hand, states themselves are usually dominated by the modern equivalent of the old burgher elites, and so there is similar resistance within the state to public activities that make little or no economic contribution. So, state power is commonly deployed to keep municipalities from undertaking initiatives that would interfere with state objectives or incite the desire for public activities of a different sort (Magnusson 1996).

In principle, the municipality offers people the opportunity to do something different in the public sphere. Unfortunately, municipalities have been victims of statist propaganda for a very long time, and so it is often difficult for people to see what they might do with the institutions of local self-government that have been permitted to them. Urban analysts have played a large part in denigrating municipalities and encouraging statist alternatives. On the left, there is particular fear of sliding toward an American system in which local authority seems to be parcelled out among various business communities and inward-looking residential suburbs (Magnusson 2005b). If those suburbs are the models for local self-government, they are not very appealing. The abandonment of the municipality as a political venue may be understandable in this context, but it is no less unfortunate for that. There is a self-fulfilling prophecy at work, one that discourages people from testing the limits of the municipality as a venue for creative action.

If we are looking for political creativity, we are liable to focus instead on social movements that organize and spread in accordance with a logic that takes limited account of institutions of local government. Such movements define their own action space. What we see in the way of local political ferment is likely to be movement-related. A question then arises about the way municipalities mediate different movements. Are municipalities venues in which movement activities are concerted and relayed, or do municipalities stifle movement activity? Obviously, municipalities may be disposed in either way, but if the movements themselves despise municipalities as venues for action there is little chance that the relay effect will occur. In the post-socialist political imaginary, there is often an emphasis on the limited character of any particular movement. No one movement can speak for all or deal with all the concerns that people might have. The multiplicity of movements is recognized as a source of strength, not weakness. The movements can complement one another, so long as they show mutual respect. In so far as movements act in accordance with this ethic, they refrain from sovereignty claims in relation to one another. In a way, municipalities are similar, in that they mark out a domain for self-government, but refrain from asserting sovereignty. Municipal action does not preclude action by the state, or by so-called civil society organizations or movements. Whereas parties that seek state power tend to mimic the sovereignty claims of states, movements are often self-limiting in ways that resonate with municipal practice. To see the political potential of municipalities and movements (and thus to recognize the possible symbiosis between them) we have to open ourselves up to an ontology that privileges self-government rather than sovereignty as the definitive political practice.

Nevertheless, to understand the city as a political production is not merely a matter of thinking about the way it works as a municipality. Municipalities do not contain the cities they purport to represent. There is always an ensemble of relatively autonomous practices at work in producing the city as we see and experience it (Amin and Thrift 2002). Some of these practices are conceived as political, others not. The labelling may be important, but it obscures as much as it reveals. We need to take seriously the idea that everything is political in some respects and in some degree. That means exploring how the various practices work as political practices, whether or not there is an obviously political intent and whether or not there is contact with organizations that we have previously assigned to the domains of politics and government. A business that builds a great office tower is acting politically, whether or not it is dealing with municipal or state authorities. The same is true of a rock musician who transfixes his or her audience. What counts as politically important is an open question. If we ask how the city comes to be and what governs its ongoing changes, and consider those questions political, then we arrive at a way of thinking that puts sovereignty issues in their place and opens us up to the fact that cities emerge mainly from ubiquitous and proliferating practices of self-government. Considered from this vantage point, all of those practices are political.

The connectedness of cities is not an incidental outcome of their dynamism. On the contrary, cities have become what they are through the spread of urbanism as a way of life. We can certainly approach an understanding of globalization through a study of inter-state rivalries and contesting imperialisms. We can also focus on the way that capitalist enterprises have both adapted to and created the opportunity to operate globally. Such approaches lead us to a certain point, but they do not break free from the conventional ontology of the political. In so far as we take cities seriously as political productions, trace the networks established between them, locate them in relation to powerful social movements, and ask how they are served by the municipality as their outward political form, we can sketch a picture that reveals things that have hitherto been hidden to us. Only urban analysts can do that. What can we learn from our predecessors in this respect?

3 Politics of urbanism as a way of life

In the 1980s, it became fashionable to approach the urban experience through the work of two figures: Walter Benjamin, the early twentieth-century German-Jewish critic, and Charles-Pierre Baudelaire, the mid-nineteenth-century French poet. Baudelaire is supposed to have captured the complexity and ambiguity of modern urban life, and his milieu, "Paris, Capital of the Nineteenth Century", provided the frame for Benjamin's further explorations of the same subject (Berman 1982, Harvey 1989, 2003, Jameson 1991). Fashions change, however. For much of the twentieth century, Max Weber and Louis Wirth were the touchstone figures. Weber's analysis of the city first appeared in German shortly after the First World War, although the book was not translated into English until 1958 (Weber 1958). German work had a decisive influence on American sociologists of the "Chicago school" who developed the discipline of human ecology, long the dominant approach to the study of cities. At the heart of early-to-mid-twentieth-century urban sociology – a discipline that had its intellectual home in Chicago – was the belief that cities of the industrial era were qualitatively different from any that humans had known before. In part this was a matter of scale and complexity, but as an orthodox Marxist might have noted there is a point at which quantitative change becomes qualitative. What had previously been agrarian societies were now urban, and so the social, cultural, economic, and political character of those societies was bound to be different. The sociologists who observed this process were worried by it. Would there be sufficient social cohesion under the new conditions? What would happen to the old values? What sort of political leadership would characterize the new urban society? What form of rule would there be? Answers differed but Louis Wirth, the most acute of the Chicago school sociologists, captured one aspect of the emerging consensus in his immensely influential 1938 article on "Urbanism as a Way of Life" (Wirth 1964). His main point was simply that urbanism is a different form of human life, which has to be understood on its own terms and not read off accounts of capitalism, industrialism, or modernity. That view was hugely influential among urban sociologists, especially in the United States. In a way, it carries through to the work of the later analysts of urban culture, even though they may have taken their lead from Benjamin and Baudelaire rather than Wirth and Weber.

There was a strong reaction against American urban sociology in the 1970s, spurred by claims that the politics of urban development was being obscured. In 1973, the year many associate with the crises that doomed the Keynesian welfare state and inaugurated the neo-liberal era, two influential books appeared: David Harvey's *Social Justice and the City* and Manuel Castells's *La question urbaine* (translated into English as Castells 1977). Harvey and Castells were inspired by leading Marxist thinkers in France: Henri Lefebvre (1991, 2003, 2008) in Harvey's case and Louis Althusser (1969) in Castells's. They offered what they thought was a re-politicized account of urban development and its associated struggles, and in the process they updated, refined, and extended the analysis that Marx, Engels, and their immediate successors had offered. What followed were many efforts to build on what Harvey and Castells had done, or to offer analyses that differed on important points, but were inspired by the same principles (*e.g.* Saunders 1986, Logan and Molotch 1987, Smith, N. 1991). At stake was the political economy of cities. Most analysts assumed that the drive toward capital accumulation was primary – and hence that capitalists set the agenda for urban development – but that the state could and did intervene in the process, often at the instance of the capitalists and their collaborators, but sometimes also in response to popular pressures. Thus, the aim of urban political analysis was to understand the city in terms of struggles over development, struggles that might be mediated by the state, but that were always over-determined by the requirements of capital and people's capacities for resistance to it. Harvey Molotch's (1976) characterization of the American city as a "growth machine" captured the general spirit, and suggested a way of thinking about cities that highlighted their importance to capitalist development – something that David Harvey (1982, 1985) analysed at length – and the challenge they posed to what Castells (1977, 1983) called "collective consumption". Could the "use value" of cities be preserved in face of the demand for increasing "exchange value", or were cities doomed to be run over as capital reconfigured itself (and the "spatial fixes" associated with each stage of its development)? There was certainly much evidence for the latter, then as now.

Although I am tempted to linger with such analyses, which have much to offer, I will not do so here because I think that something important has been lost in the effort to explain the urban in Marxist or quasi-Marxist terms. When one begins with Marx or some notion of a struggle between the dominant and the dominated, a binary conception of politics follows like night from day. On the one side are the rulers – the ruling class or hegemonic bloc or capitalist state or system of states – and on the other side are the ruled, the people, or "the multitude" (Hardt and Negri 2000, 2004). To my mind, that means that the conventional ontology of the political has been reinstated. Inevitably, cities are marginalized as objects and locales for action, and we end up seeing like a state. Detailed analysis of the political economy of cities reveals that the people are fragmented, struggles within and between communities are over many different things, various regimes emerge to mediate those struggles while maintaining capital-friendliness, and the higher authorities impose their own rules and agendas as they themselves struggle with wider changes in the economy, culture, society, and politics. Many radical critics have turned to cultural analysis because it seems to offer a way of revealing aspects of politics that might be concealed by a strict focus on political economy (*e.g.* Zukin 1991, 1995, 2010). We can see that cultural turn in Harvey's and Castells's later work (*e.g.* Castells 1983, Harvey 1989). A certain despair arises when the analyst recognizes that the people are rarely as united or as progressive as they ought to be and that things keep falling back into the old patterns, which enable the rulers to go on ruling more or less as they have done before. The analyst's despair may be offset by arbitrary calls to action – calls that echo the revolutionary aspirations of the past – but just as often the radical critic becomes a *flâneur*: drawing attention to the bizarre patterns of urban life, reminding us of our hypocrisies and misconceptions, and gesturing – sometimes with distaste and at other times with approval – at the politics of this or that. Neither the *flâneur* nor the armchair revolutionary actually engages seriously with urban politics, because they are both caught up in the idea that serious politics is a matter of challenging our rulers. Since that challenge never seems to emerge – or at least not with the strength or in the form wanted – serious politics always seems to be just out of reach. What can one offer other than an ironic comment or a curt summons to action? And, where can that lead but to a renewed sense of futility?

To my mind, the route that the Chicago school analysts took is actually more promising, because it begins from the city and takes urbanism seriously as a distinctive form of life. It does not treat urbanism as a merely cultural phenomenon or attempt to explain it away in terms of the requirements of capitalism. The flaw, widely noticed, is that it tends to naturalize urban development, rather than treat it as a political production. My aim here is to try to politicize the analysis without resorting to a binary, statist ontology of the political.[1] I take a particular cut through the work at issue, one that begins with Weber's effort to understand the city as a form of political order distinct from the state, passes through Chicago school analyses of urbanism as a way of life, makes a detour through Hayek's conception of a self-organizing society, and then focuses on ideas about street-level government and self-government, which I find in the early work of Jane Jacobs and Richard Sennett.[2] My purpose is to thread some ideas together, ideas that might enable us to see like a city without depoliticizing it or resorting to a misleading binary. Let me begin with Weber, because he was the one usually posed in twentieth-century sociology as the person who could reground our thinking in a way that eschewed Marx's utopianism (Marx 1977) in favour of a hard-headed realism (Weber 2004). On most accounts, Weber points toward the modern state as the inevitable locus of modern politics, but there is another strand in Weber's analysis that points toward the city.

Can we draw a different ontology of the political from Weber himself? Is such an ontology implicit in the work of the Chicago school sociologists? Is it echoed in the work of economists like Hayek, or in analyses of public choice? Is it grounded in the practices that Jacobs and Sennett observed? I can offer no definitive answers to these questions here, but I want to suggest that there is a way of reading this material that points toward a different ontology of the political – and that does not have the political implications that Hayek and his avatars believe.

The modern state and the Occidental city

Max Weber is famous for many things, not least his definitions:

> A "ruling organization" will be called "political" in so far as its existence and order is continuously safeguarded within a given *territorial* area by the threat and application of physical force on the part of the administrative staff. A compulsory political organization with continuous operations (*politischer Anstaltsbetrieb*) will be called a "state" in so far as administrative staff successfully upholds the claim to the *monopoly* of the *legitimate* use of physical force in the enforcement of its order. Social action, especially organized action, will be spoken of as "politically oriented" if it aims at exerting influence on the government of a political organization; especially at the appropriation, expropriation, redistribution or allocation of powers of government.
>
> (Weber 1978, vol. 1, 54)

> Since the concept of the state has only in modern times reached its full development, it is best to define it in terms appropriate to the modern type of state, but at the same time in terms which abstract from the values of the present day, since these are particularly subject to change. The primary formal characteristics of the modern state are as follows: It possesses an administrative and legal order subject to change by legislation, to which the organized activities of the administrative staff, which are also controlled by regulations, are oriented. This system of order claims binding authority, not only over the members of the state, the citizens, most of whom have obtained membership by birth, but also to a very large extent over all action taking place in the area of its jurisdiction. It is thus a compulsory association with a territorial basis. Furthermore, today, the use of force is regarded as legitimate only in so far as it is either permitted by the state or prescribed by it. . . . The claim of the modern state to monopolize the use of force is as essential to it as its character of compulsory jurisdiction and of continuous operation.
>
> (Weber 1978, vol. 1, 56)

Do these definitions suggest that the state must be on a particular scale? Yes and no. On Weber's view, a state cannot exist unless it "*successfully* upholds

the claim to the monopoly of the legitimate use of physical force in the enforcement of its order". Moreover, a *modern* state "claims binding authority . . .
over all action taking place in the area of its jurisdiction". Presumably the
latter claim must also be successful if a state is to exist in its complete
modern form.

In our own day, there has been much talk about "failed states" in Africa
and some other parts of the world, such as Afghanistan or Colombia. This
failure consists in the state's inability to maintain a monopoly of the *effective* use of physical force. Whether the loss of efficacy precedes or follows
the loss of legitimacy is less important than the fact that there are competing forces within a particular area, with varying degrees of authority,
making claims upon people that cannot be met without angering one
competitor or another. It is difficult for civilians to know what to do in these
circumstances. Even if there is a clearly superior power in a particular area,
that power may be more interested in injuring, despoiling, expropriating, or
even exterminating the inhabitants than in ruling them indefinitely. There
may be no rationality to the violence of the conquerors, especially when
the soldiers are young boys high on drugs. To talk of situations such as
these in terms of "failure" is to put things mildly. On the other hand, it is
clear that even in the better governed parts of the world states are "failing"
in some degree. If, as Weber says, a state must *uphold successfully* "the *monopoly*
of the *legitimate* use of physical force in the enforcement of its order", if
it is to *be* a state in the proper sense, which of the current states could
actually meet that requirement? There certainly are districts of every modern
city in which the writ of the state is strongly contested, and where local
"authorities" – street gangs, criminal syndicates, local elders, charismatic figures
within the ethnic community, religious leaders, or even underground armies
like ETA – have more capacity to enforce their will than the state itself.
We do not have to go to Baghdad or Kabul to see that.

States exist within a wider order of great complexity. Although each state
is nominally sovereign, some are obviously more sovereign than others. Even
the European Union is militarily dependent on the USA (as is the United
Nations, if it wishes to mobilize effective military force in its own name).
Not even the USA can sustain a monopoly of legitimate violence just when
and where it pleases, however. Sovereignty in the sense of a real capacity
to control events is even more elusive. The financial crisis of 2008 again
demonstrated how difficult it is for states to deal effectively with the economy.
So-called globalization is only one aspect of the problem, as Soviet planners
discovered. There also are other orders of culture, religion, and social identity that no state can effectively control. Science and technology have their
own momentum. Information moves through various unregulated channels.
People try to go where they think that there will be more opportunities or
more security, and it is difficult to stop them, as both the European Union
and the United States have been finding. Social and cultural movements like
feminism, environmentalism, or fundamentalist religion develop in accordance

with their own logic and spread despite the wishes of the authorities. Things keep changing in ways that vex the powers that be. The result is that efforts to exercise sovereignty in the full Weberian sense can be both farcical and tragic, like the Western military operations in Afghanistan or the European and American efforts to forestall migration across the Mediterranean and the Rio Grande.

Weber was well aware of the limits of sovereignty. Much of his analysis is designed to show that things develop in accordance with diverse initiatives, demands, ambitions, conflicts, and struggles. He attempted to classify human efforts and struggles, to make clear what was at stake in various instances, and to show why particular outcomes had occurred. He wanted to get away from simplistic accounts that obscured the complexity of social causation and the multiplicity of possible outcomes from seemingly similar combinations of factors. He was particularly suspicious of one-dimensional or teleological explanations. Unfortunately, he has often been interpreted as a one-dimensional, teleological thinker, since he was so much obsessed with understanding the origins of modernity, and he seemed to identify modernity with rationalization. It is a short, but unfortunate step to thinking that Weber offered us an apotheosis of the modern state and hence a justification for focusing our politics on the state. There is much in Weber's work – and his own political commentary – that points us in that direction, but we should not lose sight of the complexity that Weber tried so hard to understand. It should be obvious now that politics has a much wider ambit than Weber's formal definition implies and that it has other important foci besides the state itself. The territorialities of politics are diverse, and they do not conform in any simple way to the boundaries of states. Conflicts between environmentalists and waste-producers develop locally, regionally, and globally in a bewilderingly complex pattern, and the authorities that attempt to mediate these conflicts are themselves quite diverse. The same is true of struggles over the supply of drugs, the use of automobiles, the display and practice of sexuality, the rights of workers on the job, claims to intellectual property, and a host of other issues. To be "politically oriented" is to be confronted with many different issues, each with its own pattern and field of struggle. The state is always of some importance in relation to these issues, but it is rarely the case that the crucial battle will be fought on the terrain of the state itself. The winner has usually been determined by the time the state is mobilized for action. The relevant territories for politics are different from the ones determined by the boundaries for states.

Weber's account illustrates this by putting efforts to create and maintain states in the context of wider struggles to gain economic advantage, social prestige, or political power. He also highlights the importance of religious ideas and technical innovations. For him, there was no single object of struggle, no terrain of engagement that remained fixed for all time, and no agency that offered a guarantee for human progress. Weber frames his analysis – always implicitly, sometimes explicitly – in terms of a familiar contrast between the agonistic freedom of the West and the slavish dependency of the East. Thus, in his great unfinished account of "economy and society" over the ages, he stresses the difference in character between Occidental cities and their Oriental or Asian counterparts. He focuses on two periods in this context: the era of the ancient *polis*, prior to the rise of the Hellenistic kingdoms and the Roman Empire; and the era of the medieval commune, prior to the rise of the "modern patrimonial states" and their (liberal-democratic) successors. He implicitly accepts one of the key features of Western self-understanding, namely that the West has differed from the East, not by virtue of its *success* in forming great states, but the very opposite. Weber does not attribute this to any particular Western virtue, but rather to a concatenation of circumstances that had little to do with any noble motives. Nevertheless, his reading of world history draws our attention to the fact that characteristically modern ways of thinking and being originated in places that the great states could not control. These places were characterized, in large degree, by what Weber called "non-legitimate domination": political authority of a sort that was at odds with prevailing norms of legitimacy. The places concerned were definitely *urban*.

Weber recognized that a place could be a city in a sociological, economic, military or political-administrative sense, and yet not have the capacity to govern itself, even for purely local purposes.

> Not every "city" in the economic sense, nor every garrison whose inhabitants had a special status in the political-administrative sense, has in the past constituted a "commune" (*Gemeinde*). The city-commune in the full meaning of the word appeared as a mass phenomenon only in the Occident. . . . To develop into a city-commune, a settlement had to be of the non-agricultural-commercial type, at least to a relative extent, and to be equipped with the following features: 1. a fortification; 2. a market; 3. its own court of law and, at least in part, autonomous law; 4. an associational structure (*Verbandscharakter*) and, connected therewith, 5. at least partial autonomy and autocephaly, which includes administration by authorities in whose appointment the burghers could in some form participate. In the past, such rights almost always took the form of privileges of an "estate" (*Stand*); hence the characteristic of the city in the political definition was the appearance of a distinct "bourgeois" estate.
>
> (Weber 1978, vol. 2, 1226)

In Weber's view, the ancient *polis* had many of the characteristics of a city-commune.

> However, in Antiquity the concept of the "commune" was fully differentiated from that of "the state" only with the city's incorporation into the large Hellenistic or Roman territorial states, which at the same time

robbed the city of its political independence. The medieval city, by contrast, was a "commune" from the very beginning, even though the legal concept of the "corporation" as such was only gradually formed.
(Weber 1978, vol. 2, 1243)

In Antiquity, many of the inhabitants of cities were slaves, although slaves usually had a chance to buy their freedom if they succeeded in the businesses in which they were put out to work.

> The Occidental city thus was already in Antiquity, just like in Russia, a place where *the ascent from bondage to freedom* by means of monetary acquisition was possible. This is even more true for the medieval city, and especially for the inland medieval city. In contrast to all known urban development elsewhere, the burghers of the Occidental city engaged in status-conscious policies directed toward this goal.
> (Weber 1978, vol. 2, 1238)

> The urban citizenry therefore usurped the right to dissolve the bonds of seigneurial domination; this was the great – in fact, *revolutionary* – innovation which differentiated the medieval Occidental cities from all others. In the central and northern European cities appeared the well-known principle that *Stadtluft macht frei* ["town air makes free"], which meant that after a varying but always relatively short time the master of a slave or serf lost the right to reclaim him. . . . In the cities the status differences disappeared – at least in so far as they signified a differentiation between "free" and "unfree" men.
> (Weber 1978, vol. 2, 1239)

Thus, the medieval city-commune was the place where the principle that "all men are free" was first established in practical terms – for reasons that had more to do with the need for labour than with high-minded principles.

Weber traces with some care the differences between southern and northern Europe and between the Continent and England, in terms of the development of city-communes. It might seem that the relevant authority was granted "from above", as later jurists often attempted to show, but in reality there was often a seizure of power by a "sworn association" (*coniuratio*) of burghers.

> In a formal legal sense the corporation of the burghers and its author-ities had their "legitimate" origin in (real or fictitious) privileges granted by the political and at times by the manorial powers. . . . But quite often, and especially in the most important cases, the real origin is to be found in what is from the formal legal point of view a revolutionary usurpation of rights. To be sure, this cannot be said of all cases. We can distinguish a "spontaneous" and a "derived" formation of medieval city associations. In the "spontaneous" case, the commune was the result of a political

association of the burghers in spite of, or in defiance of the "legitimate" powers or, more correctly, of a series of such acts. Formal recognition by the legitimate authorities came only later, if at all. A "derived" burgher association was formed through a contracted or legislated grant of more or less limited rights to autonomy and autocephaly, issued by the city founder and his successors; it is found frequently in cases of new foundations as grants to the settlers and their successors.

The "spontaneous" usurpation through an act of rational association, a sworn confraternization (*Eidverbrüderung: coniuratio*) of the burghers, is found especially in the bigger and older cities, such as Genoa and Cologne. As a rule, however, a combination of events of both kinds occurred. In the documentary sources of urban history, which by their nature overemphasize the continuity of legitimacy, such usurpations are as a rule not mentioned at all; it is usually only by accident that one can be documented.

(Weber 1978, vol. 2, 1250)

The urban elites came to expect such autonomy, and so the superior authorities had little choice but to grant it.

Once the revolutionary usurpations had met with success in several large cities, the political lords who founded new cities or granted new charters to existing ones hurried, for reasons of competition, to concede to their burghers varying portions of the rights elsewhere obtained without waiting for the formation of formal unions. Thus the attainments of the city unions tended to spread universally.

(Weber 1978, vol. 2, 1259)

In a way, the medieval city-communes were victims of their own success, in that the burgeoning capitalist economy outgrew them. In England, the urban elites never won as much autonomy as some of their Continental counterparts, but they did succeed in achieving greater influence at the centre of the kingdom. This altered the political logic.

Here we thus find for the first time an interlocal, *national* bourgeoisie. The increasing power of the burghers in Parliament and within the royal administration . . . prevented the development of a strong movement for independence in the *individual* communes. Not the local interests of municipalities as such, but the interlocal interests of the townsmen, formed the basis for the political unification of the bourgeoisie.

(Weber 1978, vol. 2, 1280)

In any case, the economic logic was also changing. Entrepreneurs had once wanted the protection of a city-commune sensitive to their own requirements, but such protectionism was becoming obsolescent.

> [T]he traditional forms of enterprise integrated in the "city economy" no longer were the ones which could generate the really great profits, and, further, . . . both the politically oriented and the commercial and industrial capitalist undertakings simply no longer found a useful support in policies of the "city economy" type, . . . Even where these undertakings were formally located in the city, they could no longer be sustained by an entrepreneurdom tied locally to the individual burgher association. The new capitalist undertakings settled in the new locations suitable for them, and for help in the defense of his interests – in so far as he required any at all – the entrepreneur now appealed to powers other than a local burgher association. . . . [T]he great modern commercial and industrial cities of England arose entirely outside the precincts – and thus the monopoly-power spheres – of the old privileged [municipal] corporations.
>
> (Weber 1978, vol. 2, 1330–31)

Once the great territorial states had modernized their administrative apparatuses and become sensitive to urban-economic concerns, they could offer better protection to entrepreneurs than the smaller city-communes. But, even then, the entrepreneurs sought islands of freedom where they could organize their businesses as they chose.

The city-communes are but one element in the story that Weber tells. He is interested in what stimulated rationalization, and he discovers that the incentives were often religious. He insists, however, that the religious movements that fostered rationalization – early Christianity, later Protestantism, especially Puritanism – were essentially *urban*. Moreover, he notices how rationalizing practices tend to migrate from one area of life to another: from soul-searching to profit-seeking, from profit-seeking to civic administration, from civic administration to engineering, from engineering to science, and so on, in ever more complicated and variable patterns. The setting that enables this is the city: in particular, the city in which all men are nominally free and in which the particularistic ties of tribes and clans (and the cults associated with them) have been largely broken. If the modern state is the normal form of political organization at the beginning of the twentieth century, that is because modern urban society and the modern urban economy both enable and require that mode of organization. A great state is not necessarily an aid to modernization, as the early history of the West attests. As modern life – which is to say, modern *urban* life – takes shape, the rationalization and modernization of the state becomes both necessary and possible. In that context, the city-communes may lose much of their former political autonomy. Nonetheless, the rationalizing and modernizing practices of the city-communes are projected onto a larger scale, and urban life becomes possible on that bigger scale. Urban life, not the modern state, is the essential ground. If the early experience of Western cities is any indication, then the gaps in state authority, which allow for new efforts at rationalization, are crucial. The anarchy of the Occidental city – its fortuitous and often fleeting "ungovernability" – is the source of its peculiar strength, and it is that strength that has now been projected onto a wider scale. This has implications for politics that Weber himself did not see.

Human ecology and urbanism as a way of life

By the time Weber died in 1920, sociologists at the University of Chicago had already developed an approach that enabled them to understand how a self-sustaining social order emerged from the apparent disorder of cities. They called this approach "human ecology". According to Amos Hawley the term "ecology" was coined by the biologist, Ernst Haeckel, in 1868 (Hawley 1950, 1). The study of plant and animal ecology was reasonably well established by the early 1900s. Robert E. Park and Ernest W. Burgess then extended the methods of ecological analysis to encompass human settlements. Park explained the approach as follows:

> There are forces at work within the limits of the urban community – within the limits of any natural area of human habitation, in fact – which tend to bring about an orderly and typical grouping of its population and institutions. The science which seeks to isolate these factors and to describe the typical constellations of persons and institutions which the co-operation of these forces produce, is what we call human, as distinguished from plant and animal ecology.
>
> (Park in Park *et al.* 1925, 1–2)

Their colleague, Roderick D. McKenzie, elaborated on the approach in a 1934 essay.

> Human ecology differs from demography and human geography in that the main object of attention is neither the population aggregate nor the physical-cultural habitat but rather the relations of man to man. The human ecologist . . . concerns himself with the nexus of sustenance and place relations of the individuals and institutions which give the community its characteristic form and organization. Basic to the ecological idea is the concept of competition. . . .
>
> The unit of ecological study is the communal organism, which is at once an aggregation of individual persons, a geographical and cultural habitat, and an interrelated and interdependent bio-social entity.
>
> (Hawley 1968, 40)

Park grew rather mystical in applying this approach to urban analysis.

> The city . . . is something more than a congeries of individual men and social conveniences. . . . The city is, rather, a state of mind, a body of

customs and traditions, and of organized attitudes and sentiments that inhere in these customs and are transmitted with this tradition. The city is not, in other words, merely a physical mechanism and an artificial construction. It is involved in the vital processes of the people who compose it; it is a product of nature, and particularly human nature.

(Park in Park *et al.* 1925, 1)

From this point of view, we may, if we choose, think of the city, that is to say, the place and the people, with all the machinery and administrative devices that go with them, as organically related; a kind of psycho-physical mechanism in and through which private and political interests find not merely a collective but a corporate expression.

Much of what we ordinarily regard as the city – its charters, formal organizations, buildings, street railways, and so forth – is, or seems to be, mere artefact. But these things in themselves are utilities, adventitious devices which become part of the living city only when, and in so far as, through use and wont they connect themselves, like a tool in the hand of man, with the vital forces evident in individuals and the community.

The city is, finally, the natural habitat of civilized man.

(Park in Park *et al.* 1925, 2)

Park quoted Oswald Spengler favourably in this regard: "Nations, governments, politics, and religions – all rest on the basic phenomenon of human existence, the city" (Park in Park *et al.* 1925, 2). To understand the city was to understand civilizations. Darwinian ideas about competition, adaptation, and natural selection provided the means for analysing distinctively human forms of community. Human communities were different from animal communities, because humans were capable of purposive action. Nonetheless, there were limits to what humans could achieve, as was evident from the history of city planning. City plans laid down rules that were somewhat effective in determining the form of urban regions.

Within the limitations prescribed, however, the inevitable processes of human nature proceed to give these regions and these buildings a character which is less easy to control. . . . [T]he city acquires an organization and distribution of population which is neither designed nor controlled.

(Park in Park *et al.* 1925, 5)

The implication was that city plans had to take account of the natural order of cities, an order that the human ecologists were intent on explaining. Thus, Burgess described the "natural" tendency for cities to develop in concentric circles from the central business district outward. Park and others noted the processes whereby people segregated themselves into different residential neighbourhoods in accordance with class, race, and ethnicity. McKenzie focused attention on the development of metropolitan communities that transcended the administrative boundaries of cities and their suburbs. None of this was meant to suggest that government action was futile. On the contrary, the human ecologists were generally supportive of urban planning. Nevertheless, they thought it was essential to understand the natural tendencies of urban development, in order to make planning effective.

Louis Wirth was one of the younger scholars of this group. He was a German Jew by birth, but he had come to the United States as an adolescent, and had had his intellectual formation there.[3] Caught up in the Roosevelt New Deal, he played an important part in analysing the challenges implicit in urbanization. More than his predecessors, he recognized how people in remote areas were being drawn into the urban way of life.

> The distinctive feature of man's mode of living in the modern age is his concentration into gigantic aggregations around which cluster lesser centers which radiate the ideas and practices we call civilization. . . . The influences which cities exert upon the social life of man are greater than the ratio of urban population would indicate, for the city is not only increasingly the dwelling-place and the workshop of modern man, but it is the initiating and controlling center of economic, political, and cultural life that has drawn the most remote communities of the world into its orbit and woven diverse areas, peoples, and activities into a cosmos.
>
> (Wirth [1938] 1964, 60)

This had major analytic implications.

> As long as we identify urbanism with the physical entity of the city, viewing it merely as rigidly delimited in space, and proceed as if urban attributes abruptly cease to be manifested beyond an arbitrary boundary line, we are not likely to arrive at any adequate conception of urbanism as a mode of life.
>
> (Wirth [1938] 1964, 63)

Wirth set out a number of sociological propositions "concerning the relationship between (a) numbers of population, (b) density of settlement, (c) heterogeneity of inhabitants and group life". He drew on ideas from Simmel, Tönnies, and Durkheim, as well as his American colleagues. Thus, he imagined a variety of effects from urbanization: impersonal, superficial, and segmental human relationships, physical and social segregation, the separation of work and residence, an accentuated division of labour, increased competition, aggrandizement, and mutual exploitation, greater social tensions, indirect media of communication and representation, affiliation to groups tangential to the immediate community, more formal controls and routines, a sensitivity to artefacts rather than nature, heightened mobility and greater acceptance of insecurity, greater sophistication and rationality, relativism, secularism, tolerance, and anomie. Not all these effects were worrying, but many raised issues about social cohesion and political consensus.

> There is little opportunity for the individual to obtain a conception of the city as a whole or to survey his place in the total scheme.
>
> (Wirth [1938] 1964, 77)

> [T]he masses of men in the city are subject to manipulation by symbols and stereotypes managed by individuals working from afar or operating invisibly behind the scenes through their controls of the instruments of communication. Self-government either in the economic, or political, or the cultural realm is under these circumstances reduced to a mere figure of speech, or, at best, is subject to the unstable equilibrium of pressure groups.
>
> (Wirth [1938] 1964, 82)[4]

Like others of the Chicago school of urban sociologists, Wirth had a favourable attitude towards planning.

> Planning, through its emphasis upon integration and the intelligent and orderly pursuit of achievable social goals, which in a free society are not imposed from without or above but self-selected in the course of democratic interplay of ideas and wills, is at least one promising alternative to violence and chaos.
>
> (Wirth 1964, 206)

Planning had to be on a large scale if it were to be effective.

> If the planner must err, let him err on the side of taking in more rather than less of the periphery of the city.
>
> (Wirth 1964, 312)

> Just as gunpowder spelled the end of the walled medieval city, so the automobile, electricity, and the technology of modern industrial society have blasted the barriers of city charters and of the traditions and laws and grooves of thinking which have hitherto prevented a rational approach to city planning.
>
> (Wirth 1964, 317)

Wirth looked forward to the day when at least some action could be undertaken on a global scale.

> The individual members of the human family have broken the provincial boundaries of their culture and must learn to think, feel, believe, and act in accordance with the progressively enlarging sphere of a world culture.
>
> (Wirth 1964, 151)

There still are local cultures, but there is also an approximation to world civilization. There still are local, county, state, and national governments, but there are also emerging world political institutions, however feeble.

(Wirth 1964, 327)

The "emerging world political institutions" to which Wirth referred were the ones created in the years immediately before his death in 1950.

As I have already noted, the Chicago school sociologists were later criticized for "naturalizing" the political economy of urban development and attributing effects to "the urban" that might better be attributed to capitalism (Castells 1977, Smith, M. 1979). There is much merit in these criticisms, but we should not lose sight of the advantages of a "human ecology" approach. Weber and Marx tended to abstract from the natural environment in developing their analyses. The human ecologists brought the environment back in without resorting to a crude environmental determinism. What they sought to show is that the forces that determined the distribution of plants and animals were still present in human communities. Thus, an order, balance, or ecological equilibrium would tend to emerge, whether or not anyone planned for it. Moreover, the question with regard to any public intervention was what change in the equilibrium it would effect. One could not wish the natural forces or the equilibrating mechanisms away. The effect of an action would only match its intent if the actor had a good understanding of human ecology and could anticipate the reactions that his action would stimulate. Both Weber and Marx were searching for a "systemic" understanding of this sort. The human ecologists reset the analytical problem in the broader context of the evolution of life-forms. Wirth then added something of particular value, by stressing that urbanism is a particular human life-form that began to take shape thousands of years ago, before industrialism, modern capitalism, or the modern state emerged. The implication is that specifically modern forms of economics, government, and politics took shape within a form of life (urbanism) that overdetermines their possibilities. That form of life is in turn overdetermined by natural processes.

We need not embrace any of the specifics of the Chicago school analysis to see the value of the conceptual shifts they were urging. Urbanism seems to entail the humanization of the immediate natural environment. This has effects on the way that we relate to one another, as well as on our relationship to the wider environment. As we now know better than ever, human actions can disturb the natural equilibrium in ways that are highly deleterious to us, as well as other species. Our grasp of ecology in the broader sense is still quite weak, and we may never be able to predict the long-term environmental effects of some of our actions. Crucial causal relations are non-linear, and one form of order may succeed another for reasons that cannot be anticipated in advance. This applies to social life as well. All we can do is model human and human–natural interactions in ways that enable us to see the possible consequences of our actions more clearly. That is what the human ecologists were trying to do. The most pertinent criticism of their work is that it was at once too ambitious and too modest: too ambitious in the sense that it suggested that it would be easier than it is to grasp the dynamics of the whole and to suggest appropriate courses of action in relation to that whole; too modest in the sense that it tended to read back from the present order on the assumption that the present was an inevitable evolutionary outcome of the past. A more critical approach to human ecology would do much to reveal paths not taken and raise alternatives for the future. To do this with sufficient modesty is difficult, however.

The human ecologists did not offer a clear account of politics. They treated it on the one hand as one of the social phenomena they were explaining and on the other as the deus ex machina that would reform the order they were describing. In this respect, they followed Marx, Weber, and the other evolutionary sociologists. Unlike Marx and Weber, they tended to treat the moment of freedom implicit in political action as relatively routine. At stake were not the heroics of class struggle (Marx 1977) or political virtuosity (Weber 2004), but the mundane business of urban planning, a business that had to be democratic if it were to be effective. Wirth, McKenzie, and others of their generation thought of planning as an activity that had to occur on a grand scale, if it were to encompass the forces of urbanism. Hence, they thought in terms of metropolitan planning – planning for large city-regions – and tried to imagine how that might connect with planning on an even wider scale. They did not imagine that the state would simply give orders to other social actors. On the contrary, goals would be "self-selected in the course of democratic interplay of ideas and wills". This suggests that the field of the political would somehow be extended to encompass a variety of actors who would not be subordinated to the state. To put it otherwise, democratic planning would be a process from which the state and other actors took direction. Its field would transcend the state and every other institution. Although the scale of it might be limited for practical reasons, there was no reason in principle why it should stop at the boundary between one state and the next. Indeed, the transnational metropolis could only be planned on a transnational scale. The implication was that democracy, in the sense of democratic planning, had a natural field of action that transcended the state institutionally and geographically, and put the ongoing existence of the state at issue, since it was an institution that was evidently becoming obsolescent for urban society. The globally integrative effects of urbanism were such that a politics adequate to it could not be state-centric.

This was not an explicit conclusion, but it was implicit in the American sociological approach, of which "human ecology" was one variant. To imagine that there was a natural order to a free society was to believe that an alternative to "violence and chaos" might emerge even if there were *not* a "monopoly of legitimate violence". It was to suggest that social order depended less on the restraint of violence by violence than on the development of forms of peaceful cooperation. Democratic planning, as Wirth and others imagined it, was a process of peaceful cooperation, in which agreed goals could be determined. It could enhance an order that tended to emerge of itself as people pursued their own objectives. If things worked as they should, "violence and chaos" would be displaced by more fruitful practices. There need not be any direct confrontation. Even as things were, interest group pluralism provided a framework for peaceful competition. The more consensual politics of democratic planning could only enhance social cohesion. The question was, to what extent was such democratic planning actually possible?

Catallactics and the unplanned *cosmos*

In a widely and deeply influential book called *The Road to Serfdom* (Hayek 1944), the Austrian émigré economist, Friedrich von Hayek, attacked the very idea of planning, democratic or otherwise. The book drew on the work of other economists like Ludwig von Mises and Frank H. Knight. It had an immediate impact, but its delayed effects have been even more profound. It is not an exaggeration to the say that the dominant neo-liberalism of our time is Hayekian in inspiration. In later books, especially *The Constitution of Liberty* (Hayek 1960) and *Law, Legislation and Liberty* (Hayek 1973–79), Hayek elaborated a theory that challenged many of the premises of modern politics. The focus of his attack was "socialism" in all its forms, but the implication was that the nature and limits of politics had been misunderstood by most people on all sides of the contemporary debates. According to Hayek, the main error in contemporary politics was that people had come to think of society as if it were an organization (*taxis*) that could be directed in accordance with some sort of rational plan, rather than as a spontaneous order (*cosmos*) that had evolved in a way that enabled all sorts of people to achieve all sorts of objectives of different types. If the public authorities were to try to remake society with a plan for social justice in mind, they would not succeed, because they could not possibly have the knowledge required to achieve their purpose. No one could gain a synoptic view of the whole. If the authorities did try to impose an order on the basis of their own inevitably partial understanding of things, they would block a host of creative initiatives and so forestall improvements that might have solved the problems they were trying to deal with. Moreover, they would be obliged to resort to widespread coercion of a sort that would make a mockery of individual liberty. Rather than rules well known in advance, there would be directives issued after the fact to stifle initiatives that were not in accordance with the plan. People would be demoralized by this, and come to think that exercising power over others was the only way of achieving any advantage. The results would be dreadful, Hayek thought, even if they did not go to the totalitarian extremes of Nazi Germany and Soviet Russia and only resulted in the sort of paralysis that had overcome Britain.

Hayek overstates his case, but his main point is an important one. So long as there are many different human actors – as inevitably there will be – the ultimate order of things will be determined by human *inter*action, and not simply by the action of those who claim ultimate authority. Those who are under authority will react to the authority's actions, in various ways. These reactions – what Foucault was to call "resistances" – will never be fully manageable, and so the authority will have to broaden and intensify its controls in order to achieve its objectives. This will deform the authority itself, and generate further unmanageable reactions. And so it will go, until the ultimate order of things becomes very different from what was originally intended. Hayek sees the issue in cognitive terms. People can understand and control what they make, but "society" is not something humans have made. Society has grown or developed as a side-effect of things we have done for other reasons, and it is a much more complex form of order than any we could purposefully create. So, we make a category error when we treat it as an organization like an army or a business corporation that can be directed towards a specific purpose. Society is certainly an effect of purposive activity, but if we try to impose a specific purpose or set of purposes upon it, it spins out of our control. Other people substitute their purposes for ours and new modes of interaction proliferate more rapidly than we can imagine, let alone control. Although the attempt to control society can never really succeed, it can block many from things happening and make everyone's life more miserable. A sensible and sensitive approach to social order is one that recognizes limitations on what can or should be managed.

Hayek drew his inspiration from the eighteenth century, especially from the great thinkers of the Scottish Enlightenment: David Hume (1987), Adam Ferguson (1995), and Adam Smith (1991). He described himself as an Old Whig, and that is quite an accurate characterization. From Smith especially, he draws the idea of a market order (or "catallaxy") that provides for both progress and freedom. According to Smith's classic account, the principles of conduct that bring a market order into existence (and maintain it into the future) are ones that grew naturally from market interactions. These principles are the conditions of possibility for the existence of the market and as such are accepted by those who want to trade as norms or laws to be enforced on all concerned. The relevant principles have been discovered, not invented. The "society" or *cosmos* that emerges from commercial activity is not, in principle, confined to any particular political jurisdiction. In fact, the market order has emerged in large degree from interactions at the margins of existing political jurisdictions, where people have to work out for themselves the terms of peaceful interaction. Certain tried and true principles have emerged, ones that have enabled the formation of what Adam Smith called the Great Society, which encompasses people of different nations, religions, and purposes.

> The Great Society arose through the discovery that men can live together in peace and mutually benefiting each other without agreeing on the particular aims which they severally pursue. The discovery that by substituting abstract rules of conduct for obligatory concrete ends

made it possible to extend the order of peace beyond the small groups pursuing the same ends, because it enabled each individual to gain from the skill and knowledge of others whom he need not even know and whose aims could be wholly different from his own.

(Hayek 1982, vol. 2, 109)

It would seem that wherever a Great Society has arisen, it has been made possible by a system of rules of just conduct which included what David Hume called "the three fundamental laws of nature, *that of stability of possession, of its transference by consent*, and *of the performance of promises*", or, as a modern author sums up the essential content of all contemporary systems of private law, "freedom of contract, the inviolability of property, and the duty to compensate another for damage due to his fault".

(Hayek 1982, vol. 2, 40)

In Hayek's view, the Great Society is essentially a law-governed market order that has emerged as an unintended by-product of trading activities and – *as we now can see* – enables material and other forms of progress to a degree hitherto unknown. Happily, this order also maximizes human freedom. The prospect of commercial success (or, the fear of commercial failure) provides an incentive to people to rationalize their activities in a way that provides benefit to others (in the form of saleable products or services). People do not have to be ordered to do this or that. They will work out the best course of action for themselves, in light of the commercial possibilities. Thus, they will retain their freedom in an order that nonetheless guides them to do what is of benefit to others. The "guidance" is not the result of a political or religious directive. The market and its opportunities are more like natural phenomena that a person has to deal with in exercising his freedom. No one has decreed or planned that other people will spend more on good ice cream than on good poems. That is just the way it is.

In Hayek's view, the requisites of the Great Society can now be specified with considerable precision, thanks to the science that has developed in its wake, "catallactics" (or what the rest of us would call economics or political economy). In his last book, Hayek sets out a plan for preserving the Great Society against onslaughts from those who would undermine its principles of organization. The crucial principles of organization are the ones implicit in the common law of the Great Society, law that has developed over time and that embodies widely accepted principles of justice. The political authorities are not above the law: they are subject to it. The law is not the result of anyone's command. It develops incrementally, decision by decision. Judges have the responsibility to decide on the implications of the law in disputed cases. At times, however, it becomes necessary to make a more substantial change, in light of ongoing experience and changing moral sentiments. In Hayek's view, it is important that the legislators be different from those who are in charge of the government, because the latter have an entirely different role.[5] The legislators have to determine how the law is to change (if at all), and the law applies to government as much as it applies to private citizens. The law must be stated in general terms, with an understanding that it will apply equally to everyone, endure into the indefinite future, and work for cases that cannot now be anticipated. It cannot be formulated with a view to benefiting this particular person or group. The government proper has charge of the resources made available to it on principles of taxation determined by law. It has to deal with particularities when it disposes of those resources, and it needs to make regulations in conjunction with its own work. Government regulations or dispositions of resources are not "laws" in the proper sense, however, even though they may appear as such in the current statute books. Law in the Hayekian sense is of a different character: abstract and general. The traditional distinction between the executive and the legislature in modern constitutions does not provide the required separation of powers, because the main business of modern legislatures is the supervision of government. What we need, Hayek thinks, is to take the law-making power away from the democratic assemblies that supervise government and give it instead to assemblies specifically chosen for the purpose of law-making. The latter assemblies would be less partisan, quite detached from immediate problems of government, and very much focused on the long-term requirements of the Great Society.

Fundamental to the Hayekian view is that "several" or private property must be preserved. People must have confidence that what they acquire by lawful activity in the market will remain theirs. This means that they must also have the right to dispose of their property as they please, by gift or sale. It also means that they should not be subject to disproportionate taxation. Freedom of contract is implicit in the right to dispose of one's property as one chooses. So, the whole order of the market is bound up with the principle of private property. For that reason, the principle has to be embedded in the constitution.

> The basic clause of such a constitution would have to state that in normal times, and apart from certain clearly defined emergency situations, men could be restrained from doing what they wished, or coerced to do particular things, only in accordance with the recognized rules of just conduct designed to define and protect the individual domain of each; and that the accepted rules of this kind could be deliberately altered only by what we shall call the Legislative Assembly.
>
> (Hayek 1982, vol. 3, 109)

> Such a clause would by itself achieve all and more than the traditional Bills of Rights were meant to secure; and it would therefore make any separate enumeration of a list of special protected fundamental rights unnecessary.
>
> (Hayek 1982, vol. 3, 110)

What the fundamental rights are intended to protect is simply individual liberty in the sense of the absence of arbitrary coercion. This requires that coercion be used only to enforce the universal rules of just conduct protecting the individual domains and to raise means to support the services rendered by government; and since what is implied here is that the individual can be restrained only in such conduct as may encroach upon the protected domain of others, he would under such a provision be wholly unrestricted in all actions which affected only his personal domain or that of other consenting responsible persons, and thus be assured all freedom that can be assured by political action.

(Hayek 1982, vol. 3, 111)

The institutional arrangements that Hayek recommends are all designed to ensure that these fundamental rights are well protected. He recognizes that the constitution must have democratic support, but he denies that a democratic majority has the right to trench upon fundamental rights. The right of a democratic majority is to choose a government and a body of law-makers, but the law-makers, the government, and the democratic majority all derive their authority from a pre-existing body of law which they have no right to overturn. All political authority is limited by that body of law, which entrenches fundamental rights, most especially the rights associated with private property.

It takes no genius to see that Hayek is faced with a conundrum. He argues, quite convincingly, that *no one* can achieve a synoptic understanding of the Great Society, and yet he wants to say that *he understands* which of the organizational principles of that society must be preserved against the possible depredations of democratic majorities. He offers some good reasons for thinking that the principles that he and his eighteenth-century predecessors have picked out are important. These principles deserve careful consideration. On the other hand, as Hayek says with respect to civilization (or the Great Society), it is wrong to suppose that "man knows what its functioning or continued existence depends upon" (Hayek 1960, 23). Presumably, Hayek, Smith, and Hume share in this partial-sightedness. In fact, it is most reasonable to suppose that they and we have missed or misunderstood some of the crucial principles. We ought to be cautious about institutionalizing principles of order, for fear that we put things in place that stand in the way of improvement. As Hayek says,

the case for individual freedom rests chiefly on the recognition of the inevitable ignorance of all of us concerning a great many of the factors on which the achievement of our ends and welfare depends.

If there were omniscient men, if we could know not only all that affects the attainment of our present wishes but also our future wants and desires, there would be little case for liberty. And, in turn, liberty of the individual would, of course, make complete foresight impossible. Liberty is essential in order to leave room for the unforeseeable and unpredictable; we want it because we have learned to expect from it the opportunity of realizing many of our aims. It is because every individual knows so little and, in particular, because we rarely know which of us knows best that we trust the independent and competitive efforts of many to induce the emergence of what we shall want when we see it.

Humiliating to human pride as it may be, we must recognize that the advance and even the preservation of civilization are dependent upon a maximum of opportunity for accidents to happen. These accidents occur in the combination of knowledge and attitudes, skills and habits, acquired by individual men and also when qualified men are confronted with the particular circumstances which they are equipped to deal with. Our necessary ignorance of so much means that we have to deal largely with probabilities and chances.

(Hayek 1960, 29)

A market economy certainly does provide for some happy accidents, thanks to the liberties it offers. It is by no means clear, however, that market liberties are the *only* ones required for happy accidents to occur, or even that the market liberties we have are quite the right ones for the twenty-first century.

Hayek describes a catallaxy as a "special kind of spontaneous order produced by the market through people acting with the rules of the law of property, tort and contract" (Hayek 1982, vol. 2, 108). Might there be other such orders that we would do well to nourish? Hayek derives his conception of spontaneous order from Michael Polanyi, who describes it as follows:

When order is achieved among human beings by allowing them to inter-act with one another on their own initiative – subject only to the laws which uniformly apply to all of them – we have a system of spontaneous order in society. We may then say that the efforts of these individuals are co-ordinated by exercising their individual initiative and that this self-co-ordination justifies this liberty on public grounds. – The actions of such individuals are said to be free, for they are not determined by any *specific* command, whether of a superior or a public authority; the compulsion to which they are subject is impersonal and general.

(Polanyi 1951, 159, cited in Hayek 1960, 160)

Presumably, a similar order might arise if communities interacted with one another within a framework of law that had grown naturally from the experience of communal interaction. Moreover, the politics internal to these communities might develop in accordance with principles that people freely accepted, because they understood them as necessary to the peaceful settle-ment of disputes, including disputes about leadership and communal goals. Those who believe in democratic politics tend to think that widely accepted principles – such as the right of every person to have a voice in decisions that affect him or her, the need to find consensual solutions whenever possible, or the propriety of resorting to a majority vote when all else fails – *have* emerged in much the same way as the principles Hayek cites. These principles have been found, not invented, and they are more fundamental than the rules that govern particular polities. Why we should be less attentive to these principles than to the ones Hayek cites is certainly not apparent.

Ideas about democratic mutualism, which have been developed by anarchist and anarchist-influenced thinkers since the nineteenth century, seem especially pertinent in this context (Kropotkin 2006, Bookchin 1987, 1991, Day 2005). The claim is that groups, communities, and enterprises will adjust to one another over time, on the basis of mutually agreed principles. If the principles are rooted in what people will accept when they are not subject to threats and intimidation, they should be consistent with democratic aspirations. Although theorists of public choice and cooperation more generally have analysed the ways in which negotiated or cooperative solutions to common problems emerge, there is a tendency to distrust the spontaneous order that arises from democratic activities whenever it impinges on idealized market principles. If we were to recognize that democracy itself is a kind of spontaneous order, we would see that an ideal quite different from what Hayek posits arises from the claim that people can and often do work out their differences without resort to violence. The bodies that have to adjust to one another are in effect political authorities, whatever guise they may adopt. Businesses, tribes, sects, parties, charities, communities, movements, and whatever, which organize themselves in different registers, establish their own spaces, write their own histories, and contest for people's allegiance are commonplace. Such entities are often quite robust, as authorities that claim sovereignty usually discover. The challenge is to find ways of dealing with this inevitable diversity. If what Polanyi and Hayek suggest is correct, it must be the case that people have worked out ways and means of resolving differences over the years: ways and means that depend on principles that have been *found* to work, and that may be effective even in the absence of sovereign authority.

Hayek is generally reluctant to apply the same logic to the public sector as he does to the private. He is happy to recognize that the law regulating transactions in the market has evolved since the eighteenth century, and that much has been learned about how to make markets fairer and more efficient. On the other hand, he seems to suppose that people have learned nothing in the last two hundred and fifty years about how to make public services more efficient and responsive to public needs, how to ensure that citizens are not mistreated by public officials, and how to make public servants effectively accountable for their actions. In fact, public or administrative law has evolved as much as private law, and it contains a variety of principles (such as the right to a fair hearing or due process) that give considerable protection both to people who want access to services and to those who are directly involved in delivering those services. Moreover, practices of accounting, auditing, and programme evaluation have been greatly elaborated in an effort to enhance efficiency and effectiveness. Hayek admits that an increasing proportion of what we need may have to be supplied out of public finance, due to the inevitable limitations of the market. Thus, there is a huge field of endeavour in which market incentives do not work (or are very ineffective), but in which the need for "happy accidents" or creative innovations is no less apparent. The practices that have promoted honesty and efficiency in the market cannot be transferred wholesale to the public sector, because the public sector is not and cannot be governed by the market. It is *different*, as Hayek himself is at pains to point out. Given this difference, it is reasonable to suppose that the principles and practices appropriate to public sector management and service delivery are likely to be the ones that have evolved *within* that sector. These principles are not the same as the ones that evolved within the domain of democratic politics. On the other hand, they may complement principles of the latter sort, just as the principles of good market behaviour may complement principles of conduct in public life.

To have some confidence in the evolving practices of the public sector, one would have to suppose that it was there to serve, rather than to dominate. This, of course, is the premise of liberal-democratic politics: the belief that we can organize "government" so that it serves objectives that we cannot achieve privately. There are several dimensions of this. As Hayek himself notices, there are some products and services that we cannot get on the market and have to provide by means of public finance. We also have to work at amending and improving the law that governs all activities, including the activities of government itself. There are complicated problems of enforcement, matters of adjudication, and questions of efficiency and effectiveness that bear on these various forms of work. However, there are other dimensions of public activity as well, dimensions that Hayek fails to notice. Public activity is in part a matter of collective self-definition: articulating who "we" are, what "we" want to be, what norms, values, and ways of being we want to have expressed in and through the *public* action in which we are engaged together. To live freely as private individuals and to become what we want to be as individuals is one thing. To live freely as a community is another thing, for our communal or public life is something that we have to produce together. Having the freedom to be what we want to be and do what we want to do individually is not enough for most of us. We also want to be and do something meaningful as a community, and this means having a venue for public, as well as private, action. What we can do as individuals with respect to public action is important, but not as important as what we can be and do collectively. The conditions of possibility for our collective existence matter. One of the arguments for liberal democracy always has been that to organize a government "of, by, and for the people" is to establish it on principles – akin to but different from the principles of the market economy – that provide for *public* freedom. (Compare Tocqueville 1945, Arendt 1958, 1961.) The further claim is that public freedom and private freedom reinforce one another in ways that Hayek does not understand. Because he is obsessed with the role of the state as a coercive organization, Hayek has trouble recognizing that politics can be a domain of freedom.

Hayek edges closest to such an understanding when he deals with the way that the state might be reorganized. As he says, quite correctly, the state has had no monopoly on the development of valuable public services.

> It should be remembered that long before government entered those fields, many of the now generally recognized collective needs were met by the efforts of the public-spirited individuals or groups providing means for public purposes which they regarded as important. Public education and public hospitals, libraries and museums, theatres and parks, were not first created by governments.
>
> (Hayek 1982, vol. 3, 49–50)

In principle, public activity extends far beyond the domain of the state.

> The mischievous idea that all public needs should be satisfied by compulsory organization and that all the means that the individuals are willing to devote to public purposes should be under the control of government, is wholly alien to the basic principles of a free society. . . . In a truly free society, public affairs are not confined to the affairs of government (least of all central government) and public spirit should not exhaust itself in an interest in government.
>
> (Hayek 1982, vol. 2, 150–51)

Within the domain of the state, decentralization is to be preferred.

> There are strong reasons why action by local authorities generally offers the next-best solution where private initiative cannot be relied upon to provide certain services and where some sort of collective action is therefore needed; for it has many of the advantages of private enterprise and fewer of the dangers of the coercive action of government. Competition between local authorities or between larger units within an area where there is freedom of movement provides in large measure that opportunity for experimentation with alternative methods which will secure most of the advantages of free growth.
>
> (Hayek 1960, 263–64)

> To re-entrust the management of most service activities of government to smaller units would probably lead to the revival of a communal spirit which has been largely suffocated by centralization.
>
> (Hayek 1982, vol. 3, 146)

Thus, there is some scope for public enterprise even in a well-ordered Hayekian society. Governments will contract out services whenever possible, to take advantage of market efficiencies. On the other hand, they will take care not to crowd out voluntary initiatives, paid for by charitably minded people. Moreover, the state will be so organized that services remaining in its control will be provided mostly by regional and local authorities that regard themselves as "quasi-commercial corporations competing for citizens" (Hayek 1982, vol. 3, 146).

This last idea harks back to Weber's account of medieval lords offering civic freedom as an encouragement to settlement in new towns. What Hayek omits is that people may want something more than good services from public activity. To the extent that people do, the presence of strong voluntary organizations and local public authorities is vital to the development of a public life that offers possibilities for serving others, trying out new ideas for the public benefit, and working with others to articulate the means and ends of public activity, public expression, and public identity. Hayek's analysis of the implications of his own principles for the public sector is woefully underdeveloped. He cannot bring himself to admit that there is more to the unplanned order of the Great Society than what he can see when he focuses on the operations of the market. For him, public action through the state always bears the taint of coercion, and so cannot be identified with the domain of freedom. However, his argument depends on a simplistic account of freedom, in which the absence of coercion is the only thing that ultimately figures. Is the absence of coercion sufficient for freedom, or does the exercise of freedom require other conditions, which we need to specify? Is the presence of some coercion sufficient to negate freedom, or can freedom persist despite some elements of coercion in the situation people face? Can some elements of coercion be necessary to the flowering of certain forms of freedom? Hayek certainly accepts the coercion necessary to maintain market relations (and hence the private freedom associated with those relations). Why is the coercion necessary to maintain public freedom unacceptable, then? And, what of the quality of coercion? Is there no difference between rules that we impose upon ourselves democratically, and rules that are imposed by an alien authority?

Urban life poses particular problems for the analysis that Hayek is urging upon us. As he says,

> Civilization as we know it is inseparable from urban life. Almost all that distinguishes civilized from primitive society is intimately connected with large agglomerations of population that we call "cities," and when we speak of "urbanity," "civility," or "politeness," we refer to the manner of life in cities. . . . Yet the advantages of city life, particularly the enormous increases in productivity made possible by its industry, . . . are bought at great cost.
>
> (Hayek 1960, 340)

In many respects, the close contiguity of city life invalidates the assumptions underlying any simple division of property rights. . . . The general formulas of private property or freedom of contract do not therefore provide an immediate answer to the complex problems which city life raises.

(Hayek 1960, 341)

What a land owner or occupier does will have a huge impact on his or her neighbours, and so it will be impossible to protect the rights of neighbours without seriously impinging on his.

The framework of rules within which the decisions of the private owner are likely to agree with the public interest will therefore in this case have to be more detailed and more adjusted to particular local circumstances than is necessary with other kinds of property. Such "town planning," which operates largely through its effects on the market and through the establishing of general conditions to which all developments of a district or neighbourhood must conform but which, within these conditions, leaves the decisions to the individual owner, is part of the effort to make the market mechanism more effective.

(Hayek 1960, 350)

Some of the aims of planning could be achieved in such a way that certain decisions would rest with the holder of the superior right, i.e., with some corporation representing the whole district or region and possessing powers to assess benefits and charges to individual subowners. Estate development in which the developer retains some permanent control over the use of the individual plots offers at least one alternative to the exercise of such control by political authority.

(Hayek 1960, 351)

So, Hayek grasps at the idea of a super-landlord, like the Duke of Westminster or the Disney Corporation, as a substitute for a democratically organized municipality. Why we should prefer such private authority to the public variety is not apparent.

All analytic roads seem to be lead to the same set of conclusions. The "spontaneous order" that Hayek is attempting to describe is actually more complex than he imagines. The catallaxy or market order is only one dimension of a more complicated whole. Other orders are also formed spontaneously, but their principles of organization are different. Among these is an order of democratic politics. What have we learned about nurturing that order as a space of freedom? Hayek tells us little about that, because he cannot or will not grasp that freedom is multidimensional and that politics offers opportunities for the free development of human potential that cannot be provided by the market. He also identifies politics with the state, and hence not only with coercion but also with the practice of sovereignty. He thrashes about trying to conceptualize an order that can be sustained without sovereignty, but in the end he resorts to sovereignty as an emergency measure in circumstances that threaten the order he prefers. ("The basic principle of a free society . . . may yet have to be temporarily suspended when the long-run preservation of that order is itself threatened" (Hayek 1982, vol. 3, 124).) This is a familiar move, which mirrors the moment of sovereign decision in which Hayek articulates the principles that everyone must uphold if the order he wants is to be sustained. If (as he tells us) the order or orders in which we are implicated as civilized beings actually are too complex for any of us to understand fully, then we are ill advised to put our faith in sovereignty, either as an emergency measure or as a ground for order. A sovereign order is an order of violence, whereas a political order may defer the resort to violence indefinitely, in large part by deferring the answer to the question of who is sovereign. The problem with politics is not its capacity to generate a totalitarian order: it has little such capacity. The problem, rather, is the vulnerability of a political order to claims of sovereignty, violently enforced. Thus, the problem is not how to contain and defeat politics (as Hayek supposes), but rather how to nurture its better forms and thus to realize its potential for deferring and deterring violence or coercion, and providing possibilities for "happy accidents".

The uses of disorder

Not long after Hayek published *The Constitution of Liberty*, a very different critique of centralized planning appeared: Jane Jacobs, *The Death and Life of Great American Cities* (Jacobs 1961). This critique had an enormous impact on thinking about cities, especially in the United States. Jacobs was not a university-based scholar, but a journalist, architectural critic, and Greenwich Village mother with her "eyes on the street". The appeal of her book was that it seemed to be based on first-hand observation of her own neighbourhood, rather than abstract theories. Nevertheless, Jacobs understood what she saw in light of scientific work on complex systems. As she said, "Cities happen to be problems in organized complexity, like the life sciences. They represent 'situations in which a half-dozen or even several dozen quantities are all varying simultaneously *and in subtly interconnected ways*'." (Jacobs 1961, 433) This was an insight she might have taken from Hayek or the human ecologists, but she put her own spin on it. She marvelled at the way that a civilized order emerged without planning on the streets outside her New York City apartment. Not only did this order facilitate civilized interaction, but it also constrained and controlled violence.

> The first thing to understand is that the public peace – the sidewalk and street peace – of cities is not kept primarily by the police, necessary as police are. It is kept primarily by an intricate, almost unconscious

network of voluntary controls and standards among the people themselves, and enforced by the people themselves.

(Jacobs 1961, 31)

Under the seeming disorder of the old city, wherever the old city is
working successfully, is a marvellous order for maintaining the safety
of the streets and the freedom of the city. It is a complex order. Its
essence is intricacy of sidewalk use, bringing with it a constant succession of eyes.

(Jacobs 1961, 50)

The sum of such casual, public contact at a local level – most of it
fortuitous, most of it associated with errands, all of it metered by the
person concerned, and not thrust upon him by anyone – is a feeling for
the public identity of people, a web of public respect and trust, and a
resource in time of personal or neighbourhood need. The absence of this
trust is a disaster to a city street. Its cultivation cannot be institutional-
ized. And above all, *it implies no private commitments.*

(Jacobs 1961, 56. Emphasis in the original.)

From this she inferred what was missing from large areas of American cities.

We shall have something to chew on if we think of city neighbourhoods
as mundane organs of self-government. Our failures with city neighbourhoods are, ultimately, failures in localized self-government. I am using
self-government in its broadest sense, meaning both the informal and
formal self-management of society.

(Jacobs 1961, 114)

To Jacobs the key to a good city was people's capacity for self-organization,
self-management, and self-government.

In some respects Jacobs's vision was similar to Hayek's, in that it emphasized the potential for a spontaneous order, and offered sharp criticisms
of planners who thought that they could substitute their own designs (a *taxis*,
in Hayek's terms) for the form of order that would develop naturally. On
the other hand, Jacobs's conception of a civilized order was as much social
and political as economic. In her view, the informal contacts that generated
a harmonious order were not just the ones occasioned by market relations.
Even the latter had to develop into something more if a civilized order were
to emerge. People had to look out for one another in some degree and show
a care for the quality of the public space that they shared with one another.
Rules of conduct and mechanisms of enforcement would develop spontaneously under the right conditions, but these rules and mechanisms were more
complex and diverse than the ones that Hayek and Adam Smith highlighted.
The *cosmos* of the street neighbourhood could not be understood – or
effectively nurtured – just by the means that Hayek had in mind. Jacobs did

not propose that the effort to plan cities be abandoned. Instead, she advocated "planning for vitality". She wanted to

> stimulate and catalyze the greatest possible range and quantity of diversity among uses and among people throughout each district of a big city, . . . promote continuous networks of local street neighbourhoods, . . . combat the destructive presence of border vacuums, . . . unslum the slums [by encouraging people to stay put], . . . convert . . . cataclysmic uses of money [to more stabilizing investments], . . . [and] clarify the visual order of cities.
>
> (Jacobs 1961, 408–9)

This would require city-wide action, as well as some coordination at the district level, but the aim would be to facilitate the sort of spontaneous order at street level that would emerge if people had appropriate freedom. In later works – especially *The Economy of Cities* (1970) and *Cities and the Wealth of Nations* (1984) – Jacobs emphasized the importance of diverse, small-scale businesses that would employ local people effectively and mobilize their innovative capacities. She was as suspicious of the dead hand of national or multinational business corporations as she was of the dead hand of the nation-state. Implicit in her analysis was a call for the political, social, and economic revival of cities that had been stifled by larger-scale institutions. Ideally, urban autonomy would work its way down to street level.[6]

A few years later, the young social and cultural historian, Richard Sennett, offered another perspective on the problem of urban order. He tried to differentiate his account from Jacobs's, but in many ways he built on her critique of contemporary planning and reinforced her call for a kind of creative disorder in urban life. Whereas her focus was on the need to plan for dense, diverse, mixed-use neighbourhoods (with, for instance, short blocks to facilitate movement, and a mixture of businesses and residences to ensure twenty-four-hour use of the streets), his attention went to the homogeneous suburbs where people had been going to escape the risks of city life. He did not put all the blame on the planners (or capitalist entrepreneurs) for the way the suburbs had developed, for he understood that many people wanted the security of communities in which they did not encounter any significant differences. Unfortunately, such communities were characterized by a withdrawal from public life into the family, the repression of deviants within the community, and an often violent reaction to differences within and between communities. "This kind of reaction, this inability to deal with disorder without raising it to the scale of mortal combat, is inevitable when men shape their common lives so that their only sense of relatedness is the sense in which they feel themselves to be the same" (Sennett 1970, 45). Sennett wanted "survival communities", in which people were forced to deal with one another in order to address their common problems (as had once been the case in agricultural areas and older industrial neighbourhoods). Such communities, he said, "do not arise spontaneously, nor are spontaneously maintained, but instead have to be created and urged into being" (Sennett 1970, 127). Fortunately, this was largely a matter of throwing the responsibility for community issues back onto the communities themselves, and refusing to use sovereign authority to solve community problems.

> What is needed in order to create cities where people are forced to confront each other is a reconstituting of public power, not a destruction of it. As a rule of change, the situations creating survival encounters would be as follows: there would be no policing, nor any other form of central control, of schooling, zoning, renewal, or city activities that could be performed through common community action, or, even more importantly through direct, nonviolent conflict in the city itself.
>
> (Sennett 1970, 115)

> [P]olice control of much civil disorder ought to be sharply curbed; the responsibility for making peace in neighbourhood affairs ought to fall to the people involved.
>
> (Sennett 1970, 133)

The aim was to induce order through a form of "disorder" that would bring people out of their homes to deal directly with others in their own communities. Such encounters would help people overcome their adolescent fears of difference and uncertainty, and make them more open to reasonable accommodations with others.

> The great purpose of city life is a new kind of confusion possible within its borders, an anarchy that will not destroy men, but make them richer and more mature.
>
> (Sennett 1970, 92)

> [We need to abandon the] assumption that the planning of cities should be directed to bring order and clarity to the city as a whole. Instead of this idea, whose basis is found in mechanical ideas of production, the city must be conceived as a social order of parts, without a coherent, controllable whole form.
>
> (Sennett 1970, 116)

Sennett, like Jacobs, favoured denser cities with "socio-economic integration of living, working, and recreational spaces" (Sennett 1970, 129). Although he wanted "the removal of central bureaucracies from their present directive power" (Sennett 1970, 132) and talked of the need for "a new anarchism", he still thought that strong public authorities were essential. There would be decentralization, but the centre of state authority would remain.

> We . . . need to explore how a centralized state apparatus can be made compatible with decentralized ends. . . . Conceivably through social experiment we can learn how to distribute centralized resources to create decentralized, uncontrolled social situations.
>
> (Sennett 1970, 133)

Thus, the idea was to plan for the wanted diversity. The difficult of doing this is fairly evident, however. As Sennett himself acknowledges, many people want what homogeneous suburbs have to offer, and so a democratic central government would find it difficult not to provide for that choice. If the majority of people lived in the suburban way, they would not be very sympathetic to policies premised on the claim that their way of life was wrong. So, centralized democratic "planning for diversity" would be difficult to sustain politically (Sennett 1977). The Hayekian "thin theory" of the *cosmos* is in many ways easier to sell politically, because it suggests that people should be free to choose between diverse neighbourhood communities and homogeneous ones. The "public choice" theorists, who drew on Hayekian ideas, gradually elaborated on a theory that suggested that each neighbourhood should be free to buy the range of public services that it wanted (Tiebout 1956, Ostrom *et al.* 1961, Bish and Ostrom 1973). They said that such neighbourhoods could compete for citizens in the way Hayek suggested, and offer differentiated environments and public services mixes that would appeal to different sorts of people. Thus, a variegated urban order could emerge as a result of the marketing of different neighbourhood environments. There would not need to be the "centralized state apparatus" to which Sennett referred, if we were to abstain from social engineering and let cities develop in accordance with the preferences people expressed in the market.

Of course, in practice Hayekians have been as attached to social engineering as anyone else, if not more so. The most obvious example of this is the reconstruction of the local state in Britain from the 1980s onward. The ostensible aim was to give people more choice: to own their own homes, rather than live in public housing; to use private rather than public transport; to send their children to schools supported by like-minded parents; to use recreational facilities restricted to those who had the ability to pay; to buy premium health care; to work in businesses free from state control. To achieve this aim, the Thatcher government broke up the islands of local socialism that had been established in parts of Britain. It also broke the power of the unions, deregulated the City of London (to give the bankers there the freedom they thought they needed in order to maintain the City's pre-eminence as a global financial centre), and facilitated the de-industrialization of the world's first industrialized country. These policies were intended to revive Britain by making it into an "enterprise society" on the Hayekian model. For the British Conservatives and later for New Labour, "America" was the model. The supposed freedom and dynamism of American cities was associated with private sector initiatives, public–private partnerships, market-based solutions, and all the other policy nostrums that have since become nause-atingly familiar. The overall "plan" – which is what it was – was the same one already implicit in American public policy, the one that was exported to poorer countries under the aegis of the Structural Adjustment Pro-grammes demanded by the International Monetary Fund and the World Bank (Davis 2006). It is hard to think of a grander or more destructive scheme of social engineering than the one that has been effected over the last thirty years or so under the guise of encouraging enterprise and giving people more choice (Harvey 2005, Lipschutz 2009).

Others have written at length about the hypocrisies and hardships involved, and so there is no reason for me to repeat the analysis here. Instead, I will just note how an ostensibly anti-statist theory like Hayek's turns into its opposite – just as Marx's did, it might be noted – when it is embedded in the conventional political imaginary. If things are not going as they should, blame falls either on the rulers or on the people or both. In this case, the people are blamed for being insufficiently entrepreneurial and the rulers for indulging this slovenliness and profiting from it. The new order, initi-ated by the Hayekian revolutionaries, is to be imposed by the power of the state, a power that is supposed to be self-limiting because it will wither away once a properly entrepreneurial Hayekian society is established. One can hear the echoes of earlier revolutionary projects in this initiative: not only the ones marshalled under the banners of communism and national socialism, but also the ones justified in terms of the "white man's burden". A certain culture or way of being in the world is presented as the best and other possibilities – in this case, ways of living and acting that challenge the order generated by the market – are actively suppressed. Fortunately, there has been a good deal of resistance to the Hayekian order in the form of local public initiatives (dare we say socialist ones?), alternative economics, green regulations, communi-ties of commitment, sanctuaries for the excluded, trans-local movements, and so on. Considered globally, urban life has not been susceptible to close control, and instead has generated possibilities and problems that are not easily understood on a Hayekian register.

Sennett and Jacobs refer back to ideals of planning that we find among the Chicago school sociologists like Wirth. As such, they themselves nod at the rationalizing power of the state. Ideas like theirs have informed efforts to diversify city neighbourhoods, encourage street life, promote multicultural-ism, and capitalize on the vibrancy of cities for a variety of purposes, especially economic ones. Since the 1990s especially, the idea of the vibrant global city has held the imagination of many urban planners, local business leaders, and municipal politicians, often as a counterpoint to the narrow Hayekian vision of a market-based social and political order. Implicit is a sort of communitarian neo-liberalism that posits the global city as an integrative order (or community of communities) that brings the world in and lets the people out in an explosion of creativity and inter-communal good will that capitalizes on the discoveries that people make when they are obliged to negotiate their differences in close proximity to one another – and actually find opportunities for personal development and social solidarity in the process.[7] As I noted in Chapter 1, speculations about a wider global order – the global city on a global scale – tend to refer back to these possibilities, rather than to the ones favoured by Hayekians: not least because the security required for a generalized Hayekian order can only be generated (if at all) by a super-state that deploys extraordinary military power. The possibility of building global order out of the street-level practices of self-government that Sennett and Jacobs discuss seems much more appealing. How this might happen is a difficult question, but we will not get far in working out the answers if we keep resorting to a statist political imaginary rather than thinking the political through in a different way.

4 The art of government

Does a different ontology of the political actually emerge from the analyses that I have just been considering? If so, it situates politics in the practices of government and self-government that enable urban life. As Jacobs and Sennett notice, such practices emerge in the street, according to no one's plan. As Hayek argues, the order that results from mutual adjustments is ultimately global and not radically dependent on state authority. Although Hayek tends to identify this order with the market, Wirth and the other Chicago school sociologists make it clear that the relevant order takes shape through the normal practices of urban life. Weber emphasizes that modern civilization actually emerged in cities where the writ of the sovereign was suspended in favour of local authorities. Although Weber would want us to think of politics as an activity related to the state, the field of the political is evidently wider and more complicated than he indicates. Political authorities of some significance may be formed outside the state, or in and against it, as the communal authorities in late medieval Europe seem to have been. Moreover, there are many authorities like churches and businesses that are rule-making and rule-enforcing bodies with substantial resources, great organizational capacity, and high legitimacy. Such authorities certainly look political to me and many other people, even if analysts like Weber and Hayek insist on putting them in a different category. In any case, there are authorities of a different sort, such as interest group and social movement organizations, which are clearly political in their purposes. Many important authorities, including religious bodies, multinational corporations, and organizations of other sorts, operate in action spaces incommensurate with the state system. To be effective, states themselves have to operate in such spaces as well. If the business of politics is government in the broadest sense of that word, it includes even what we do to ourselves as individuals so as to fit into the communities where we live and the activities in which we engage. We govern ourselves in large degree, but – as Jacobs and Sennett notice – we are also involved in governing others. If the field of the political is coextensive with the field of the governmental, it really does encompass the whole of human life, and the relevant political authorities are extremely various, including even the self-governing individuals liberals prize.

Now, we can adopt a utopian vision of things as Hayek does, and imagine that the magic of the market will generate the order we want. Things rarely go in accordance with our plans or expectations, however, and the temptation is to resort to sovereign authority to fix the resulting problems. The Hayekians and other neo-liberals have been doing just that for the last few decades, with many baneful results. If any alternative has been articulated, it has been in the spirit of Wirth, Jacobs, and Sennett: referring to notions of democratic planning, collaborative governance, and networked authority on the one hand and self-government and local initiative on the other hand. Wirth's reference to democratic planning seems antique now that planning has lost its cachet in face of criticisms in the Hayekian style. On the other hand, the demand for democratization in face of oligarchical modes of collaborative governance and networked authority seems highly pertinent. Moreover, the idea of planning suggests that market-based rationality might be put into relation with other things, including other rationalities. Although it might be difficult to articulate a singular ideal in relation to the one that Hayek and his followers have put forward, the possibility of living and thinking differently is certainly pertinent. Perhaps we could even live socialistically or in environmentally friendly, multiply gendered, culturally receptive ways. Who knows? If social diversity, variety in ways of life, differences in conceptions of the good, and divergent standards of judgement are all to be valued, then there is much to be said for an urban order that transcends both the market and the state. In any case, it seems that we will have such an order whether we like it or not.

How should we understand this order? I have been arguing that we need to look at it as a political production, but not interpret it in binary, statist terms. Other urbanists have been inspired by people like Henri Lefebvre (1991, 1996), Gilles Deleuze (Deleuze and Guattari 2004), and Paul Virilio (2005) – or by anglophone analysts like Doreen Massey (2005) and Ed Soja (1996) – who have helped us see how the space of the urban is produced. Elsewhere I have followed this line of inquiry myself, trying to understand the relationship between the space of the urban and the space of the political. I concluded that we are best advised to think of the urban as a hyperspace of many dimensions, each of which is produced by political action and related to the others politically (Magnusson 2000a). I have no more to add to that thought, and in any case I suspect that efforts to analyse things spatially take us away from more important issues, which are not well posed in spatial terms. Perhaps I should add immediately that switching from the spatial to the temporal is less of an alternative than sometimes imagined, because spatiality is always already posed in relation to temporality and vice versa. I want to do something different here, and that is to focus on the *practices* normally associated with politics, especially the practices that politics supposedly puts at issue. What are these practices? How do they relate to the practices that enable urbanism? So far, I have made the assumption that these practices have something to do with government or at least self-government, even if I have challenged the idea that they are necessarily associated with ruling.

But, how are such practices to be understood? What is involved in treating these practices (or challenges to them) as political?

In addressing such questions, I find it helpful to turn to the work of Michel Foucault, who introduced the term "governmentality" to describe what he called the "art of government". Foucault's work is particularly useful because he puts himself at a distance from this art and analyses it critically without resorting to simple condemnation. As is well known, most of his work relates to matters that are quite different from the ones I am considering here. I have nothing to add to the extensive commentary on those aspects of his work. Instead, I will focus on the sequence of lectures that surrounds his discussion of governmentality, a discussion that spawned a whole school of "governmentality studies" in the English-speaking world after the lecture in question was published in English in 1991 (Burchell *et al.* 1991). Only recently have the related lectures been published in full (Foucault 2003, 2007, 2008), and it is easier now to put his analysis in contexts other than the ones that seem to interest most of the commentators on his work. In these lectures, given at the Collège de France between 1976 and 1979, he addressed himself more directly than anywhere else to what we might call the standard problematic of political science – the problematic that I associate with a statist ontology of the political – and in the course of that offered an account of liberalism and neo-liberalism as successive iterations of the art of government. One of Foucault's key claims is that this art, previously associated with the family and the church, came to be understood as a central function of the state in the modern era. Modern conceptions of politics and government – the ones I have been relating to the statist ontology of the political – are bound up with this understanding, as are the social sciences and moral and political philosophy. Of particular significance for me is the fact that Foucault connects the modern art of government to the problem of the city. One might say – although Foucault himself is not so explicit about this – that it is the city that makes government as we know it necessary. As he makes clear, government is not the same thing as sovereignty, although there may be a connection between the two.

Does a Foucauldian analysis of governmentality point toward a different ontology of the political? If so, is it the one implicit in seeing like a city? For me, these are the ultimate questions, but there is much else in his analysis that is pertinent. He offers us a different way of thinking about statism, neo-liberalism, liberalism, government, and politics, and it is worth getting a sense of his analysis and the critiques that follow from it before re-posing the problem of the city, as I will do in the final section of this chapter. Where might we go, if we were to follow Foucault?

Beyond the problematic of the state

Foucault's political judgement was far from perfect – whose is? – but these lectures show him at his most astute. Although the last of them were given early in 1979, before Margaret Thatcher and Ronald Reagan took office and before anyone thought that there was a "Washington consensus", Foucault sensed that the issue of the moment was not the "growth of the state" but the advance of neo-liberalism. He criticized the then current – and, I would say, always present – "phobia of the state", a phobia with which, unfortunately, he himself has been (quite mistakenly) identified. He remarks that "what is currently challenged, and from a great many perspectives, is almost always the state: the unlimited growth of the state, its bureaucratic development, the state with the seeds of fascism it contains, the state's inherent violence beneath its welfare paternalism" (Foucault 2008, 186–87). In these critiques, he suggests,

> there is the idea that the state possesses in itself and through its own dynamism a sort of power of expansion, an intrinsic tendency to expand, an endogenous imperialism constantly pushing it to spread its surface, and increase in extent, depth, and subtlety to the point that it will come to take over entirely that which is at the same time its other, its outside, its target, and its object, namely: civil society.
>
> (Foucault 2008, 187)

Moreover, he says,

> The second element . . . in these general themes of state phobia is that there is a kinship, a sort of genetic continuity or evolutionary implication between different forms of the state, with the administrative state, the welfare state, the bureaucratic state, the fascist state, and the totalitarian state all being, in no matter which of the various analyses, the successive branches of one and the same great tree of state control in its continuous and unified expansion.
>
> (Foucault 2008, 187)

The result, he says, is an "inflationary" critique of the state, one that "encourages the growth, at a constantly accelerating speed, of the interchangeability of analyses. . . . For example, an analysis of social security and the administrative apparatus on which it rests ends up, via some slippages and some plays on words, referring us to the analysis of concentration camps" (Foucault 2008, 187). So, "something like a kinship or danger, something like the great fantasy of the paranoiac and devouring state can always be found" (Foucault 2008, 187–88).[1]

Ironically, something akin to this "fantasy of the paranoiac and devouring state" can be found in some of the later writings that evoke Foucault's name. By contrast, in Foucault's own lectures (particularly the later ones) we find, if not a view of the state exactly comparable to Gandhi's assessment of Western civilization ("it would be a good idea"), a number of ideas that could be read in similar terms. Foucault attempts to avoid polemics. His aim is to understand, rather than to praise or condemn. But, he evidently believes that what he calls "liberal governmentality" – and what others might describe as the standard forms and practices of modern liberal democracy – is in many respects better than most of the obvious alternatives, not least the "party governmentality" of Nazism and Communism (Foucault 2008, 190–92). He is far from condemning constitutionalism, the rule of law, human rights, or any of the other things that liberals value, but he senses that we have far less understanding of these things than we usually suppose, and that we need to stand back and look at things differently if we are to make sense of the actual currents of our own time and orient ourselves politically. In particular, he thinks that both the state and civil society have been misunderstood, and that political theory and political philosophy largely bypass the debates that actually animate contemporary politics.

As ever, Foucault's method is indirect. He offers no "theory of state", because he thinks that any such theory would suggest that the state has some sort of eternal essence that persists across space and time. If, for him, there is any essence or constant with respect to these matters, it is simply that there is a field of possibilities, in which there are countless plays of power and authority, struggle and initiative, strategy and tactics. Almost nothing can be deduced from human nature, or anything else: as he says, "history is not a deductive science" (Foucault 2008, 77); we have to discover what people have done, how, and why. What we can see, evidently, is the emergence sometime in the distant past of something that we could describe as "the state". We can also see that there have been many changes in the way people have reacted to the state, tried to use it, or come to think about it. To understand the state, we have to see it in relation to a wider range of possibilities, and that means distancing ourselves from the preset categories we normally use in our analyses. The most crucial move that Foucault makes in these lectures is to distinguish between three different aspects of ruling: what he calls *sovereignty*, *discipline*, and *government* (Foucault 2007, 107) respectively. Most crucial is his idea that "government" is something distinct. He believes that our age, the modern age, is characterized by what he calls "the governmentalization of the state" (Foucault 2007, 108–9), a change in its disposition that we are liable to miss if we approach the state as if sovereignty were its most important feature.

Now, let us be clear. Foucault is *not* challenging the idea that sovereignty is a defining feature of the state. He is happy to accept the latter assumption for the purposes of his analysis, although he is at pains to remind us that the character of sovereignty – sovereignty of whom, in relation to what? – is bound to change over time, and moreover that *modern* sovereignty has distinctive characteristics that we need to analyse. In any case, sovereignty is not really his subject here, nor is discipline. He thinks that it is the third thing, government, which requires our attention, because the balance between the three aspects of ruling – sovereignty, discipline, and government – has clearly shifted in favour of government in the modern era. How are we to understand that? What are its causes and effects? Foucault's analysis is in many ways tentative and preliminary, and he has much less to say about causation than others would like. Nevertheless, he offers fundamental insights. If he is right, we cannot take our familiar analytic categories – such as the state and civil society or economics and international relations or rights and freedoms – as given, for these categories have particular origins that are bound up with shifts of understanding that occurred in the context of earlier political struggles. We need to look backward from the present to see what we are dealing with, and to look, not so much directly at our objects of study, as at the fields in which those objects are constituted. Although Foucault's ostensible subject in these lectures is "biopolitics", he says much less about that than one might expect, and much more about neo-liberalism, which he apparently sees as the latest iteration in the modern art of government.

One of the many surprising moves that he makes in his lectures is to begin his account of neo-liberalism in April 1948, with a speech by Ludwig Erhard, who was later Minister of Economics in the post-war government of West Germany and who ultimately succeeded Konrad Adenauer as Chancellor (Foucault 2008, 80–81). Erhard was immensely important. As Paul Martin was to Jean Chrétien or Gordon Brown to Tony Blair, so Erhard was to Adenauer – even in his political deficiencies. Whereas no one would say that Brown and Martin are great thinkers, Erhard was formidable intellectually: a thinker in his own right, who was part of the group of "ordo-liberals" so crucial for German and later European political development (Foucault 2008, 77–121). There is nothing unusual about Foucault's recognizing Erhard's importance. What is unusual is the connection that Foucault makes between what he calls German neo-liberalism and American neo-liberalism. After all, the German model – with which Erhard was strongly associated – was and is often presented as an *alternative* to the American model, an alternative that turns on the idea of the "social market economy", an economy that seems to be of a different sort from the one recommended by American neo-liberals. The American – or, after Thatcher's election victory in Britain – the *Anglo*-American model of neo-liberalism is often taken to be *the* model of neo-liberalism, in relation to which Germany offers the main counter-example. That is not the way Foucault saw it, however. For him, the German and American models were variants of the same thing: the neo-liberalism that needed to be understood.

It seemed obvious to Foucault that neo-liberalism had to be analysed in relation to two things: the recent rationalities of government to which it was responding, and the older form of liberalism which it was replacing. To understand the first, one had to go back to the 1930s and 1940s. To understand the second, one had to go back to the late eighteenth century, when liberalism as we know it was taking shape. Foucault does not make an explicit argument in this regard, but he treats the high point of classical liberalism – the nineteenth century – as a less interesting period, one in which ideas that had been adumbrated earlier were being put into practice.

In retrospect, at least, we can see that his analysis of neo-liberalism has a similar character. We have been living, as he did not, through the period in which the principles of neo-liberalism were put into effect on a global scale, but he well knew that those principles had already been worked out in an earlier era. In any case, the neo-liberal order that most directly affected him was already in place in the form of the European Community (later the European Union), an order that had been established on the sort of principles that Erhart articulated back in 1948. Of course, this is not to say that things are ever implemented exactly, but what Foucault saw is that Erhart was looking for a way to embed German sovereignty in the market (rather than the other way around, as earlier liberals had tended to do). Although Foucault does not say so explicitly, that is an obvious way of understanding the whole project of European Union, beginning with the European Coal and Steel Community in 1950.

So, what were the ordo-liberals, the pioneering German neo-liberals, responding to in the inter-war period? The easy answer would be Nazism and Communism, but the truth is more interesting and complicated than that, for the ordo-liberals were also reacting to trends within liberalism itself, such as the New Deal in the USA, the Beveridge plan for the welfare state in Britain, and Keynesian economic interventionism. They were riled by the then popular idea of planning, either as a means to social justice or as a way of overcoming the irrationalities of the capitalist economy. They denied that there were inherent irrationalities, and instead claimed that the apparent irrationalities were effects of state intervention. On their view, each intervention created more irrationalities, which induced more interventions and further irrationalities in an endless cycle. The ultimate outcome, even of the seemingly benign liberal interventionism associated with Keynes, Beveridge, and Roosevelt, would be some kind of totalitarian state. In many ways, their analysis was similar to Joseph Schumpeter's, who suggested that although capitalism was the best economic system, it generated social effects that led to an inevitable reaction. Schumpeter thought that the reaction could be moderated, so that the future socialist state would not be characterized by the abuses of Nazism and Communism, even if it lacked the excitements and benefits of capitalist freedom. The ordo-liberals were at once more pessimistic and more optimistic. As Foucault says, they thought that a new capitalism could be established, one that would avoid the ills that had accompanied the old capitalism, not least the "mass society" identified by Werner Sombart at the beginning of the twentieth century and exploited by the Nazis during their rise to power. The neo-liberal alternative was not a return to "laissez-faire", but an effort to create and sustain an "enterprise society".

Foucault remarks that, "All those who share in the great state phobia should know that they are following the direction of the wind and that in fact, for years and years, an effective reduction of the state has been on the way, a reduction both of the growth of state control and of 'statifying' and 'statified' governmentality" (Foucault 2008, 191). His immediate reference is to neo-liberalism, but no doubt he was thinking of the longer history of liberalism, a history that he traces back to the eighteenth century. For others, liberalism begins with the critique of absolute sovereignty, a critique that is grounded in ideas about natural right and the social contract. For Foucault, such an analysis is misleading, for it misses the connection between liberalism and the emergent "art of government". As he sees it, the idea that rulers had to *govern* took shape quite gradually, but once it did there was recognition that the key to good government was a proper understanding of political economy. From that followed the idea that the best – which is to say, the most effective – government was one that governed as little as possible, that respected the freedom of the governed and indeed encouraged them to use it, that, to the extent that it intervened, helped to produce the sort of people who could use their freedom for the benefit of themselves and others, and that acted liberally as a matter of *policy*, quite apart from any question of right or rights. As Foucault sees it, eighteenth-century liberalism dissolved the question of right into the question of interest: what was in everyone's interest? The liberal answer was that it is in everyone's interests to be governed in accordance with the principles of liberalism, principles that derived not from an analysis of right, but from a consideration of the requirements of government. A liberal economy, it was said, was simply better from everyone's perspective than a police state. It would be more productive, and so healthier, wealthier, and wiser than a police state. It would certainly be happier, and more loyal to its rulers or to the system of government through which they were ruled.

In Foucault's analysis, the key connections are between *liberalism*, understood as an "art of government", *political economy*, the science that generated that art, and *raison d'Etat*, the analytical frame within which that science developed. In brief, the idea that there was a *raison d'Etat* distinct from any other form of reason took shape in the sixteenth century. The argument, essentially, is that the ruler had to focus, first of all, on maintaining his own position, or "state". As Machiavelli explained, that would mean doing things that might be at odds with morality or religion: what was necessary for maintaining the state had to be worked out on its own terms. In the sixteenth and seventeenth centuries, there was a shift of emphasis from the ruler to the state itself, conceived as an enduring entity in a competitive situation. Ideas about the Second Coming and the restoration of the Empire faded, and analysts began to consider seriously how the state might be strengthened in relation to other states. That involved a more careful analysis of the state's resources: most especially the people it had. What shape were they in? What were their occupations? Were they healthy? Did they have the necessary means of life? Were they contented? Were they producing a surplus that could be taxed? Sons who could serve in the army? Statistics were needed to make sense of all this. But, once the statistics were collected, movements and distributions had to be detected. How could the people best be governed? How could their strength be fostered for the benefit of the state? The original idea was that greater things could be achieved by regulating the population more strictly than had been done in the past. This was the idea of the police state, which took shape in the seventeenth and eighteenth centuries. To police the population effectively was to develop its strength. This is where the liberal critique came in, through political economy. The political economists argued that state interventions were usually counterproductive. Not only did they waste the resources of the state, but they actually frustrated the state's own purposes. Better to leave the people alone if you wanted them – and your state – to be strong; or, at least, that is what the liberals argued.

There were two key liberal concepts: the economy on the one hand, and civil society on the other. We know the idea of the economy – of a self-subsistent realm governed by the laws of the market – primarily through the work of Adam Smith and his successors. Less known, but equally important was Adam Ferguson's conception of civil society. Both Smith and Ferguson – and many of their contemporaries: they were not alone in this – were using old terms, namely economy and society, in new ways. The key claim was that the thing at issue was generally present (not localized in a family or community), self-subsistent, more-or-less orderly, and as much rooted in nature as it was in society. In fact, the distinction between what was natural and what was an effect of society made little sense from this perspective. Society had always existed in one form or another. On the one hand, it was natural for people to live in societies, and, on the other hand, it was equally natural for people to separate themselves from one another into distinct societies. The civilizing influences, the ones that inclined people to deal peacefully with one another, were the ones implicit in commercial transactions, which occurred for mutual advantage rather than reasons of pure sociability. As Foucault sees it, Kant, Ferguson, and Smith were all on the same page in stressing the possibility that a new world order could emerge from liberal governmentality. Whatever might be said of right, the key question was one of government. How might government be constituted so that the competitive relation would work to mutual advantage, whether in terms of the relationship between individuals or the relationship between collectivities, such as the ones that were formed into states? From this liberal perspective, the problematic of good government was what linked political philosophy to international relations, and it did so through the medium of political economy, understood as a nascent science of society or, more accurately, of *governing* society.

Foucault suggests that the idea that the major task of rulers was to govern their subjects was new. Previously, the focus had been on sovereignty: keeping the subjects in order by dispensing justice and punishing wrongdoers; maintaining the integrity of the state by forestalling or overcoming internal and external threats (Foucault 2003, 36). There was also the idea of discipline, which became increasingly important in the early modern era. Foucault had given much attention to discipline in his earlier works, but here he suggests that there is something else that goes beyond discipline and has a different logic: that is government. Foucault thinks that the idea of government took shape in different contexts, at one remove from the state itself: in the household and in the church. The good father governed his family well. The church, more particularly the bishop, had a pastoral responsibility in relation to his "flock", the members of his diocese. The model of course, constantly invoked, was of the good shepherd tending his sheep, watching out for the benefit of each and all and giving of himself for that purpose. The focus was on the sheep rather than the shepherd. In this view, the virtues of the shepherd were incidental to the well-being of the sheep, and the issue certainly was not whether the shepherd's position could be maintained. Foucault is interested in the way ideas about good government, originally associated with problems of pastoral care (or the care of families, in the case of fathers) migrated from those spheres to the sphere of the ruler. The argument, essentially, is that the new understanding of the state, and hence of *raison d'Etat*, implicit in what international relations theorists call the Westphalian system, changed the question that rulers and their advisors had to address. Sovereignty was less of an issue, because it had been placed on firmer foundations. On the other hand, the question of government loomed larger. Government could not be just left to the bishops and the heads of household if the question was now how to maximize the state's resources and mobilize them for the ruler's purposes.

Foucault refers to the process as the governmentalization of the state, rather than the statification of government, because he recognizes that the initial move toward more intensive policing soon reversed itself. If the aim was to govern well, then the institutions of government had to be subject to careful scrutiny. Statification was a means, not an end, even from the vantage point of the rulers. But, of course, the shift of focus from the ruler to the state enabled another shift, from the state to the people it governed. What of their benefit, their interests? As we know – although Foucault mentions it only in passing – the argument from the eighteenth century onward was that a government chosen by and accountable to the people it governed would be the best: not only the best in terms of the people's welfare, but the best in terms of the strength of the state, since a well-governed people would produce what the state required. And, what would the state require? What it needed would be to maintain itself – and hence that society as a distinct society – in a competitive situation in which other states sought to strengthen themselves for their own purposes. The logic is familiar to us. What Foucault adds to the standard analysis is recognition that the problem of government is what links domestic politics to international relations, and hence political philosophy to security studies. Political economy is the linking knowledge.

According to Foucault, every knowledge – without exception – is an apparatus of domination (although of course it is never *only* that). Other knowledges are subjugated, repressed, excluded, or marginalized by knowledge of the art of government. To insert ourselves in the debates about how people should be governed is to involve ourselves in these practices of subjugation. Moreover, we ourselves are caught up in a problematic that generates the objects of knowledge to be considered. Are we obliged to be instruments of such practices? Foucault implies that, at the very least, we can be much more self-critical than we usually are. For political scientists, that means being especially suspicious of political economy, for political economy presents itself as the discipline that turns the idealism of political theory and the realism of international relations into a science rooted in the hidden realities of society. What appears in the first instance is the economy, regulated by its own internal mechanisms. Then other social phenomena appear, diagnosed by sociologists, anthropologists, and others. The data about economy, society, and culture provide the stuff for social scientific analysis. Political economy wrestles these data back into the field of the political, and as such into the domain of government. The impetus of political science is to interpret these data in terms of the problem of government, and so to pose them as problems of policy or diplomacy. To the extent that they appear as political problems of a different sort, there is normally a reference back to the state and hence to the problems of governing associated with the state. This keeps things in a familiar field where sovereign right – the right of the state in relation to society and the right of the state in relation to other states – remains an ordering principle. Thus, a science that may appear to be taking us past the state and rooting itself in the realities of society brings us back to the state constantly.

Foucault grew up and lived his life in an intellectual environment dominated by Marxism and phenomenology. The positivist orthodoxy of the Anglo-American world is something that he encountered at a distance. These lectures make a double move in that while analysing that positivist orthodoxy, and so putting it at a critical distance, they do not relapse into one of the other orthodoxies familiar to Foucault. In a sense, he treats Marxism and phenomenology as derivatives of the positivism he wants to understand, a positivism that he describes not as such but as *political economy*, embedded in a modern art of government geared to a *raison d'Etat* that on the one hand explains how states must operate to survive in an international order and on the other hand says how those states must be organized to satisfy the needs of their own people. What becomes positivism in the nineteenth century follows from the earlier moves in which analysts identified a society and an economy at one remove from the authorities (the state), which could improve things and strengthen themselves by governing as they should. In the end, everything pointed back toward the problem of government and hence toward the vantage point of the state. Marx's critique of Hegel, which followed on from Hegel's critique of Kant, which in turn followed on from Kant's critique of Hume, did not really shift the vantage point or displace the problem of how we might be governed ideally. To be sure, a certain historicization was involved, which enabled Marx to develop his account in terms of an age-old struggle of the oppressed that would culminate in the redemption of humanity itself. But, this was really a variant of what the other political economists were doing, and have done ever since. In that sense, Hayek, Keynes, and Marx are brothers under the skin who offer different accounts of how the problems posed by the early political economists are to be resolved. The phenomenological take on this does not alter the problematic, any more than logical positivism does. For Foucault, the only moves that can actually change the questions are ones that de-centre the problem being addressed. That is what his work as a whole attempts, and that is the spirit in which he approaches the triad of political philosophy, political economy, and international relations.

Foucault's work in these lectures is exploratory. He would not want to be read as having set out a complete theory that deals with every relevant issue and can stand without revision. Instead, we should be looking for uninflationary critiques that enable us to see things we may have missed, things that put the state, government, and politics in a different context.

Uninflationary critiques

One such critique can be derived from Foucault's inversion of Clausewitz's dictum to the effect that war is an extension of politics by other means. Foucault suggests that it was Clausewitz who actually inverted a long-standing analysis to the effect that *politics is war by other means*. According to Foucault, the latter analysis had first taken shape in Europe early in the seventeenth century, and it had informed much of the critical commentary in subsequent years. The key idea was that there were two peoples or two races within the bosom of the same society, one of which had subjugated the other. In England, this idea was linked to the Norman Conquest: the Normans had supposedly subjugated the Saxons.[2] The idea went through many variations, some of which enabled a critique of absolutist monarchy in the name of the ancient rights of the Saxons, and others of which identified the oppressed common people with those whose rights had been usurped at the time of the Conquest. The idea of a race war was transmuted into the idea of a struggle between people of different estates or classes, and that idea obviously played itself out in the revolutionary struggles of the seventeenth, eighteenth, nineteenth, and twentieth centuries. However it is iterated, this idea of an ongoing war within the very bosom of civil society challenges the practices (to which Clausewitz is obviously attached) by which war is pushed to the margins of the state, where it comes into play, if at all, between states. More significantly (at least in Foucault's analysis), it challenges the whole problematic of "right", the one that suggests that the war can be resolved within a system of right that somehow redeems the injustices of the past and present. Foucault points out that the analyses to which he refers turn not on the right, but on the relation of forces. Whoever is stronger will get to determine the right.

Foucault's (2003) commentary on this in *Society Must Be Defended* is quite unsettling, because he talks of the "race war" and seems to approve of the

critiques – or, more accurately, "insurrections of subjugated knowledges" –
associated with it. His approach is deliberately unsettling, of course. He argues
that the dominant discourses – philosophical accounts, histories, moral and
political reckonings – are geared to the question of sovereign right: what the
king is to be, what the king is to do, how the king is to relate to his subjects, what authority he has, what the sources of his legitimacy are, what
limits there might be to what he can do, and so on. Replacing the king with
the nobles or the people or some combination of them does not change the
basic logic. The presumption still is that there is or can be a sovereign right
that, as it were, resolves everything and provides for justice itself. The
"historico-political" discourses to which Foucault refers are not based on
such abstract reasoning. They are geared to the particularities of the past
and present, the particular injustices or oppressions from which *some*
people are suffering or have suffered and from which *others* are benefiting.
Although in some versions there is a claim that the victory of the oppressed
will inaugurate an era of universal right, one that somehow redeems all
past and present injustices, this connection between force and right is itself
forced. We can see that forcing in various stories of historical progress, including the philosophically sophisticated dialectics of Kant, Hegel, and Marx.
Foucault shows how these stories respond to earlier ones, especially in France,
which celebrated the capacity of the strong to dominate the weak and effectively erased the distinction between force and right. What Foucault forces
us to see is that the connection between force and right is *always* forced, that
claims of universal justice or the rights of the people always refer back to
a war that the people have won or must win, and to an "other" that must
be contained, repressed, marginalized, excluded, or simply destroyed. The
prettiest accounts of universal justice cover over a desperate struggle whose
motivations are far from pure, a struggle that will *continue* in some form,
perhaps in a form that is scarcely recognizable to the original combatants.

Foucault's point is *not* that there is a different and better way of thinking about these things, an approach that will somehow resolve all the
contradictions. His point is exactly the opposite: we are deceiving ourselves
if we think that there is or can be such a resolution. All systems of right are
systems of domination – and vice versa, one might say – and it is foolish to
suppose that it could be otherwise. What we need to do is to keep the contradictions in view, trace the way that the dominant discourses dominate,
follow the insurrection of subjugated knowledges, and, as it were, keep the
issues in play, rather than burying them by making claims to universal truth
like the ones posed by the social sciences or the dominant forms of political
theory. On the one hand, the thematic of "race war" leads to state racism,
be it in the form of apartheid, Nazism, Stalinism, or eugenics. On the other
hand, it gives us the struggle of the common people against their oppressors,
colonized peoples against the imperialists, women against male chauvinists,
people of colour against white supremacists, cultural minorities against the
dominant culture, sexual minorities against compulsory heterosexuality,

and so on. We may give the struggles we consider "good" the cover of universal right, but those struggles are actually rooted in something different: the particular claims of people who consider themselves a race apart. We should not delude ourselves about what we are doing when we attach ourselves to those particular claims.

A second critique is implicit in this first one. What Foucault (2007, 2008) makes increasingly clear in the later lectures (*Security, Territory, Population* and *The Birth of Biopolitics*) is that there is a particular approach to the problem of right in liberal societies, one that depends on assimilating right to interest. What follows from the sort of analysis developed during the Scottish Enlightenment by people like Hume, Smith, and Ferguson is that rights – and indeed right itself – only make sense in so far as they accord with our interests. If it is in our best interests to submit to a tyrant, so be it. The overarching claim, developed by the later utilitarians and implicit even in the earlier iterations of political economy, is that the question of right really is subordinate to the question of interest, which means to say that all of us – kings or the subjects of kings, aggrieved nobles or common people, imperial masters or colonized subjects, male chauvinists or feminists, heterosexuals or homosexuals – need to look to our interests before we act politically. The utilitarian claim is that we simply *are* creatures of interest, and act as such when we are being rational. Claims of right that go beyond our own interests are simply irrational. We may have an interest in a system of rights or a system of right, but we can only judge that by analysing our interests. That we must do realistically, in context, although of course we may posit improvements that might be for our benefit or in the general interest. Political economy or the social sciences more generally reveal what is in our interests, and so teach us what to want. In so far as we learn the lessons of political economy or the social sciences we become more governable subjects, who can be offered more extensive rights because we know how to use them responsibly. In fact, we can progress peacefully by becoming more attentive to our own interests, learning how they intersect with other people's interests, and acting together to further our mutual interests. That is what liberal society promises.

Foucault is reminding us that the key to actually existing liberalism is not the system of right articulated in the seventeenth and eighteenth centuries but the practice of government developed from the late eighteenth century onward. That practice of government has always been understood in terms of political economy, which is why the shifts and changes associated with the latter are so important. The abandonment of laissez-faire and the moves toward a more interventionist state associated with Roosevelt, Keynes, and Beveridge, as well as the subsequent shift toward a neo-liberal governmentality of the sort advocated by Erhard, Von Mises, and Hayek (and now associated with Reagan, Thatcher, and the Washington consensus), are crucial, not because "the economy" is dominant but because they entail such profound changes in the way we are governed. The question of how we should be governed is constantly posed and re-posed. Neo-liberalism just happens to be the discourse that became most powerful from the 1970s onward, a discourse (Foucault reminds us) that was already well articulated by 1945. In Foucault's analysis, political economy as a way of understanding the problem of government is not separate from the philosophical reinterpretation of the individual as a "subject of interest" or the re-framing of *raison d'Etat* as a question of the state's interest in its own survival. There is a common intellectual understanding and a common set of political commitments implicit in the efforts of political economists, political philosophers, and international relations analysts to work out what is in everyone's best interests, individually and collectively. The quandaries of rival interests – including rival claims of right – are well known, but the implicit hope is that peaceful solutions can be reached if people come to understand what their best interests are. That violence might be required in the general interest (or indeed in the interests of particular individuals or communities) is always recognized, and always regarded as a worrying problem.

There are two important implications of what Foucault is saying. The first is that discussions of right or rights tend to beg the question in so far as they avoid the problem of interests. This is not just a philosophical problem. We could say, with Hume, that rights are always a matter of interests and should be analysed in those terms. But, that is not the main point. The point is that liberalism, the system of right that purports to offer extensive rights, is actually geared to a system of government, an "art" of government, which puts interests first and understands rights and right itself in relation to interests. Interests are understood in terms of a balance of forces, and so point back toward the analyses we have just considered, the ones that suggest that politics is an extension of war by other means. This way of understanding things is what enables us to make sense of *raison d'Etat* in the same terms that we analyse economic competition or contentions in the courts of law or Parliament. Liberalism, the social sciences, and political philosophy are all in fact geared to the question of interests. This is what gives them a common "grid of intelligibility". So, there is a certain naïveté involved in discussions of right or rights – except, of course, in so far as they serve as cover for something else, namely a form of domination. If we keep Foucault's analysis of the relation between right and domination in mind, it is easy to see not only that the discourse of right can conceal interests, but that the discourse of interests is a way of concealing domination. We are expected to become creatures of interest, rational economic actors, and so on. This expectation is enforced upon us in the context of endowing us with rights. The neo-liberal discourse that gives this endowment a particular interpretation – we are to be entrepreneurs of ourselves – is only the latest iteration of something that has been going on for a long time and that will probably continue far into the future.

The second implication of this part of Foucault's analysis is more comforting to liberals. His complaint about "the phobia of the state" has many dimensions, but one of them is that analyses of this sort ignore the fact that the modern state has been posited as a way of restraining, modulating, and rationalizing the exercise of power by our rulers. Efforts at perfection may be futile, but that is not to say that nothing has been achieved or that the other things on offer are better. There is a good deal to be said for the idea that we should all become governable subjects who look to our interests, consider them rationally, take the long-term view, think of what we have in common with others, and so on. A more peaceable kingdom or world order may well follow from that sort of thing. So, hysterical attacks on liberalism are scarcely in order, although such attacks may occur regardless. It is helpful in this context for us to understand what liberalism offers, what it actually requires, what forms of domination it entails, what it represses, and what it generates in the way of oppositional discourses. Foucault actually encourages more measured reflection on liberalism (although this may not be evident from the tone of what he says in other contexts). His own edginess is bound up with his commitment to critique, not with an antagonism to liberalism per se.

A third uninflationary critique arises from his idea that the main aim of government as we know it is security. When Foucault talks about security, his main reference is to political economy, and hence to the liberals and neo-liberals who argue for the security of property, the security of contract, the security of the person, and so on. Liberals have long argued that the main purpose of government is to secure people so that they can go about their own business. If people cannot count on the fruits of their own labour, why should they put any effort into it? Why not just take what they want from others, using whatever violence might be required? How can we expect people to be peaceable, productive, hard-working, and cooperative if they have no security? The beauty, as far as liberals are concerned, is that relatively little has to be done to make for a healthier, wealthier, and wiser society. Just make sure that people have a modicum of security in their own possessions, that they can go about their occupations without being disturbed, and that they can grow or make things for sale and count on getting money or goods in return as agreed. If you do that, the liberals say, things will go surprisingly well for everyone. People will be more productive, there will be more to go around, there will be much less violence, and everyone will be happier and more loyal to the state. Security is mainly about establishing an economy that actually works. Given that, questions will then arise about whether anything more can be done to improve things. Is the security necessary for markets to function sufficient, or should there be social security in a broader sense: a minimum income, food, clothing, and shelter, health care, aid to the young, old, and disabled, opportunities for training and education, protection against exploitative employers or deceptive sellers, controls on pollution, environmental protection, traffic safety, disease control, and so on? Virtually every question of public policy is a question of security from a liberal perspective, because it always comes back to whether people, individually or collectively, have what they need to go about living healthy and productive lives, lives that they certainly want and that are in any case of the sort that strengthens the state and makes it more secure in relation to its own people, other states, and outsiders.

Foucault is well aware of the violence implicit in liberalism. As we have noted, he stresses the fact that any system of right, including liberalism, is a system of domination and hence a system that mobilizes violence in one way or another to sustain itself. But, in reminding us how liberalism works as a security system, Foucault is drawing our attention to its peaceable face. Liberalism is a theory of how security can be achieved with a minimum of violence. Security is what economy and society may lack in the absence of the state, but the state is dangerous because it may overextend itself, wreck things, and even wreck itself. Keeping the right balance is what the art of government is about, an art that extends from the domestic to the international. The art is keyed to the understandings developed within political economy (and the social sciences more generally) and it is *that* which tells us what the key threats to security are, and how they can be met. It cannot be stressed often enough that the central idea of liberalism, an idea that arises from the problem of government as it was posed in the eighteenth century and that has been constantly posed and re-posed ever since, is that security is achieved by nurturing and developing a society and economy that always already exists. The problem is not anarchy, but inadequate security. The solution is not violence but nurturing and developing the economy and society. What is required – as Machiavelli explained five hundred years ago – is an economy of violence, an economical use of violence, a certain restraint that leads to wise, carefully measured, and highly limited deployments of violence, a policy that recognizes that the people's security and the state's security are one, and that violence is most effective when it is used least. The idea of governing less, which is the key to liberal thought, is actually an idea about what is involved in carrying Machiavelli's dictum into effect. A liberal society is one that achieves security – and hence health, wealth, and wisdom – because it knows how to govern itself with a minimum of violence.

One implication of this Foucauldian way of thinking about security is that the traditional divide within international relations between "realists" and "idealists" means almost nothing. Realism and idealism are the necessary polarities of an art of government that extends indifferently from the domestic to the international. One can be a realist or an idealist about the practicalities of government in any setting, and this antinomy necessarily informs any debate. The problem of the international is somewhat different from the problem of the domestic, but only in minor degree, for "the war" (or threat of it) is everywhere, ominipresent, and ongoing, and hence there is a set of problems that is recognizably similar in every setting. The liberal claim is that the best strategy for dealing with these problems is always the liberal strategy, the one that gives ultimate priority to economy and society and hence to measures which secure people as the sort of folks who can behave sociably and be rational and productive economic actors. In other words, a sound economy is always the first objective of rational government, an objective that once achieved will probably lead to lasting peace. All else is irrationality. The question for liberals is how this irrationality is to be quelled, contained, displaced, repressed, or destroyed with a proper economy of violence. That is an important part of the art of government, but the locus and scale of activity is incidental to the main purposes of government. The separation between the domestic and the international, like the separations between public and private or between the political, the social, and the economic, occurs within a field of vision (or grid of intelligibility, as Foucault describes it) that is established (produced, called into being) through the art of government. All problems are conceived as problems of government, and that is what these separations tend to conceal.

Is the liberal ideal of an economy of violence to be scorned? Scarcely. In fact, critical security studies and human rights theories are complementary *liberal* discourses that articulate criticisms of the state for intervening *too much* in people's lives and failing to give them the security they really need to go about their proper business as productive, socially connected people, operating in a free society and a free market. These criticisms are akin to the ones Erhart, Hayek and the others articulated in their critiques of state economic interventionism. The issue is always the same in that respect: the state governing too much. So, the currently popular leftish critiques are actually in the spirit of neo-liberalism, in that they suggest that we have not yet been liberal enough. We need to make our liberalism that much more thoroughgoing if we are to govern ourselves as we should and could. To put it so will make many critics uneasy, since they understand what they do as something opposed to neo-liberalism. In a way, the opposition is real enough, in so far as it is connected to defending social welfarism and Keynesian economic interventionism against the neo-liberal critiques. There may also be a real opposition that turns on differing estimates of the character and extent of various threats to liberalism, external and internal. Nevertheless, there is a common ground, a shared grid of intelligibility, which the disputes tend to obscure. That ground or grid is inherent in the problem of government, and the liberal view of how that problem is best handled remains predominant, generating a series of critiques that feed into one another, complement one another, and reinforce this particular way of seeing things.

All of this points towards a fourth and final critique of the uninflationary kind, one that turns on the relation between political theory, political economy, and international relations. Foucault's analysis reveals how these three fields are connected to one another through the art of government. The problem of political theory is how the state should be constituted, given the requirements of the art of government. That this *is* the problem is concealed by analyses that suggest that questions of justice or right come first and that ideas about how the state should be constituted can and must be derived from answers to those fundamental philosophical questions. Foucault reminds us that those fundamental philosophical questions have already been answered or dismissed in accounts that derive from the claim that we are fundamentally creatures of interest (or at least that we should be considered in this guise for purposes of political, social, and economic analysis). That premise, that we are creatures of interest, is what informs liberal governmentality, and hence the whole edifice of modern thought that suggests that we are best governed by being governed as little as possible. The latter idea, not any conception of human rights, is the important one, for human rights will always be trumped by the necessities of government when there is a conflict. In this sense, liberalism is always a matter of realism, a doctrine that suggests that we have to be realistic about human nature, the balance of sociability and unsociability it entails, the possibilities of cooperation and conflict, and so on. The theory is that both the state and the society it governs – and indeed the whole system of states underpinned by a common market civilization – can be strengthened by *restraining* the state appropriately, reining it in, regularizing its activities, framing them within a system of laws, securing the governed as much as the government, and so on. What political theory suggests is how this can be achieved, given what we know from political economy and international relations.

Are political economy and international relations simply empirical disciplines with no particular normative dispositions? Scarcely: both of them refer back to the problem of government, and focus on the objects of study and action that appear when we come to understand human affairs in terms of the problem of government. The things that political economists and international relations scholars study are not just there. They are called into being by the practices at issue. Hence they appear to be objects of study and action that have a certain unquestionable reality, and in relation to which knowledge can be generated. The knowledge concerned is what is relevant to the art of government and hence to political theory, understood as a theory of how things should be constituted if government is to be as it should be. Each of the knowledges at issue – political economy, international relations, and political theory – feed into the others, and ground them in ostensible reality. We know that political theory is realistic if it withstands the tests of what we know from political economy and international relations. But, what we know from the latter takes for granted that the state normally has the form proposed by political theory, both in terms of its relation with other states and its relation with society or the economy. There is a circularity whereby each of these sub-disciplines of political science serves to ground the others, so their credibility depends not on what they are like in isolation, but on how they work together as an ensemble. This ensemble is rarely recognized, however, and even more rarely criticized, because it appears as "common sense": just the way the world happens to be, rather than the way that it happens to have been formed and sustained in and through the disciplines which offer the means of analysing it.

Towards a different political science?

So, how might we take these insights and redeploy them in articulating a different ontology of the political, one that avoids the binary divisions of the statist ontology and capitalizes on other insights that flow from urban analysis? Note that the city has a special place in Foucault's own account of the emergent modern art of government. It was the problem that the early police state developed in France and elsewhere in the seventeenth and eighteenth centuries was supposed to resolve, but could not. Cities could not be managed by sovereign authority as it had previously been conceived, because city life was a matter of flow and transformation. A city, it was discovered, could only be governed at a distance, indirectly, because the people who inhabited it had their own projects, as well as the means to realize those projects in and against the state. People would put up resistance, find gaps, and establish their own enterprises regardless of what the state did. The state had to respond to this by taking account of how people actually behaved, or would behave if the conditions under which they operated changed. This was the essence of the liberal insight into the problem of government. It led to two related ideas: that economies and societies were largely self-subsistent and self-organizing, and that rational government was largely a matter of securing the framework for individual and collective action.

We might add several things to Foucault's analysis. If Weber is right about the peculiar character of late medieval cities, then it seems that the modern art of government emerged there, as local authorities struggled with questions of public health, civil order, poor relief, transportation, drainage, fire protection, dispute resolution, and a host of other issues. At first, the rulers who claimed sovereignty were not immediately relevant when it came to solving these problems. They were more like a nuisance or a threat. When states began to take a greater interest in government in general and the government of cities in particular, many of the relevant rationalities had already been articulated. Since then, many new rationalities have been articulated, most of them at one remove from the state, as Hayek would have expected and as Foucault shows in other contexts. Although we may associate the art of government with the state, its field of practice is actually much larger and the authorities involved much more various. It is not just the state that has posed the problem of government for itself. The problem of government – often disguised in recent years as a problem of organization and management – has been posed and re-posed incessantly in the modern era, in recognition of the fact that people tend to escape control, as they do in the city. People can be disciplined, and the discipline can be made more effective by self-discipline. Nevertheless, disciplined people are still free to act – in fact, they must be free to act if they are to accomplish anything – and so the question of how they are to be governed will reappear. Is *self*-government enough? The insistent claim from most of those who purport to understand the art of government is that external government and hence sovereign authority is also required. On the other hand, economies, societies, communities, religions, families, and even individuals all tend to exercise their freedom and put sovereign authority at a distance.

The eighteenth-century discovery of a more-or-less self-subsistent economy and society was actually an appreciation of the realities of urban life, considered in its intensity and extension. The global market or "empire of civil society" (Rosenberg 1994) was an effect of the links between cities and between them and the countryside. The mode of production that Marx and others were to call capitalist was quite evidently urban in the way that it colonized agriculture and turned the wilderness into a standing reserve of natural resources. Because cities were linked to one another through trade routes, networks of communication, and flows of capital, they could establish a global presence. Not only did they colonize what was outside, but they brought the outside in, and made the cities themselves places of extraordinary intensity. Of crucial importance was the fact that people of different clans, tribes, villages, nations, and religions were drawn together, and bound to find ways of living together despite their differences. So, as I have already suggested, what is most notable is *not* that cities fall apart in the absence of sovereign authority. It is the opposite: cities are remarkably resilient, hard to erase, and capable of generating a kind of order in the most unlikely conditions. Cities look a lot like self-organizing systems. They are characterized (if I may quote myself) by "proximate diversity, complicated patterns of government and self-government, a multiplicity of authorities in different registers, the infinite deferral of sovereignty, self-organization, and an emergent order that, though chaotic, is by no means anarchic".[3]

Whereas the economy and civil society are defined in relation to the state, as orders that emerge prior to the state or just beyond its reach and that pose for the state the central problem of government, the city (or what Wirth called urbanism as a way of life) is defined in relation to the countryside (or the rural way of life it supplants). Moreover, the city tends to generate its own political authorities, in accordance with its own needs and opportunities, regardless of the concerns of the state. Thus, the city is on a different register from the state, although it is no less political for that. If the state emerges in response to the problem of sovereignty, the city has different origins and a different political order is immanent in its own rationalities. If the state requires a monopoly of legitimate authority to persist as a state, the city as city does not. The city depends on the intricate pattern of government and self-government that Jacobs and Sennett observed, and hence on multiple authorities in different but not necessarily inconsistent registers. The effect of the city is to hold sovereignty in suspense, defer its application, and perhaps render it redundant. In fact, the suspicion that sovereignty may not be necessary runs through liberal thought, a form of thought that seems to be implicit in urbanism as a way of life.

Most analysts of urbanism as a way of life hold the state at a distance in order to get a better sense of what urbanism entails on its own. That analytical move may be necessary as a first step, but it tends to have the double effect of depoliticizing urban analysis and abstracting the city from the state in an unrealistic way. The two registers, city and state, do not exist in splendid isolation, but rather as a complex ensemble. The standard ontology of the political situates the city at the boundary between the state and civil society, as an element of what is to be governed – society, the economy, a complex of local but globalizable communities – and as an element of the state itself, in the form of local government. I have been suggesting that the state has to be understood in relation to the various political claims advanced inside and outside urbanism or "the city", the way of life that has become predominant globally. Seen this way, the claims to sovereignty that characterize the state are just that: claims that have more or less effect on the political situations we have to analyse. The claims of the state certainly do not exhaust the field of the political, nor are they determinant in any simple sense. As I will be suggesting in the next chapter, our understanding of the city as a political order is a kind of subjugated knowledge, worth uncovering and articulating at greater length.

This stab at an analysis of urban order is not Foucault's: on the contrary, I am extrapolating from where he begins through a complex literature that has many nineteenth-, twentieth-, and twenty-first-century formulations, some of which I considered in the previous chapter. What I mean to suggest is that there is a different way of thinking about what we confront already implicit in the moves that Foucault is considering. Foucault follows the double-movement that constitutes the state as the other of civil society (or economy and society), the latter conceived as a more-or-less natural order and the former posited as what can rationalize or improve what is already there. A minoritarian view of this is that what we are actually considering is not the dualism of state and civil society, but a more complex object, in which political and governmental practices appear in many different guises, at various scales, and in different rhythms. To think of government simply from the vantage point of the state, or to suppose that politics is only about government, is not only to oversimplify, but to subjugate knowledges that we already have. The reaction that many of us have to neo-liberalism is not just that it is oppressive, demeaning, and ultimately unjust, but that it models our world in the crudest of fashions and offers banal and unworkable solutions to complex problems. As I have said, we need to see like a city. Foucault helps prepare us for that task, but there is much more to be done if we are to challenge standard-form political theory.

5 Seeing like a state, seeing like a city

A naïf might imagine that the object of political theory was to explain politics. Judging from what self-described "political theorists" do in most countries, nothing could be further from the truth. Efforts to *explain* politics generally come from outside political theory: from politicians and bureaucrats, historians and journalists, sociologists and economists, psychologists and biologists, geographers and anthropologists, and even occasionally "political scientists". Unlike scientists in most disciplines, *political* scientists rely very little on the theories that theorists in their discipline develop. Political theorists generally operate in splendid isolation, at one remove from political scientists and at another remove from politicians and political activists. Many devote their efforts to the activity Hegel warned us against: giving instructions to the world. These instructions consist of constitutional principles, norms of conduct, ideological orientations, or laws and policies, for which some sort of philosophical rationalization is offered. In some cases, the mode of intervention is more of a lament: this world will never learn to be the way that political theorists think that it should be! In the circumstances, it is not hard to sympathize with the realists who turn away from this moralistic idealism in favour of an examination of what is actually done. In that context, Machiavelli appears to be the exception that proves the rule: a canonized political theorist who actually makes *politics* his main object of study and claims that a proper understanding of politics must precede any effort to lay down principles of conduct or issue prescriptions to participants.

Much of the unrealism of contemporary political theory can be attributed to the way that political theory has become attached to the state. There are two aspects of this attachment. To a great extent, political theory is *about* the state, or, more particularly, about the way the state might be better organized, differently conceived, repositioned in the world, and so on. The *rechtstaat* – the well-ordered state – is an ideal that intrigues many if not most political theorists. Much of their work is oriented toward that ideal and grounded upon it. Even theorists who are doubtful about the state often attend to it, because they think that the state is here to stay. Theorists, like others, think that they must assume the enduring presence of the state in order to be realistic. So, there is a double attachment: a normative link, arising from the belief that a well-ordered state is the ideal, and an empirical link, arising from the belief that the state, like the weather, will always be with us. Hidden in these latter two beliefs is a third: that the state, where present, ultimately structures the political field so as to determine its possibilities. In other words, there is a belief that sovereignty actually is effective. Many political theorists are deeply suspicious of politics, because politics – as opposed to law, reason, or morality – is a source of disorder. Politics involves plays of power, clashes of interests, differences of identity and value, moments of instantaneous decision, waves of emotion, sudden shifts of opinion, violent conflicts, efforts at domination and liberation, aspirations to justice or glory or redemption, and venal concerns about wealth and status. It is never what we would want it to be, and so it is tempting to look to the state (or another authority imagined to be sovereign) to fix it. Law is usually the means imagined. It is supposed that, if politics gives way to law, disorder will give way to order: an order that flows from the power of the state. The power of the state is doubly authorized: by its seemingly inevitable presence on the one hand and by the way it embodies sovereign authority on the other. In principle, sovereign authority can override bad politics and institute the right and the good.

Of course, as we all know, sovereign authority has that capacity only in our imaginations. Political theorists are caught up in their own version of the myth of the "good tsar". Russian peasants are said to have believed that the tsar himself was a benevolent figure who would address their problems if he knew of them; unfortunately, landlords and local officials kept the truth from him. In the political theorists' version of this, actual states are akin to the local landlords and officials, locking up the truth of the state, and preventing others from bringing the *rechtstaat* into being. Political theorists, like charismatic peasant leaders, seek only to free the state and bring it back to its true purpose. Stated so, the project of political theory sounds ridiculous – and well it should. We know that actual politics conforms to no one's ideal, and that the crucial problems of politics cannot be resolved by the exercise of sovereign authority. And yet, we are tempted always to theorize in relation to the imagined community of the state – or, at least, in relation to an imagined sovereign authority – rather than in relation to politics proper. Politics proper has shifting and uncertain boundaries; it is invested with irresolvable conflicts; it is fraught with uncertainty; it brings us as low as it does high. To theorize in relation to politics is to deal with a chaotic field, in which order is always partial, relative, and temporary. The political is always in transformation. The effect of a political intervention is always uncertain.

So, what is there to say, theoretically? Must we retreat into silence? I think not. For political theory to be realistic, however, it must attune itself to the complexities and uncertainties of politics. As I have been arguing, one way of doing this is to learn to see like a city rather than a state. To envision the political *through* the state is to see it in terms of the practices of sovereignty and hence of law. To envision the political through *the city* is to see it in terms of complex practices of government and self-government, practices that always involve multiple authorities in different registers. In the city as city, sovereignty and hence the law is always in suspense, but order is nonetheless generated by the various practices of government and self-government. We know something of the latter, thanks to the work of sociologists and anthropologists. Nevertheless, the real world of politics – politics seen through the city – remains woefully undertheorized. In Foucauldian terms, the relevant knowledges are subjugated to state-centric political theory.

Seeing like a state

Political theory as we know it developed in the shadow of the state. When the discipline began to take its present shape, in the late nineteenth-century United States, it was in the context of an effort to improve higher education by bringing American institutions up to the level of the most advanced ones in Europe: namely, those in Germany.[1] The newly familiar scholarly divisions that separated political science from economics on the one hand and sociology on the other were overlaid by the distinction between the social sciences generally (of which *political* science was one) and the humanities, including philosophy and history. The social sciences were supposed to bring a new rigour to the study of human social life. From the beginning, the assumption was that political science would be focused on government and more generally upon the state: hence, upon the comparative study of constitutions or more particular political institutions, public administration and public policy, and also the contest between parties and other groups for control of governmental institutions, the exercise of political leadership, the contest of political doctrines, and so on. One might study the sociology of politics, or indeed its psychology. One might also study political economy, as people had been doing since the time of the physiocrats. But, what made political science distinctive is that it took the state, rather than society or the economy, as its object of study. Within political science, all analytical roads led to the state, because the state is what political science had to explain. Sociologists or economists might try to explain it, but in the end they lacked appropriate tools. If they tried to explain the state away, as an effect of society or an effect of the economy, they ultimately failed, because the state was *sui generis*: something that emerged over time and would develop into the future as a result of distinctively *political* struggles that had to be understood on their own terms. The insistence on the need for a distinctively *political* science was bound up with the recognition that human affairs were not simply social or economic in character: they were also political, and had to be analysed accordingly by a separate discipline. What came to be called "political theory" was related to that discipline of "political science".

If a political scientist was interested in explaining the way things were, a political theorist was interested in how they might be; or, so most political theorists thought. Political struggle was always about ideas, in the sense that political actors put forward different ideas about the way people should be governed and for what purposes, the bases of legitimacy, and the constitution of the political realm. These matters could be studied empirically, but it was also important to work out what made sense and how. Of necessity, that meant that current political ideas had to be put into a context that was both historical and philosophical: historical in the sense that ideas had to be traced to their origins and connected to other ideas; philosophical in the sense that those same ideas had to be subjected to rational assessment. Knowledge of consequences would never be enough, since political ideas were always bound up with notions of how people *ought* to live and hence with claims about the right and the good. To some analysts, this implied that political theory had to be part of moral and political philosophy, rather than political science. That move has been resisted, of course: on the grounds that the political is different from the moral or even from the ethical, and hence that the *political* ought is different from the *moral* ought. Machiavelli is not a moral philosopher of any consequence, but he is a major political theorist. His way of drawing the line between morality and politics may not be to everyone's taste, but it raises an issue of central concern to political theory. More generally, the findings of political science, which a moral philosopher may choose to ignore, are of central concern to political theory in so far as it is a discipline concerned with the form and disposition of the state. If one accepts reason of state – broadly or narrowly conceived – one can fancy oneself a realist.

Among political theorists, the common view is that the ancient Greeks first saw the problem with which we have to contend. For there to be a settled way of life in which humans achieve the most of which they are capable, there must be a political order that determines what is lawful and what is not, and protects lawful citizens and the lawful order itself against internal and external threats. The right to interpret and enforce laws, as well as to make new laws as needed is implicit in the concept of such an order; so too is the right to use violence when necessary to maintain the law and the order which gives rise to and flows from that law. The Greeks are interesting because they saw that reasons could be given for preferring one form of order to another and that most if not all the reasons could be assessed without recourse to religious precepts. Modern political theorists are inspired by this humanism-*avant-la-lettre*, as well as by the ideal of the Greek *polis*: an order in which free and equal citizens govern themselves by deliberating and deciding together on the most important issues, delegating lesser matters to ordinary people chosen by lot, and filling the highest offices by electing the best to those positions and holding them to strict account. In the *polis*, we see the germ of the modern extensive republic: the liberal-democratic nation-state now regarded as the norm of political order.

It is well known that Enlightenment thinkers looked back to Greece and Rome for models. By the early twentieth century, many serious thinkers believed that the political achievements of the Greeks and the Romans actually could be surpassed: that an extensive republic based on the rule of law could be established and maintained indefinitely; that everyone – rich and poor, black and white, male and female – could be given the benefits of citizenship; that there could be open debate and democratic decision on public issues; that officials high and low could be elected and held to account; and that a federation of republics could be established to maintain peace among the nations. In thinking then and now, the United States of America had pride of place, since it was arguably the first and obviously the most striking example of a modern republic: one that offered a model to emulate or a point of reference in articulating something better, something freer, more democratic, and more egalitarian. Although in the first half of the twentieth century there were many intellectuals who reacted against the idea of liberal democracy, such voices have been muted in the past fifty or sixty years as political institutions in different parts of the world have been remodelled in light of the ideals of modern republicanism. Whether there has been real democratization is a matter for dispute. What is not in dispute is that a particular form of the republic – the liberal-democratic nation-state – is taken to be the norm. If political order in some part of the world departs from that norm, that is thought to be a problem. The presumption is that the liberal-democratic nation-state must be universalized if we are to move successfully toward the best political order.

The two junctures of modern republicanism – nation and state, liberty and democracy – are both distinctive, as is the third juncture, the one that fuses the nation-state with liberal-democracy. That there can be no democracy without liberty has long been accepted, although there is much dispute about the form of liberty that democracy requires. More interesting are the other two fusions, of nation with state and of nation-state with liberal-democracy. These fusions have received much less attention from political theorists, because they are not so easily analysed within the Graeco-Roman–Enlightenment tradition. Whether a nation exists or not is largely a matter of how the people concerned feel about it. There is no obvious reason why people should identify as a nation if they do not; nor is there any reason why they should not, if they do. But, the strength of nationalist sentiment seems to be such that it requires the division of the world into separate states, *and* helps to sustain those states as autonomous political entities once they are created. So-called "constitutional patriotism" is the Enlightened version of nationalism: it enables a double loyalty, to one's own state and to the system of states that maintains and qualifies state autonomy. What renders everything intelligible is the principle of state sovereignty, which suggests that there must be an ultimate authority in every part of the world in order to maintain a lawful order there, and that in the world as a whole the ultimate authorities must be related to one another as equals. Either might will make right through the balance of power, or the right will be empowered through mutual recognition.

For philosophers, the principle of sovereignty is attractive, because it suggests the possibility of enforcing an ideal: if not universally at least locally.

In so far as the principle of sovereignty is accepted, the ordering impulse of moral and political philosophy – the one that leads to prescriptions for morality, ethics, law, government, and politics – comes to seem practical. In writing or speaking, one's implicit appeal is to the sovereign: the one who has the capacity to implement the principles being advanced. The effect is a sort of complicity with sovereign authority, a complicity that is often unacknowledged. Among political theorists, this complicity may take a slightly different form in that it is often tied to the claim (usually unarticulated, but often implicit) that *state* sovereignty is inevitable in the modern era and hence that state sovereignty must be taken as the ground on which theorists have to work. Behind that is the idea that without sovereignty in some form there can only be chaos, lawlessness, and violence: thus, the defeat of every plan for betterment and every scheme to vindicate the right.

So, in these ways and others, we political theorists are trained to see like a state, but even more completely and thoroughly than Scott's (1998) analysis suggests.[2] We think from the vantage point of the state about the realm we are to govern in our minds. We attempt to reduce it to a uniform field, imagine the political subjectivities that might be brought into being and put in order, and orchestrate things (in our minds, at least) so that everything will fit together as we think it should. We are the philosopher kings or enlightened monarchs or great redeemers or popular liberators of our own imaginations. Sovereignty in general and the state in particular is the condition that we assume to assure ourselves of our own sanity: we are not megalomaniacs, but only advisors to those who could implement our dreams.

Seeing like a city

We can start to sense the possibilities for a different way of seeing if we return once again to the ancient *polis*. It is typical now to think of the *polis* as a miniature state: hence, the increasingly common tendency to translate the term *polis* as "state". We know that the *polis* was not a state, and indeed that the idea of the state did not really take shape before the sixteenth century of the common era, about two thousand years after the heyday of classical Greek philosophy. But, we tend to set that knowledge aside, because we scarcely know how to think of political order, except in terms of the state. For us, the state is normative in the sense that all other forms of political order are simply defective versions of it. What makes the *polis* recognizable for us, as a state, is that it is not simply the effect of religious or tribal traditions. It is a kind of rational order, intelligible in terms of human needs and possibilities conceived in the most general terms, without reference to the particularities of religious belief or cultural tradition. In principle, it is an order appropriate for all humans, especially in so far as it meets needs and realizes possibilities that are suppressed by particular religions or cultures. Thus, the *polis* is the embodiment of a universal truth, a truth realized in a different, perhaps higher, form within the modern state.

To see the *polis* in this way is to obscure its character as a city, however. Plato and Aristotle, the most influential of the Greek thinkers, were not comfortable with the *cityness* of the *polis*. They feared its disorder, its openness, its variety, and its multiplicity of contending authorities. I use the term "authorities" in the broadest sense here to refer to the presence of many different forms of authority and claims to authority: a condition in which the question of authority is never really settled. The condition that Plato and Aristotle particularly feared is one in which efforts to impose an overarching authority tended to generate a reaction that produced yet more authorities to contest the authority of the existing ones. One might argue that what typifies the city is not the imposition of an overarching authority, but the multiplication of challenges to existing authorities of all sorts. Hence, the medieval maxim that "city air makes free". To embrace the city is actually to embrace a condition that problematizes claims to overarching authority by generating rival claims. The rival claims are, in modern parlance (De Landa 2000), "attractors" that generate forms of order that may be sustained for some time, but that are liable to be displaced by other attractors that produce new forms of order. So, the city is not a stable order, so much as a field of possibilities generated by diverse human efforts. One sign of this is that the modern city transcends its own bounds, so that it no longer makes sense to think of a city as a self-contained entity. The Aristotelian ideal of self-sufficiency is unsustainable.

Weber realized that the medieval European city was even more interesting than the *polis* in some ways, because it developed at one remove from sovereign authority. As I have noted in previous chapters, he described the medieval city in terms of "non-legitimate domination" – or, as I would put it, a domain in which authorities emerged that were either unauthorized by the sovereign, recognized by the sovereign only after the fact, or constituted in direct defiance of the sovereign. What enabled a distinctively civic order to exist was not the grant of the sovereign, but the production of effective authorities from within the civic order itself. Authorities emerged, not in accordance with an overarching plan or established rules of recognition, but rather in accordance with the opportunities and necessities of the time. People claimed and exerted authority in various forms and for various purposes, under various circumstances. Authorities thus proliferated, with various political rationalities in play at the same time. Some of these rationalities were religious, dynastic, or tribal/national. Others were partisan/ideological. Still others were attuned to a logic of class domination. And some were tied to projects of civic improvement or moral reform. Cities were generators of possibility that attracted the ambitious, but they tended, thanks to their ideational and organizational fertility, to resist or subvert efforts to reduce them to any uniform order. Not that reduction to a uniform order was impossible: that was what Weber thought had happened in Oriental cities. But, in principle, the city was a form of order resistant to and/or subversive of sovereignty.

To see the city so is to recognize that it is not a miniature state, but rather an order of an entirely different type. It is not organized on the sovereignty principle, but instead on the principle of self-organization, which in turn implies a multiplicity of authorities operating under conditions of rivalry and inter-dependence. The most influential account of the city on these terms is the one that projects the market (a civic institution) onto a global scale and theorizes it as a self-organizing "economy". We know this account in its various iterations from Smith to Hayek. We also know the analyses that show that mutual adjustment is possible even when the entities in competition with one another are rivalrous governments and not just competing businesses. One need not go into these accounts in detail or accept the ideological cant associated with them to see that there is a larger point at stake. A kind of order can emerge even when there are rivalrous authorities.[3] Moreover, a secondary politics attuned to the form of that order is likely to be gener-ated when the form appears disorderly or disruptive to people's desires and expectations. The point is not (whatever Hayek might have thought) that the order of the city projected globally conforms to an ideal, but rather that it *is* an order of sorts that can be analysed on its own terms.

Another insight comes from the work of urbanists like Jacobs and Sennett, who have elaborated the implications of proximate diversity. The idea is that the city can generate *civilized* order by bringing diverse activities together: by making them proximate to one another. Out of that idea has come a con-ception of urban order that challenges many of the presumptions of statist urban planning. One need not idealize the processes at issue to see that there are street-level practices of government and self-government that enable markets to function, traffic to flow, people to move about, goods to be pro-duced, services to be provided, gods to be worshipped, books to be written, ideas to be circulated, and so on. These are the primary processes of government and self-government: the ones that make "civilization" in any form possible. The familial, tribal, cultural, and religious loyalties that bind people together in other ways are not necessarily helpful to urban order. In fact, they often lead to conflict that brings the city as a city to a standstill. Often this is the pretext for the assertion of sovereignty. In so far as sovereign authority suppresses conflict and facilitates "civilized" activities it can be regarded as the *sine qua non* of urban life. But, this view of it – the Hobbesian view – is misleading in so far as it conceals the origins of civilized life. Sovereignty may secure civilized life, but it does not create it. To the extent that people learn to live with people who are not of their own family, clan, tribe, village, religion, culture, or nation, it is through the every-day negotiations of life: the ones that enable people who are otherwise strangers to live beside one another as neighbours, to pass each other peacefully on the street, work together, do business with one another, or even come together in joint projects for mutual benefit. It would be wrong to suppose that the ordering practices of urban life are generated just from the bottom up. It is not that simple. People live on many scales simultaneously, and there are always ideas about the wider order or orders of life that inform what happens on a smaller scale – and vice versa. There is no simple way of describing how it is that masses of people who are otherwise strangers can come together and produce a relatively civilized urban order. What is clear, however, is that the imposition of sovereignty is at best one element in the generation of such an order.

Is sovereignty *necessary* to urban order, however? There certainly are some reasons for thinking so, but they are not as persuasive as most analysts take them to be. No doubt people want to be secure in their own homes, and to be able to go about their business without threat of violence. Theft, robbery, extortion, and intimidation are not welcome: to say nothing of rape, assault, and murder. Cities can scarcely exist without policing in some form, and so the necessary forces have to be mobilized, organized, and applied in one way or another. How this is done has varied a great deal, however: only in the last couple of centuries has the modern system of policing become the norm. Although sovereign authority may have become important in this regard, effective policing still depends on an organic relation between the police and the population, and that usually means keeping the state at a distance and allowing local authorities to assert control. So, the policing function is as much an effect of self-organization as is everything else in the city. Police forces under local control may still be operative even if sovereign authority collapses. Urban order is robust, not just because of the way people organize themselves in their dealings with one another, but also because of the way local policing continues in face of the most extraordinary challenges.

That said, the effectiveness of the police may not be as pressing an issue as the effectiveness of the army. The premise of most political theory has been that an army is necessary to secure the ground on which civilized life – including civilized policing – develops. How can we be secure without an army, and how can there be an army without a commander-in-chief or sovereign? There is no easy answer to such questions, except to say that an answer might not be required. In the city as city the problem of sovereignty is infinitely deferred. To use Schmittian language (Schmitt 2006, 2008), sovereignty is the exception postponed, evaded, deflected, subverted, and ultimately transfigured. If a city is threatened by an invading army or gangs of lawless rioters, a would-be sovereign may promise to repel the invading army or suppress the riots. The would-be sovereign will certainly expect obedience in return, but the bargain involved – which is not really a bargain, since people have no choice but to accept it – is just a moment in the reorganization of the city. Ultimately, the would-be sovereign is incorporated as an element in the life of the city. The sovereign is not so much the rock on which the city is built, as a part of the rubble the city transforms into the structures of urban life. The processes that renew civic order in the wake of war are the ones that made civic order possible before the war. Once the vibrancy of urban life is restored, the sovereign's authority is increasingly tamed, contained, and incorporated into the ordinary ways of the city. For the city to flourish, sovereign authority must be transformed into the exception that proves the rule.

To see like a state is to suppose that the most important political problems are resolved once sovereignty is established. This supposition is very much at odds with experience. Often as not, the effort to establish a stable state generates violent conflict or exacerbates existing conflicts, because one claim to sovereign authority is being advanced at the expense of others. If things go well, a particular sovereignty-claim may be accepted and then made increasingly irrelevant politically as the various actors adjust to a situation in which they must offer nominal allegiance to certain principles. Things do not always go well, however. Another way of achieving a kind of civil peace is when rival sovereignty-claims are moderated or held in suspense as people with radically different views work out ways of living side by side. The latter way is more akin to the other practices of urban life. When we see like a state, we assume that the state is the necessary solution to the problem of sovereignty, and miss the fact that this purported solution may be part of the problem. Even to suppose that *some* form of sovereignty – not necessarily state sovereignty – is necessary to political order is to beg the question. It is not clear that the problem of sovereignty has to be resolved. What Weber noticed about medieval cities is of more general interest, for these were places where sovereignty claims were displaced, evaded, held in abeyance, or otherwise rendered ineffective as urbanites got on with what they wanted to do. Such suspense is not necessarily ideal, but neither is a forced resolution of the suspense. In any case, a resolution is liable to be temporary.

I make these remarks with recent experiences in Iraq, Afghanistan, Somalia, Congo, and other places of apparent disorder in mind. I am not an expert with respect to any of these places, but from what I can tell from afar peaceful order is always a matter of reviving the practices that enable cities to work as cities. There is no magic elixir for this, and the presence of an army with overwhelming firepower – as in Afghanistan or Iraq – is clearly not sufficient. Indeed, in these instances, it seems to cause more problems than it solves.

To see like a city is to recognize that political order is not something that can be fixed in any simple way. A political order is always in the process of being overcome, and the challenges to it may arise from any quarter. In this context, the threat of adverse change provides the excuse for efforts to establish and maintain sovereignty. There is always a widespread desire for the certainty, fixity, security, and control that sovereignty promises, but it exceeds any need that sovereignty might serve. In the circumstances, it is well to be suspicious of any claim to sovereignty, on the grounds that it is likely to be as excessive as it is ineffective in relation to the securities it is supposed to provide. To see like a city is to accept a certain disorderliness, unpredictability, and multiplicity as inevitable, and to pose the problem of politics in relation to that complexity, rather than in relation to the simplicity that sovereignty seeks. To put it bluntly: to see like a city is to grow up politically.

Seeing like a theorist

The simplicity that sovereignty seeks is related to the simplicity that philosophy has often sought: as Plato recognized, philosophy and kingship must coincide if a certain form of order is to be implemented. The simplicity of such an order is implicit in its form of determinacy: governed by linear equations, the unfolding of such an order can be predicted in advance. The city, on the other hand, is a complex order, whose unfolding is non-linear. Outcomes cannot be predicted with any certainty. A type of authority that had been considered irrelevant – such as religious authority – may suddenly reappear in a new form, with new force. A form of economic enterprise that no one had imagined – Google or Facebook – may transform scientific inquiry or social relations, as well as undercut established businesses and open up new opportunities for the accumulation of wealth. Armies or police forces can be destabilized by insurgents using new forms of deployment and unconventional weaponry. And, political alliances can be formed between groups and for purposes that were never contemplated a few years before. There is a homology between the city and politics that contrasts with the homology between the state and sovereignty. In binding itself to the state, political theory connects itself to the latter pair, and abandons the former. This is a mistake. It would be better to abandon the state to the philosophers and claim politics – and hence the city – for political theory.

What are the implications of this? The first is that the form of politics can never be anticipated in advance of its emergence. We cannot say in advance what the main problems of the immediate future will be. We can extrapolate trends, of course, and by doing so predict that certain familiar problems will continue and others emerge and become salient. But, there will be surprises, and some of those surprises will be such that they throw most of our calculations off kilter. So, we can never be very confident about our ability to anticipate the field of political activity to which our theories must relate. We may accept parameters that have no force, and theorize about problems and patterns of politics that fade into insignificance. As Hegel recognized, we can scarcely comprehend our own time in thought, let alone project ourselves into the future. The second implication follows from the first. We cannot say in advance that the key theoretical issues are axiological, epistemological, or ontological. The persistent axiological emphasis of Anglo-American political theory – the demand to be normative – arises from the belief that there is a known field of the political to which our prescriptions might relate. But, in fact, the field is *not* known, and we are faced, as theorists, with the persistent challenge of comprehending something that is shifting and changing before our eyes. To suppose that our main problem is to work out appropriate moral axioms is actually to avoid the task at hand, which is to make politics intelligible. The third implication also follows from the first. We must be modest in our claims and expectations. The God's-eye view is not available to us: we can offer only partial understandings that may be helpful in limited ways.

To shift from the state to the city has other implications for our thinking as well. Any concept of the state involves related concepts that denote the domains to which the state relates. The state governs society. It has a relation to the economy, culture, religion, and nationality. It has a relation to other states. Relations among states and between state and society are governed by the principle of sovereignty. Thanks to that principle, which appears to be operative in the world, we have an analytical starting point that enables us to effect a division of labour among social scientists and that specifies the boundary issues with which we have to contend as analysts. Is the disposition of the state determined by the economy, or vice versa? Does a disjuncture of nation and state foredoom the latter? Can a system of secularized states contain religious wars? Such questions seem good until we realize that they presuppose the political order that renders them intelligible. It is not clear that *that* is the political order with which we have to contend. To envision the world *through* the city and *as* a city is to see its constitutive relations and boundaries differently.

One immediately thinks of the city in relation to the countryside, or of the urban in relation to the rural. Thus, a certain geography is invoked, but it is not the geography of the state system. As Wirth argued long ago, a different *way of life* is implicit in urbanism, a way of life that can be distinguished from agrarianism or hunting and gathering. As Lefebvre (2003) argued more recently, urbanism as such is different from industrialism and is implicitly global. The frontier of the urban is not at the boundary between one state and the next; nor is it at the boundary between state and society. Instead, it is at the boundary of the rural, the natural, or the un-urbanized: a boundary that can be understood both historically and geographically. At that boundary, questions of nature and culture are acutely contested. From one point of view, the city is understood as what civilizes us – transforms us from tribesmen or villagers into citizens – and what civilizes our environment – changes it into a safe, comfortable, but stimulating and interesting home for humans. From another point of view, the city alienates us from both nature and culture: despoils the environment even as it degrades the rich variety of cultures that give meaning to human life. We need not accept either of these polar visions to see that citification or urbanization or civilization – whatever you want to call it – involves transformations of the greatest political significance. How we are to understand ourselves in relation to our own natures or own cultures or in relation to what is not of human making is clearly of central concern. The issues at stake are more sharply posed when we see like a city rather than a state.

When we see like a city we quickly recognize that our trajectory is not something that can be controlled in any simple way. And yet the city is not ungoverned. This is as true of the global city as it is of the local city: that is, it is as true of the urban world as a whole as it is of particular cities, like Vancouver or Los Angeles. To see the world as a global city is to recognize immediately that it is characterized by a multiplicity of authorities in different registers (states, municipalities, religious bodies, for-profit corporations, NGOs, charismatic figures, and so on), each of which governs within its own domain, but each of whose efforts at government are checked, regulated, or challenged by others. The principle of state sovereignty is everywhere contested, not least by sovereign states. Locally, we can see a similar pattern: as one gets closer to the ground, as it were, the more apparent it becomes that the actual configuration of political authority is extremely complex and that it is poorly represented in models that assume the centricity of the state. One must explore the ground without too many preconceptions if one is to see what is actually there. About all we can say in advance is that the pattern of government and self-government is both complex and variable, over time and space. Nevertheless, it is clear that government and self-government – and, one must note (with the Foucauldians) that the one always involves the other – enable the city to exist locally and globally. We really cannot understand this in terms of the relation between state and society or state and economy, for those categories do not capture the complexities of authority production and inter-authority relations. So, if we think of the key political questions as being about the kind of authorities that we do or should have and how those authorities do or should relate to one another, then it becomes clear that we need to investigate the city, locally and globally, with great care if we are to understand what the most relevant questions are.

The most powerful argument for seeing like a state is that the most important political identities in the modern world are the ones produced at the intersection of nationalism with the state system. The doctrine of sovereignty seems to imply that any self-respecting nation should seek its own state, in order to enjoy equality with other nations. Clearly, the nexus of nation and state is important, as is the doctrine of sovereignty, but when one examines matters *through* the city it becomes clear that identities, like values and interests, are protean. They tend to proliferate. Particular identities that have little to do with nation and state can come to the foreground and generate pressing political problems. We all know this: it is part of the stuff of everyday politics. If we see like a state, we can lose sight of the fact that the politically important identities (and politically important interests and values) are not necessarily the ones bound up with the nation-state; nor are they necessarily the ones that can be vindicated by an act of state sovereignty. We are always already engaged in a more complex politics, in which questions of nation and state certainly appear (and sometimes demand resolution), but in which other questions often overshadow them. The latter questions often cannot be resolved by the exercise of state sovereignty, because they relate to forms of authority that are resistant to state control. Ironically, one of the major impediments to state control is that states are generally too small to encompass the activities they are supposed to regulate. This reflects the fact that people are connected to one another through globalized urban networks. Urban life – and the identities it preserves, generates, or revives – actually transcends individual states and in fact the entire state system. So, it is hard to put nation and state in context if one fails to see like a city.

What holds many of us back from re-envisioning our field of study is the sense that what cannot be brought under the sign of the state is at best chaotic and at worst dangerous, violent, and disorderly. This reflects the antique view that the absence of the state entails "anarchy". What we learn from studying cities is almost the opposite. In the absence of the state, forms of political authority – and hence forms of government and self-government – tend to proliferate. The consequence may not be "good government", but it is certainly not anarchy. Self-described anarchists are actually interested in understanding the practices of government and self-government that emerge when the shadow of the state retreats. To my mind, that means explaining how cities are actually governed: the latter is not a topic in which state-centric theorists are much interested. So, ironically, anarchists are the realists in so far as they attempt to identify practices of government that emerge from the self-organization of people in and through cities. State-centric theory tends to be hopelessly idealist, in that it wishes the world to conform to a certain pattern to make things easy for the analyst. To see like a city is to recognize that order is relative, temporary, and localized, but no less real or meaningful for that. Law in various forms emerges, but it is not necessarily coordinated into a coherent whole. The resultant complexity may not be susceptible to full understanding, but that does not mean that we can have nothing of value to say about it.

In short, the city beckons us to see like political theorists who are in the midst of a world that exceeds our understanding, rather than like political philosophers who stand outside the world and judge it. The judgements of the philosophers are like regulations of the state, which many people will choose to ignore, often for good reasons. If we invest ourselves in the city, we can allow ourselves to think politically and hence to illuminate the practices that we are attempting to theorize. This means de-subjugating knowledges that have been suppressed by statist political theory, and politicizing urban analysis without reimposing the conventional statist political ontology. As I will be arguing in the next two chapters, a more critical stance in relation to urbanism becomes possible once we begin to see like a city.

6   *Oikos, nomos, logos*

To this point, I have been presenting urbanism in a generally positive light. I have been working against the view that the state, or sovereignty in some other form, is our salvation politically. I have been making two points simultaneously: that urbanism actually works after a fashion to generate a more-or-less civilized order, and that it is from within urbanism that we have to act politically. In making these moves I get dangerously close to celebrating things that I do not mean to celebrate, embracing political agendas that are far from my own, and obscuring problems that need to be highlighted. Perhaps I should be calling the white knights of progressivism to my rescue, but my point is not that the urbanism we have is good, or that it automatically generates solutions to the problems it creates. The deficiencies of capitalist urbanism are legion, and there is not much need to go through the list once again. More pertinent is the fact that it is easier to see those deficiencies through the city than through the idealized structures of the state, and to articulate responses that take advantage of the opportunities urbanism offers. Our problem is to think the city politically, and our resources for doing that have been obscured by the accretions of statism.

In this chapter, I want to change my focus and consider the implications of two other modes of modern thought, economics and ecology, both of which refer back to the *oikos*, household, or home that Aristotle (1996) distinguished from the *polis*, and both of which suggest that we can and should be governed otherwise than politically: in the one case by the *nomos* of the market and the other by the *logos* implicit in the natural ordering of things. Ecological thinking has become more prominent as our sense of environmental crisis has intensified, and a contrast is often drawn between thinking in narrowly economic terms and adopting a broader ecological perspective. The shift in perspective is important, but both ways of thinking refer back to the same idea: that by attuning ourselves to the requirements of our *oikos* or home (properly conceived) we can become better than we are now. We are supposed to fit into something that is given in the natural order of things, an order that is not just out there in the natural world or urban life, but in here among our own needs and desires. That means submitting to an overarching rationality that may be different from the rationality of the *rechtstaat*, but that nonetheless governs us quite strictly (Luke 1997). Is this at odds with urbanism, or are economy and ecology the rationalities implicit in urbanism itself? If the latter, is urbanism just another form of oppression?

As I note in Chapter 7, I live in a place where questions of "home" are particularly unsettled. American warships pass by on their missions for "homeland security"; Indigenous people act to recover their homelands; immigrants and refugees try to establish new homes even while sustaining old ones; everyone worries about the growing number of "homeless" people; workers and would-be workers are unsettled by unemployment; young people are lost in the suburbs; habitat for wildlife disappears as forests are destroyed; and both in my neighbourhood and where I work, people and their plants are beset by invasive species. Many people understand their situation as being caught up in a way of life – urbanism – that they find oppressive, colonialist, imperialist, and profoundly destructive. They want to create alternatives, and they have to do so from within urbanism, however much they may despise it. For most of them, ecological thinking is much more appealing than economic thinking, but they are nonetheless haunted by the ideal of the *polis* as a locus of self-government. Some sort of practice of democracy is wanted, but found wanting, and the urban appears as more of a problem than an opportunity. How are we to understand this?

Logos/nomos, oikos/polis

For the Greeks, a key aspiration was to bring the *nomos* – the law or custom – of the people in line with the *logos*, or rationality itself. Aristotle argued that the *polis*, the supreme human community, was qualitatively different from the *oikos* or household. Whereas the latter could provide for certain human needs – ones that men shared with their wives and children – only the *polis* could enable the deliberation among equals that brought out human excellence. That excellence was a matter of reason or *logos*, enacted in speech of a kind of which animals were incapable. Thus, the *nomos* of the *polis* was in principle logocentric: articulated in speech, through reason, and agreed by the men who joined together in this community. Aristotle believed that the *polis* was in principle self-sufficient, able to provide for all its needs from within and to secure itself from dangers without.

The subsequent view has been that the scale of the *polis* is inadequate to human purposes (Gellner 1983, Held 1996). This inadequacy relates to two different conceptions of scale: size and measure. On the first count, the *polis* seems too small to be self-sufficient, since it exists within a wider world from which it must draw goods, services, and ideas, and on which it must rely for its own security. Even intellectually, the space of the *polis* is too confined, as Aristotle's own life indicates: there is a wider world of ideas or republic of letters in which men must participate if they are to make the best of themselves. The *polis* is also insufficient materially and militarily, because of its small size. But, the question of scale is also one of measure. On what scale or measure is the life of the *polis* to be judged? The confined scale of the *polis* and its inherently antagonistic relation to the outside world are problematic in this respect. Must we not measure ourselves against what is best in humanity at large? If the *polis* enlarges men in relation to the *oikos,* does not the wider world enlarge them further, and hence bring them closer to the *logos* of the *cosmos* as such? If so, the *nomos* of men must transcend the *nomos* of the *polis*.

But, this raises an interesting question. If the *polis* is not the proper home for men, how should the home for men be conceived? Aristotle's initial analysis suggests that the *oikos* (in the sense of the household) may be adequate as a home for women and children, but not for men as such. We can reformulate the point in terms that are not so androcentric. Some human needs can be met within the household, but not all of them. Men, women, and children all need the wider world, not least as a place where they can exercise their capacities as free human beings, rather than as people who are already locked into family relationships. But, it may be that the wider world can be conceived as an *oikos* that transcends the *polis*: a homeland whose *nomos* is in accord with the *logos*. That, at least, appears to be the implication of both "economy" and "ecology", modern ways of thinking that have developed in response to the Greek idealization of the *polis* (and the Roman idealization of the republic). Graeco-Roman notions have not been fully displaced, as we shall make clear in a moment, but let us pause to consider the twin logics of economy and ecology.[1]

Whereas Aristotle was full of scorn for trade and the unlimited accumulation of material possessions and monetary means that it seemed to imply, modern economists have developed a theory that suggests that global order can arise from peaceful commerce among people (and peoples) who have no other connection to one another but a concern for material advantage. Each can put on offer what it has in surplus, and receive in turn what it lacks. All that is required is respect for one another's property and willingness to abide by agreements undertaken. What follow are a division of labour and a free exchange of goods and services. There may be antagonism, but that antagonism is transformed into peaceful competition, regulated by the need to cooperate for mutual advantage. Thus, the world functions like a household in at least two important respects. In the first place, people are governed by their concern to provide for domestic needs: food and drink, shelter and clothing, but also the comforts associated with home. Moreover, the requirements of caring for children, providing for the elderly, helping one's near relations, and securing domestic happiness loom very large. What sits ill with this – notably the glories of war – is suspect. The second way in which the economic world mimics the household is that it depends on a "natural" division of labour. People do the things for which they are best suited or for which they have the most resources. In the world as in the household, people sort themselves out, so that everything needful gets done.

This is an idealization, of course, which abstracts from the realities of physical violence, coercion, and emotional exploitation. Nonetheless, it is contained in the modern idea of the economy: a world order, whose *nomos* is given in the fact that we are all, ultimately, of the same household or *oikos*, although we may be divided into many different families or peoples. We are united by virtue of the fact that we share an economy, which is to say a *nomos* inherent in the *logos* of the *oikos*.

Ecology challenges economy, in so far as it locates people in an *oikos* that includes non-human beings and suggests that we are subject to an over-determining *logos* that transcends the merely human.[2] The *oikos* relevant to ecology is not a scene of comfortable domesticity, but an environment within which various beings – plant and animal – interact with one another. Although humans may have a unique capacity to alter the environment, they are subject to limits that can only be understood ecologically. There are interactions among species, physical changes in the biosphere, and impacts of the former on the latter and the latter on the former, which are often beyond human calculation. Hence, notions of human mastery are out of place. People must adapt to the ecological niche appropriate to them, which is to say that they must bring their *nomos* into line with the *logos* of the non-human world. The relevant *oikos* is a home that we share with other beings whose purposes are different from ours, and that is governed by natural laws that are not of our making and not for our benefit. Other beings are not neces-sarily our friends, and changes in the environment can threaten us and them both. So, to think and act eco*logically* may not be the same as to think and act eco*nomically*.

Whereas economic thought begins from the human and moves outward, ecological thought goes in the opposite direction. To think ecologically is to suggest that the human *oikos*, however conceived, is only one element in an *oikos* for all beings, an *oikos* that has a *logos* for sure, but not a *telos* that includes the preservation of any particular species such as ours. The implication is that the androcentrism or humanism of Western thought since the Greeks is a testimony to our own vanity. To be realistic, we must gain a better sense of our own limitations. But, even in economic thought, the order appropriate to us emerges behind our backs. Our immediate pur-poses are self-interested and materialistic. To the extent that we act nobly, or generate forms of life or human expression that give effect to rationally articulated ideals, we do so within an order that is not itself the expression of an ideal. Unlike the *polis*, which is a purposive order (at least in Aristotle's conception of it), the economy is an order that makes us peace-able, cooperative, and productive despite our violent emotions, competitive spirits, and unproductive habits and jealousies. The economy civilizes us despite ourselves, not because we seek to live more rationally. Similarly, ecology brings us up against other species as well as the limits, rhythms, cycles, reactions, and transformations of the natural world in general. Human purposes may be relevant, and they may be organized economically to achieve a rationality beyond anyone's immediate intentions, but that rationality is overdetermined by another rationality that is not ours and that can never be subordinated to human purposes.

Ecological thought, as it has developed since the days of the "human ecologists" of the Chicago school, puts relatively little faith in the natural ordering capacities of humanity. People may sort themselves out in relation to one another, but like other species they may reproduce in such numbers or trench on the natural environment in such a way that the habitat for humanity collapses in specific places or more generally. Civilizations have a tendency to destroy themselves. Only in so far as we attune ourselves to the iron logic of ecological balance will we actually survive as a species. Where I live, ecological ideas are often invoked in relation to the traditions of Indigenous peoples, which were articulated in relation to specific places and with a profound sense of the limits on what humans could do in making themselves at home in a world that was not simply theirs (Atleo 2004).[3] Reinforced in this way, ecology is definitely a discourse of limits, in relation to which the expansiveness implicit in cosmopolitanism – or is it urbanism as a way of life? – appears to be a threat. Is it a threat to be contained by practices of government and self-government? Are we somehow to attune ourselves to the specific places where we live, internalize the spirit of those places, and live accordingly? Or, are we already out in the world in a way that requires us to adjust to its limits, the limits of a *cosmos* understood ecologically? Either way, our aspirations to live large in the world are contained within certain bounds.

Economy and ecology offer twin challenges to politics, in that they suggest that the *nomos* and *logos* to which we must attune ourselves are rooted in the *oikos* not the *polis*, and hence in something that is not the effect of human rationality. Whether it be the earthy and emotional demands of the household or the equally earthy pressures of the natural environment, we are bent to the necessities of an existence that mocks our capacity for self-determination. So, the ideal of autonomy – in both its Aristotelian and Kantian versions – is at odds with the fact that we need to be governed, and are governed, by forces inside of us (the ones that drives us toward the comforts of the household) and beyond us (in the natural environment). The ethics of economy and ecology demand that we submit to certain necessities, and allow ourselves to be governed by them. As such, these ethics seem to be odds with the ethics of self-assertion or self-expression that are supposedly characteristic of liberalism, in both its ancient and modern versions.

Eco-governmentality, urbanism, and republicanism

When we think economically or ecologically, we become interested in the problem of government, as opposed to the problem of politics. (As Foucault suggests, economic and ecological thinking developed in a context in which problems of state came to be understood largely as problems of government.) Government is a problem of behaviour: both our own behaviour and the behaviour of others. If people behave properly, conflicts disappear, projects get accomplished, productivity is increased, waste is avoided, and the most needful appears. This will not happen unless people are willing to be governed and to govern themselves appropriately. On the other hand, motivations are less important than conduct. If people behave properly, we may not have to worry about their reasons. Thus, as the economists have long argued, the self-interestedness of individuals, families, and larger social groupings is not necessarily a problem – indeed, it can be a benefit – if people in general submit to the governing logic of the market. A civil society can be created by channelling people's self-interested behaviour, without worrying overmuch about their motivations. If successful economically – that is, in terms of producing domestic comforts – such a society can be self-reproducing. To think ecologically rather than economically makes a difference, but the problem of human behaviour, and hence of government, remains central. Ecologists hope that the economy (and thus human behaviour in general) can become ecological, attuned by self-regulating mechanisms similar to the ones that bring supply and demand into equilibrium.

Modern republicanism purports to bring politics into line with governmentality. It does this by establishing the problematic of government as the a priori of politics. On this view, politics itself must be governed, so as to facilitate government. It may generate demands or pressures *upon* government and determine who will lead it, but it is not proper to government itself. The rationalities of government are determined by the problems at hand, and good politicians are expected to accede to those rationalities and get their supporters to submit to them. In fact, the key purpose of politics in relation to government is to secure consent, and hence the governability of the population. A secondary purpose is to enhance the rationality of government by improving the flow of relevant information. The limits on government, characteristic of modern constitutionalism, are designed to ensure that the government keeps to its proper task, which is to govern rather than to dominate. The modern republican ideal is of a government that cannot be *over* the people, because it is embedded *in* the people, a people who are to a large extent *self*-governing. Such a people can be governed lightly but rationally by orchestrating their practices of self-government appropriately. In the modern republic, government and self-government are supposed to bleed into one another and rationalize politics in relation to the rationalities of government. Ideally, government is depoliticized, because the people themselves have been depoliticized.

Most of the rationalities of depoliticized government flow from economy and ecology. Government in the ordinary sense is about making the world homely, comfortable, and productive, and ensuring that people do not overreach themselves and destroy their own environment. What Foucauldians have called biopolitics is largely an extension of the rationalities of economy and ecology. This becomes clear once we recognize the third term in the equation: the city or the urban. An implicit assumption of Graeco-Roman thought is that civilization and urbanization are the same things. To say that we are intended for life in the *polis*, that we can only be complete if we make the *polis* our home, and that the *polis* must ultimately be our *oikos* is to suggest that we must become urban to be civilized. And, of course, to be civilized is to have become self-governing in a certain way: governable through our myriad practices of self-government. The miracle of the city is that it works despite or because of the fact that it is a gathering together of strangers. Its governability flows from people's efforts to make the city a home or *oikos* for themselves. Whoever cannot or will not make their efforts consort with the strangers around them poses a threat, or perhaps just a challenge in terms of the problematic of government. Although criminals, madmen, and fanatics certainly create difficulties for others, strategies and tactics have been developed to render such people governable or to neutralize the threats they pose. This is part of a general effort to make the city habitable, productive, comfortable, and congenial. Since the nineteenth century, the city has ceased to be an isolated entity, and instead become a form of life that has spread into the countryside and encompassed the globe. The problem of economy and ecology is essentially a problem of organizing the city in this larger sense, the city as globalized urbanism. And, in so far as urbanism simply *is* the ensemble of practices of government and self-government that enable people to live together in great numbers, it has become the form through which we come to understand the problem of government, however little we acknowledge it.

The implicit urbanity of modern thinking is often obscured by appeals to the rural, the pastoral, or the tribal as heterotopias. These counter-ideals have shadowed modern thinking and coloured it so that the ideal urban community is often understood as a village, a rural retreat, or lately a tribe sharing a lifestyle. Nevertheless, the burden of modern thinking is that we are destined to be urban by virtue of our economic efforts, and that we need to learn to rationalize these efforts as best we can. A crucial aspect of this is the recognition of ecological limits. We can easily undermine the quality of our own lives if we do not limit or manage what we do to our environments, locally and globally. Thus, to think ecologically is (at least up to a certain point) simply a matter of rational self-interest. That idea has always been implicit in urban planning, which has been from the beginning a way of posing the city in relation to the environment as a problem of government. To plan the city is to rationalize our activities in relation to one another within a confined space, but it is also to think of how that space is to be reshaped as a sustainably habitable, productive, comfortable, and congenial place. Although grand plans to produce new cities or reshape old ones capture people's attention, most of the day-to-day work of urban planning is about facilitating and adjusting to economic development, with certain ecological principles in mind. Urban planning is eco-governmentality; or, to put it otherwise, what Foucauldians have called eco-governmentality is urban planning writ large. Significantly, planning has always been a way of rationalizing politics by rendering it governable.

To render politics governable has been a key aspiration of modern republicanism. This is evident in both the restrictions and the inclusions of the republican order. The familiar restrictions are the ones associated with the rule of law, bills of rights, and constitutionalism more generally. The implicit assumption is that government must be limited, so that people can go about their lawful business without arbitrary interference. The people are presumed to be self-governing for the most part, in need of only occasional restriction or guidance. Public enterprise is taken to be the exception to the rule of private initiative – and uniform action over a wider field to be the exception to more localized efforts. But, the effort to keep government within its proper bounds is complemented by the effort to include everyone within those bounds by making everyone a citizen. This universalism may have been resisted at first, but the problematic of government demands it. Whoever is excluded cannot be well governed; so, government becomes more effective when the excluded are included. This means extending political rights universally, but on condition that those rights are subordinate to the necessities of government. Everyone is free to participate, but in a system governed by the logic of government, itself attuned economically and ecologically to the reproduction of the city as the human *oikos*. Thus, urban planning or eco-governmentality carries the logic of modern republicanism forward.

Modern republicanism also entails a particular form of the international, which fudges the problem of sovereignty by locating it in a certain space of appearances. The sovereign state is the condition of possibility for the international, which is in turn the condition of possibility for the sovereign state. Thus, the actual locus of sovereignty – the state or the system of states – is always indeterminate. A similar indeterminacy is implicit in the state itself, especially in its republican form. The sovereign individual and the sovereign state are the twin conditions of constitutional or republican order, but the one always threatens to subvert the other, in much the same way that the state and the state system do. So, sovereignty is actually suspended, while acting as the principle that ostensibly secures relations between disparate authorities. This enhances the focus on government, which is a practice that does not depend on resolution of the problem of sovereignty. The hope is to keep the problem of sovereignty in suspense – between the individual, the state, and state system – in order to free up government. This does not mean freeing up "the government". Quite the contrary, "the government" must be constrained by the constitutional order that stretches from the individual to the system of states, so that the more complex practices of government and self-government can be articulated in accordance with the immanent rationalities of economy and ecology, as inflected through the urban.

The implication is that the "right to the city", as Lefebvre (1996) described it, is available only on certain terms. We notice the terms that are mediated by the state – the ones that determine who is a citizen, what rights attach to citizenship, and how citizens can go from one state to another – but we may not be so conscious of the terms implicit in the very character of the city, terms that impose themselves on anyone who lives in it or moves through it. Where to sleep, how to eat, how to dispose of one's wastes: all these questions and more are thrust upon anyone who becomes involved in urban life. As I have suggested in earlier chapters, we are all involved now whether we like it or not. That means that we are caught up in the practices of government and self-government that enable urban life, and hence are confronted with the immanent rationalities of ecology and economy. The latter may be interpreted in critical terms, demanding a different form of the urban or a limit to it, but the pressure still is to governmentalize our conduct, so that it conforms to these external rationalities.

Politics and violence

The moment of the political is one of disruption, when the regular routines of government are challenged by something that does not compute with them. The hope of modern politics is that everything and everyone can be made governable. This is in large part a matter of modulating forms of self-government, so that everything done contributes to a benign order or at least does not detract from it. But, completely smooth functioning is unimaginable. This means that whatever threatens or subverts the ensemble of governing practices must be isolated, contained, or destroyed. Although applications of force can themselves be subject to the rationalities of government, a limit is always reached, where the course of action can no longer be determined by those rationalities. Similarly, although the hope is that the rationalities of government will govern everyone's politics, we know that this will often not be true. The urge to dominate is strong, people are suspicious of one another, they seek to display their superiority, they are jealous of one another's advantages, and of course they have different ideas about the way we should live. Even if we were infused with good will toward one another – as we rarely are – we would have much to dispute. Moreover, if we were to take our cue from the Greeks, we would say that our freedom inheres in our capacity to transcend the smooth routines of government and self-government – which is to say, the logic of economy and ecology – and posit alternatives that do not flow from their rationalities. So, there is always this other possibility, a possibility of opening that is always attended by the threat of violence.

In the modern republican order, violence is supposed to be channelled through the nation-state. The state is supposed to mobilize, contain, and deploy violence to preserve the republican order. On the other hand, both nationalism and statism threaten that order, even though they are demanded by it. National identity and state sovereignty are pillars of modern republicanism, supposed to restrain non-state violence and give politics a proper outlet. But, both nation and state are ciphers that can be freely interpreted to suit a variety of purposes. So, xenophobic identities and aspirations for domination are commonly concealed within claims about nation and state. This is part of a more general problem, which is that the rationalities of republicanism, like the rationalities of government more generally, abstract from processes of domination, identity-formation, and human longing for a different world. The problematic of government encourages us to take the world as it is, with its existing modes of domination, patterns of identity, and ensembles of larger purposes. We are encouraged to work with what is *there*, keep our focus on the mundane concerns of economy and ecology that are bound up with urbanism as a way of life, and avoid the issues that might lead us to war (be it civil or international). Nation and state are there to tame the furies and give them outlet, but the main thrust of modern republicanism is toward civilization through governmentalization. The more we become self-governing and hence governable in the modern republican way, the less likely we are to resort to disruptive violence. But, this assumes that the furies can be and should be quieted.

The furies, of course, are not just that. They are also the emotions associated with demands for justice, equality, freedom, human rights, and much else that has been connected with modern republicanism. And, they are the emotions associated with economy and ecology: concerns about prosperity and domestic comfort on the one hand, and environment and natural flourishing on the other. So, what can burst the bounds of governmental rationality are not just the dark spirits of contempt for the other or the quest for superiority. Nor is religious zealotry the only form that zealotry can take. People have many ideals that can lead them to reject the rationalities of government. Some of those ideals are already expressed in the rationalities themselves, but appear twisted by historical legacies that defy correction except by challenge to the premises of government. Politics is inherently disruptive in that it brings out whatever cannot be contained within the rationalities of government. From a modern republican perspective, the role of the politician is to absorb these challenges, domesticate them, and bring people back to what can be achieved through the rationalities of government. But, it is not clear that that can be or should be enough.

The politics that inclines us to think in terms of economy and ecology is one that leads us toward a problematic of government. If it challenges modern republicanism, it is by shifting the focus toward the *oikos* (hence the city) and its immanent *nomos* and *logos*. But, this intensifies the governmentalization of politics that is already inherent in modern republicanism. The intent of modern republicanism is to governmentalize everything, including the nation and the state, so that politics itself can be rationalized. Shifting the focus from the *polis* to the *oikos*, as both economists and ecologists urge, tends to intensify the demand for politics to become orderly and rational – domesticated perhaps, or at least contained and limited in relation to an ecological order whose rationality transcends human purposes.[4] So, an eco-politics may be different from a politics of glory, and hence more peaceable, but like any politics that is centred on something and contained by it, it is an inherently limited politics that may be overridden by the energies it summons or seeks to exclude. It is through politics that we challenge the ways in which we are governed, and so the hope of modern republicanism, reinforced by the shift toward economy and ecology, can never be fully realized. If our politics were to become simply an eco-politics, it would be exceedingly brittle.

Freedom or freedom from freedom?

Hannah Arendt (1961) identified politics with freedom, but for reasons that Foucault explained freedom is always subject to governmentalization. In fact, governmentalization is about the organization of freedom to certain ends. As I have already suggested, modern republicanism involves the governmentalization of politics. The shift toward economy and ecology as the natural ground for politics shapes politics in a particular way and intensifies particular governmentalities. We are domesticated and embedded in our natural environment. The obvious concern is that we not break out of our routines in awkward and disruptive ways. We are to be tamed beasts, or at least men who understand our proper place in the order of things and behave accordingly. Although this does not sound much like freedom, the magic of governmentalization is that it makes resistances productive of the very order that restrains and manages those resistances. The economy is a model of this: it incites us to be bold entrepreneurs who break all the rules and rewards us for being innovative in productive ways. Ecological rationality works similarly, at least in the ways that it is often understood, bringing ecology under the sign of economy through eco-governmentality. So, where does this leave politics, or more generally our freedom?

A statist ontology of the political encourages us to pose this problem in relation to the state, but it is not clear that the state is the most important issue. A double offer of freedom is already implicit in the idea of the state: freedom for the citizen under the laws of the state, including an opportunity to voice concerns about those laws, advocate for change, vote for officials who will exercise state power, and hold those officials to account; and freedom for the state within the international system, including the right to organize things domestically and defend the state's interests internationally. Is this enough? Scarcely. If both states and citizens are bound by the principles of economy and ecology, understood as the principles of rationality itself, the freedom on offer is obviously constrained. It is difficult to assess those constraints if we assume that the key issues must appear along the line that takes us from the citizen to the state, from the state to the state system, and back again to the citizen. When we are invited to think economically or ecologically, we are asked to set politics aside in favour of the rationalities of the *oikos* writ large. The constraints implicit in this are not just about the way we relate to the state or the way states relate to one another. They are much more general than that. To think in terms of economy and ecology is to put our whole way of life into question. That means questioning all the ways we relate to one another from the smallest scale to the largest, in private and in public, in the cultural and the social, among our own and with others. Nothing is set aside, and there is no single axis of interaction.

When we see like a city and so adopt a political ontology of urbanism as a way of life, it is much easier to see the stakes involved in submitting to the rationalities of economy and ecology. As I have been arguing, cities exist by virtue of the practices of government and self-government that enable strangers to live together in great numbers. In a way, the principles of economy and ecology are interpretations of what is required to rationalize those practices. Obviously, there is much to be said for such rationalization, for our becoming civilized by internalizing these principles and giving effect to them in our practices of government and self-government. I have been trying to suggest that people can and do sort themselves out in cities, not least by creating the political authorities that they need, and that sovereignty may be redundant and in any case unachievable. The implication is that the ideals of modern republicanism are better served by nurturing the practices of government and self-government implicit in urbanism than by resorting to sovereign authority as the solution to our problems. Nevertheless, limits will be reached, not only in the sense of limits of what we can achieve, but also in the sense of limits of our own ideals. What I have been discussing in this chapter are ways of re-posing familiar ideals, ones associated with the *polis*, through some conception of the *oikos*, some idea of what the human homeland or household is or should be. However that homeland or household is conceived, and whatever principles of rationalization or lawful conduct are advanced in relation to it, the posited order will limit what people can be or do.

Is such a limitation appropriate or tolerable? I have been suggesting that much of what we seek is actually achieved without resort to sovereign authority, or – to put it otherwise – that the ideals of modern republicanism are better served by nurturing the practices implicit in urbanism as a way of life rather than by calling on the state to fix things. But, when I see like a city, I begin to notice what I am inclined to leave out of my own idealizing vision: on the one hand, the violences and irrationalities of the forms of urban life I find acceptable, and on the other hand, the exercises of freedom that challenge the rationalities and pacifications to which I adhere. There are bound to be challenges that I do not like, that I think are irrational, or that I simply do not understand. So, what then? Do I appeal to the sovereign to eradicate these challenges? The fixations of sovereignty are appealing, and I have to keep reminding myself that things cannot be fixed by such simple means, because urban life is so overwhelming. When I see like a state, I imagine that things can be fixed, but when I see like a city I realize that my own wish to fix things in a certain way is part of the problem.

Political theory often disguises itself as something else. In so far as people appeal to economic or ecological rationality, they tend to pose what they are saying as non-political or post-political in the hope of avoiding debates about whose interests are being served, which goals are being advanced, what ideals are being articulated, and what violences are required to make things work. Usually, the state is somewhere in the background, as the ultimate righter of wrongs and enforcer of reason. If we recognize that economy and ecology are being offered as principles of civic life, we can see more clearly that a certain vision of the city or the urban global is at stake, and that a bid to make all of human life governable has been advanced. The Foucauldian idea of freedom is one of incessant problematization, always (it is hoped) one step ahead of governmentalization. Freedom in this sense seems to be an aspect of urbanism, but urbanism also domesticates this freedom and makes it cohere with the practices of government. Ideas about economy and ecology, like ideas of modern republicanism, are keyed to hopes of coherence, hopes that are often underpinned by faith in the state as our potential redeemer. Like it or not, the city is never really settled in any particular form. Not only is it always in the process of being rebuilt, but it is always changing to accommodate new people, new cultures, new ventures, and new political arrangements. The implication is that the city cannot be governed in accordance with a singular logic, be that the logic of economy and ecology, the logic of the state, or anything else. When we focus on the city as city, we can see that it will always be excessive in relation to the principles advanced and the practices of government associated with them. On the other hand, the form of the city is such that it turns exercises of freedom into practices of government and self-government. People cannot achieve their ends, be they individual or collective, unless they adjust themselves to the freedom of others, and this means that they are always involved in governing themselves and attempting to govern others. So, it seems that the political is on this plane, and not just on the axis between states, citizens, and the system of states.

Where I live, I can see this most vividly when the claims of Indigenous peoples are articulated, because they undercut my own sense of being at home here. I am repositioned as a "settler" on someone else's land, intruding in a homeland that is not my own. I am also called to account for disrupting the natural ecology of the region, and living in accord with an economics that destroys people's livelihoods, undercuts the material basis of their cultures, and rules out ways of life that are perfectly viable. Moreover, I am reminded of the fact that the state that provides me with citizenship and that calls me to action within the space it offers for "politics" is violent, and that my participation in it is an embrace of its violence. All this makes me uneasy, but not entirely in a bad way. I am impelled to rethink where I am, and put my own notions of *oikos* and *polis*, *nomos* and *logos* at issue. Here as elsewhere, Indigenous peoples have been claiming their own "right to the city", and that forces me to reconsider my own right, not only in relation to them, but in relation to the millions of migrants whose right to the city is being denied or curtailed almost everywhere, not least in my own country. What are the conditions of possibility for everyone to have a home and to live large in the world? Can urbanism as a way of life actually provide the freedom it promises? If not, is there any alternative to it? Surely, these questions are more pressing than the future of the state.

7 From local self-government to politics

Throughout this book, I have been arguing that the dominant ontology of the political draws our attention to the state – or, more generally, to whatever we perceive as the sovereign centre, the locus from which we are governed – but that the problems we have to address are better understood in terms of the proliferating practices of government and self-government that enable our way of life. Some of these practices involve the state. Others do not. Some need to be resisted. Others do not. Because our lives are actually governed by a multiplicity of authorities operating in different registers – some of them calling themselves businesses, others religions, and still others charities, activist groups, social networks, or even gangs – and those authorities are organized on various scales, the spaces in which we are called to act are various. Moreover, the narratives that account for things are equally various, and so we are confronted with a multiplicity of imagined histories. We all negotiate these spaces and times differently. One aspect of politics (as we normally understand it) is the effort to get us all to think of ourselves as being in the same place, at the same moment, confronting the same problems. Fictions of the latter sort can be potent. Many of us imagine ourselves as being in the modern world at a particular moment of crisis that summons everyone to political action. As I suggested in Chapter 5, a kind of megalomania is encouraged by this way of thinking. We neglect what we can actually deal with, what we can actually do, in favour of a kind of fantasy life filled with evil potentates and great redeemers.

One advantage of seeing like a city – that is, thinking of the world *as* a city and approaching it *through* the city – is that it encourages us to think about what is *here*, all around us, rather than frightening ourselves with visions of what is *there*, in the big, bad world. Most of us – certainly virtually everyone who reads this book – live in relatively orderly places where people go about their business without having to worry very much about getting gunned down in the streets. The latter worry is certainly there for many people, and there are cities or parts of the world where the situation really is dire in this respect. But, if we want to figure out what works and what doesn't – in terms of providing security, advancing social justice, or allowing for greater freedom – we are well advised to begin with the world that is already familiar to us, rather than with those imagined spaces elsewhere where the bogeymen live. The bad things will come into view soon enough, but we will probably get a better sense of their forms and proportions if we approach them within contexts that we already understand to some degree. The contexts that we know may be sites of oppression, exclusion, alienation, injustice, and violence, but they also are sites at which people have been able, in some degree, to lead meaningful and productive lives. How are we to understand such sites except through the particular places that we know?

If this line of analysis is correct, then we have to focus our political attention on what people do by way of governing themselves and governing other people. So, *local self-government* – in the broad sense I am about to explain – is a crucial issue. How does it work? What are its forms? How do people engage with it politically? What are its possibilities? What are its dangers? The implication is that we will see politics differently if we approach it through the ubiquitous, proliferating practices of government and self-government that we can see all around us, and in which we are all involved already. When we are panicked, we demand that the state reduce these practices to order, but when we overcome that panic, we can see that there are multiple orders in being that already restrain us and a vitality to life that we would do well to nurture. In any case, there is much to understand and much to do politically with respect to the sites near us. These sites are local, but that does not mean that they are parochial: quite the contrary.

Understanding local self-government

Personally, I have always been attracted to the ideal of local self-government, because it is connected in my mind to democratization. I have never quite believed the story of the modern state, because it leaves out what the Greeks had in the *polis*: namely, a space where people could assemble and decide how to govern themselves. Such spaces do exist within some modern states, notably New England and Switzerland, but the town meeting form of local self-government has never been popular amongst theorists of liberal democracy. De Tocqueville seemed to praise it in *Democracy in America*, but he undercut that praise with reference to the necessities of the urban-industrial society then emerging. Famously, John Stuart Mill picked up on many of de Tocqueville's ideas about the way that private and public freedom in the USA energized the people and encouraged them to be entrepreneurial and innovative. He wanted there to be strong institutions of local self-government, but on the representative model that he advocated: one that would involve the mass of the people, but under the tutelage of the wiser and better educated.

To the extent that there is a theory of local self-government implicit in modern republicanism, it is a variant on what de Tocqueville and Mill suggested: to wit, that it is important to involve people in their own government, but not in a way that might impair its rationality. Mill put it this way:

> The authority which is most conversant with principles should be supreme over principles, while that which is most competent in details should have the details left to it. The principal business of the central authority should be to give instruction, of the local authority to apply it. Power may be localized, but knowledge, to be useful, must be centralized; there must be somewhere a focus at which all its scattered rays are collected, that the broken and coloured lights which exist elsewhere may find there what is necessary to complete and purify them. . . . [The central authority] ought to keep open a perpetual communication with the localities: informing itself by their experience, and them by its own; giving advice freely when asked, volunteering it when seen to be required; compelling publicity and recording of proceedings, and enforcing obedience to every general law which the legislature has laid down on the subject of local management. That some such laws ought to be laid down few are likely to deny. The localities may be allowed to mismanage their own interests, but not to prejudice those of others, nor violate those principles of justice between one person and another, of which it is the duty of the State to maintain the rigid observance. If the local majority attempts to oppress the minority, or one class another, the State is bound to interpose.
>
> (Mill 1991, 424)

He thought of the virtues of local government not just in terms of the adaptation of policy to circumstance, but also in terms of the education or improvement of the people.

> It is but a poor education that associates ignorance with ignorance, and leaves them, if they care for knowledge, to grope their way to it without help, and to do without it if they do not. What is wanted is, the means of making ignorance aware of itself, and able to profit by knowledge; accustoming minds which know only routine, to act upon, and feel the value of principles: teaching them to compare different modes of action, and learn, by the use of their reason, to distinguish the best. When we desire to have a good school, we do not eliminate the teacher.
>
> (Mill 1991, 425–26)

Modern republicanism as we know it is informed by such ideas. Neo-liberal notions about enforcing responsibility – requiring people to take care of themselves by eating properly, keeping physically fit, becoming educated and entrepreneurial, being active, innovative, and diligent on the job, practising safe sex and limiting their families so that they can care for their children and their parents appropriately, driving carefully and responsibly, reducing their wastes and recycling and reusing them where possible, volunteering in their communities, and of course following public affairs, voting regularly, and holding public officials to account – take forward the ideas that Mill and de Tocqueville had. In such conceptions, local government as Mill understood it does not have pride of place. The practices at issue are much more diffuse. They concern what people do when they are on their own, having sex, dealing with their children, walking down the street, going to school, looking for a job, developing their work skills, and so on. The totality of society or the economy is at issue. The whole culture is at stake. What occurs in every nook and cranny of life is important. There is not just one locale where the right modes of acting and interacting have to be developed. People are to become rationally self-governing in every aspect of their lives, and are to be so individually and collectively on every scale and in every dimension of human life. The implication – widely understood, but never quite articulated as such – is that *local self-government is the very principle of modern republicanism.*

I admit that this is an odd way of putting it, since the idea of "local self-government" has generally been articulated as a principle that concerns the autonomy of "local communities" *vis-à-vis* the state as such. That is what Mill was thinking about in the passages cited above, and that is what the International Union of Local Authorities (IULA) (1993) has in mind in its "World Wide Declaration of Local Self-Government":

> The principle of local self-government shall be recognized in the constitution or in the basic legislation concerning the governmental structures of the country. Local self-government denotes the right and the duty of local authorities to regulate and manage public affairs under their own responsibility and in the interests of the local population. This right shall be exercised by individuals and representative bodies freely elected on a periodical basis by equal, universal suffrage, and their chief executives shall be so elected or shall be appointed with participation of the elected body. Public responsibilities shall be exercised by those basic units of local government which are closest to the citizen.

As the Declaration makes clear – following as it does the principles contained in the "European Charter of Local Self-Government" (Council of Europe 1985), and hence the doctrine of "subsidiarity" articulated within the European Union – these responsibilities are to be exercised *within* the framework established by the state, and are to be subject to the general laws of the state.

Nevertheless, it is easy to see that this interpretation of the principle turns on a particular and rather arbitrary notion of what counts as local. The White House is a locality, as is the United Nations building in New York, or the European Commission headquarters in Brussels. When people talk about local self-government, they are not usually thinking about empowering localities of that sort, although partisans of the state may think that they should. The state system empowers some localities in relation to the rest: the localities where the "statesmen" (or is it the "politicians"?) and their advisors do their work. A type of local self-government is the organizing principle of the state system. Every nation, or at least every nation that commands sufficient respect, is supposed to be self-governing. If it is, it can be recognized as a sovereign state. This means that the locality or localities at the apex of the state – the executive, the legislature, and the courts – can wield a kind of plenary authority within the realm concerned. The individual states are themselves local authorities, however, confined to particular territories, and their law is municipal law in relation to the international law that establishes the rules of conduct for states. Whoever or whatever establishes and enforces the rules at the international level is in effect the "central authority". But, as we know, on a global scale, the central authority is weak, and the local authorities (states) – or at least some of them – are strong, and so nothing is as well rationalized as it might be. Nevertheless, the aspiration is towards an ubiquitous (global) rationality enabled by appropriate kinds of local self-government: treaty-based relations between states, collaborative multinational agencies, independent courts interpreting the law, independent media of communications, autonomous professions and institutions, enterprises governing themselves within the law, charities raising their own money and establishing their own purposes, social movement organizations advancing their own causes, parents raising and governing their own children, and individual people making their own decisions about what to do, where to live, and whom to be with. Liberals like to highlight the freedom involved, but equally important is the way that the different entities are expected to restrain themselves in the process of governing themselves and others rationally. As in Kant's vision of autonomy or in Hegel's conception of the state, it turns out that "freedom" involves many restrictions, some of which are imposed on us, some of which we impose on others, and some of which we impose on ourselves.

Much of the critical attention to neo-liberalism in recent years focuses on the way that practices of "freeing up", deregulating, contracting out, and so on mask an effort to orchestrate things for the benefit of the most powerful peoples, businesses, and classes. Although we should pay careful attention to this, it is important not to overemphasize the role of the state. If one begins from a statist ontology of the political, one's attention is focused on the state as an agent, but the agency at issue – in so far as it is an agency of domination, exploitation, and exclusion – is much more diffuse. Obviously, one must pay close attention to the role of capital – or "business" if you prefer. But, to stop one's analysis there, or to focus exclusively on the nexus that led Marx to describe the modern state as "the executive committee of the bourgeoisie", is to miss much. When we think of the world as a city, and examine the relevant practices through the city, we begin to see that the capacities of the executive committee are limited, and that many other agencies are involved in producing the form of order with which we are familiar. When I think of David Cameron and his "Big Society" (or George Bush, and his "thousand points of light"), I think of all the other fashions in government that have come and gone in my lifetime, almost all of which gesture at the fact that the state as such has limited capacity to do things. Since the eighteenth century, we have been told again and again that the only way to govern people effectively is through their freedom. Perhaps that is right: that we have to live in and through the world or "city" people have created, and that, although we can enjoy various forms of local self-government, we will suffer from them as well, and neither we nor anyone else will ever really be masters of this world in which we live.

Years ago, Robert Dahl (1967, 959) suggested that

> [W]e drop completely the notion so dear to the Greeks and early Romans that to be legitimate a unit of government must be wholly autonomous. With autonomy we also drop the belief that there is a single sovereign unit for democracy, a unit in which majorities are autonomous with respect to all persons outside the unit and authoritative with respect to all persons inside the unit. Instead we begin to think about appropriate units of democracy as an ascending series, a set of Chinese boxes, each larger and more inclusive than the other, each in some sense democratic, though not always in quite the same sense, and each not inherently less nor inherently more legitimate than the other.

His image of Chinese boxes or Russian dolls captures the conception of scale implicit in the state system and more generally in the statist ontology of the political. The biggest of the boxes, the one on the largest scale, is the one that encompasses the world as a whole: the global or the international. Within that is the state, within which is the province or region, within which in turn is the locality that enjoys local self-government on the model articulated by the IULA. There is a current literature on "the politics of scale" that suggests that authority is being shifted upward, downward, and outward from the state, for the usual nefarious reasons (Brenner 2004, Keil and Mahon 2009). Be that as it may, what I notice is that this statist political imaginary involves conceptions of scale and hierarchy that are quite at odds with what anyone can observe anywhere, and that tend to obscure the problems that we have to address. Is action on AIDS in Africa local or global? If an improvised explosive device (IED) explodes on the road between Kabul and Kandahar, what makes it a global rather than a local event? That it kills Americans or can be attributed to the people resisting NATO forces? Does it become a merely national event when only the Afghan army is affected? And, does it become merely "local" when some poor peasant gets killed? Or, what if the significance attributed to the event is that it will affect the

American elections? Does that make it local or national in a different way, or has it become essentially global? How can we talk so freely of "levels" and "scales" when an event in the same locality can appear global, national, regional, and local all at once, and then change its character in accordance with the various politics at stake?

It should be obvious that there are *various* politics at stake and hence that *various* temporalities and spatialities are relevant. There is no fixed spatial hierarchy, and thus no neat set of Russian dolls or Chinese boxes. New spatialities and temporalities – the Internet is an obvious one, eco-regions are another – are established through our own activities, and old spatialities and temporalities may fade into irrelevance.[1] And yet, we like to imagine that there is a settled order of things, because the statist ontology of the political suggests that there *must* be such an order for there to be a world in which we can act rationally. We hold on to this belief even as we acknowledge the complex practices of government and self-government that actually produce the world to which we relate, that generate a myriad of problems for us, and yet also appear to us as means for solving problems. We all know that bombing people into submission is not a very good way of going about things. Robust order arises otherwise. We also know that people make connections and produce "goods" – both private goods and public goods (Ostrom 1990) – in bewilderingly complicated ways that we scarcely know how to track. When we think in terms of the imagined order of the state system, or of the global as the scale of greatest or highest significance, we misrepresent the world in which we actually live.

Let me illustrate this by talking about what I can see from my own neighbourhood. It is not a fashionable place. There is nothing here to interest the guns and bombs crowd: no blood on the streets, no IEDs, no gunfights, nor even any mass demonstrations. Nothing has been settled or is likely to be settled here with respect to the current monetary crisis, fiscal crisis, environmental crisis, crisis of civilization or civilizations, or whatever crisis you would like to talk about. My neighbourhood is not the Archimedean point at which our sovereign lord (is that you, me, or someone else?) might act to redeem the world. It just happens to be where I live, of no more or less interest than the place where you live. I am acutely aware of the fact that I am not supposed to write from here, that I am supposed to project myself to somewhere more interesting. (That said, I am reassured by the current fashion for Swedish detective novels, a fashion that suggests that we already know that the world can be examined from anywhere.) I live in Victoria, a mid-sized city at the south-eastern tip of Vancouver Island, the large Canadian island that hugs the mainland of North America for about three hundred miles north of the US–Canadian border. More specifically, I live in the Fairfield-Gonzales neighbourhood. What can I see from this inconsequential place that tells me anything of general interest about the world, or more specifically about the relation between local self-government and politics?

The places of local self-government

The area where I live consists mostly of single-family homes, although there are many secondary suites rented out to cover mortgage costs. So, it is a predominantly middle-class neighbourhood of homeowners, with many renters (including students) on lower incomes. If I walk in one direction, I go up a small hill to a lookout over the Strait of Juan de Fuca – named in honour of a Spanish explorer – toward the Olympic Mountains (no prize to guess where that name came from) in the State of Washington (ibid.) There is a marker there with arrows toward various points of interest on the other side, including the City of Seattle – named after a local Indian chief – the city of Starbucks, Boeing, and Microsoft, and hence a centre of the global economy as it has now become, dependent on computer technology, air travel, and endless cups of coffee. If I go downtown – five or ten minutes away by car – I can catch a seaplane that takes me the eighty miles to Lake Washington in Seattle, and be at Bill Gates's doorstep within an hour. If I want to connect instead to a less global and more national enterprise, I can take a harbour flight to downtown Vancouver and be there even quicker: the flight itself takes about fifteen minutes. On the other hand, I can connect to the other obvious reality of the global city by walking over to the cemetery near my house. It's not just that I can look at all the graves of Canadian soldiers killed in the First World War. I am likely to encounter one or more of the homeless people who find refuge in the cemetery, both at night and during the day. The homeless, like the middle-class people in the adjacent neighbourhood, generally keep themselves to themselves. Nevertheless, their presence is felt not only in downtown Victoria – ah, that name: we do have to distinguish ourselves from the Americans, don't we? – but in the nearby neighbourhoods, like mine.

The real centre of my neighbourhood is Fairfield Plaza, across the road from the cemetery, and just a few blocks from my house. It is a busy place, since it has a popular grocery store, hardware store, drugstore, liquor store, and other amenities. The "binners" amongst the homeless return bottles to the liquor store and the grocery store to collect the refunds that provide them with a bit of cash. The Plaza, like the neighbourhood as a whole, is a peaceable place. I find this unremarkable, and not just because of the particular characteristics of my neighbourhood. In my experience, shopping centres, shopping streets, and open-air markets are generally peaceable. There may be fights or robberies occasionally – and of course in some parts of the world a bomb might go off at any time – but people are generally disciplined by the very business of buying and selling. We, the customers, need to get stuff, and we behave in a way – in relation to one another and in relation to the merchants – that enables us to get what we want. This is a social site – I often run into friends or acquaintances in the grocery store – but it is mainly a site of commercial exchange. We all – even the criminals amongst us – have an ideal of what such a site should be like if it

is to work for us, and the social pressures, the micro-practices of government and self-government, that enable us to do what we want and need to
do at this site are generally quite effective. We all know that the police visit
occasionally, and that they could be summoned at short notice, but to
attribute the order we produce to *them*, the police, is to mistake the whole
process. The police, as they themselves insist, are there to serve the community.
If they didn't exist, the merchants would establish their own security system,
as they do in many malls, not only to protect their own interests, but to
meet the demands of customers who expect to be able to shop without being
robbed, threatened, harassed, intimidated, or even jostled. Again, as the police
themselves would say, policing is most effective when it complements
practices of government and self-government that people follow anyway.
To impose order on a disorderly population or on a population that rejects
that form of order is difficult.

Anyone coming to Victoria would not only notice its suburban middle-
class feel, but also how "white" it is. The people Canadians euphemistically
call "visible minorities", who constitute about 40 per cent of the population
in Vancouver and Toronto, are notable mostly for their absence here. On
the other hand, the Aboriginal presence is palpable. There are eleven Indian
Reserves in the greater Victoria area. The total population on the Reserves
is relatively small – only about 5,000 – but the Reserves are nonetheless quite
noticeable. Most of the people who identify themselves as First Nations
or Métis live off-Reserve, and many of them are not "Status Indians":
which is to say that they are not recognized by the Canadian government
as people having the rights assigned to "Indians". Victoria has always been
a gathering point for First Nations people from "up-Island" and elsewhere
on "the Coast". So, the First Nations presence is diverse, and is becoming
more diverse, although the people concerned generally recognize that this
is Lekwungen or Coast Salish territory. The Victoria Native Friendship
Centre (http://www.vnfc.ca/) serves about 15,000 people living in greater
Victoria and the nearby communities on southern Vancouver Island. By
comparison, there are about 35,000 people in greater Victoria classified by
Statistics Canada as "visible minorities". The latter figure is about 10 per
cent of the overall population, and so one would think that First Nations
would be less visible in this overwhelmingly "white", English-speaking city.
That is not so, however. It is increasingly difficult for anyone who is at
all sensitive to the issues to ignore the fact that we are living on "occupied
territories" never ceded to the Crown or to the state called Canada.[2] All the
state-based institutions on which we depend and with which we identify are
obviously illegitimate in that they arise from arbitrary claims of sovereignty.
Originally, there were four imperial powers that made claims in this area:
Spain, Britain, the United States, and Russia. It wasn't all sorted out
between them until the 1840s, when this place became British and Fort Victoria
was established. The people who actually lived here, and whose ancestors
had lived here for untold generations, were of course not consulted. They

ended up living under British and later Canadian occupation, mostly without benefit of treaties of the sort negotiated elsewhere in North America. In recent years, the absence of treaties has become more and more of an embarrassment for the governments of Canada and British Columbia – and more and more of a nuisance as the courts have ruled that there must be Aboriginal rights of some sort that have to be taken into account. How those Aboriginal rights are to be taken into account is a huge issue that makes "property-owners" nervous, especially in British Columbia.

When the Hudson's Bay Company – a company that once claimed much of what is now Canada as its exclusive territory, by virtue of a grant from the British Crown – established its fort here in 1842, it developed a number of home farms, one of which was Fairfield. That is the area that eventually became my neighbourhood. (Gonzales was a Spanish explorer, and one of the bays of the Strait of Juan de Fuca is named after him.) When I wander around the neighbourhood, I cannot find much evidence of Native habitation, but the camas lilies that appear here and there in the spring are a reminder of a crop widely cultivated before the British came. There is a Chinese cemetery, different from the one I just mentioned, where bones were once collected from across Canada before they were shipped home for proper burial in China. Victoria's small Chinatown is actually the oldest in the country, dating back to the days of the Cariboo gold rush in the late 1850s. The other cemetery, where veterans' graves, the graves of Victoria's British elite, and various homeless people can be found, also has markers for African-Americans, who were amongst the first settlers in the wake of the US Civil War, and Japanese-Canadians, who were deported from the area during the Second World War. But, the most palpable presence in the neighbourhood as a whole are just the houses built during the various waves of settlement, from Ross Bay Villa (1865), which is now under restoration, to ones like mine that were built in the pre-First World War housing boom, and the later houses of the 1940s, 1970s, and onward. It is not a neighbourhood being rebuilt at the rate of Manhattan, but there is always something happening: usually a small house being torn down in favour of a bigger and fancier one, but occasionally a house being replaced by a small apartment building or townhouses. The Fairfield-Gonzales Community Association keeps a watchful eye on such things, and has a formal role in land-use planning in the area. Land-use planning is mostly a matter of responding to rezoning applications, but it connects with a number of large issues about the supply of low-to-moderate income housing (housing costs in the Victoria area are amongst Canada's highest), the preservation of established "communities" (that's of course the term of art for an area like mine), and the quality of the natural environment.

The neighbourhood is notorious environmentally, because the Clover Point sewage outfall is just past the cemetery. There, Victoria's "liquid waste" passes largely untreated into the Strait of Juan de Fuca, to the annoyance of environmentalists and the embarrassment of those who want to advertise this as "The Garden City". The provincial government promotes the province as a whole as "SuperNatural British Columbia", and there is widespread recognition of the fact that this whole region – with its mountains, forests, wildlife, and seashore – is an attractor for tourists, retirees with money, and (possibly) businesses that want to offer a high "quality of life" to their most valued employees. A certain environmental sensitivity is thus incumbent upon us. There are ongoing controversies about "unspoilt" natural areas on the fringes of the city, as well as about areas previously logged that the forestry companies would like to sell off as prime residential real estate. Moreover, there is a provincially instituted Agricultural Land Reserve that is supposed to protect farmland from the encroaching suburbs. So, questions about the environment are always there, along with questions about "heritage", which refer back mostly to the settler heritage – in its built form heavily influenced by styles first established in California and British India – but also gesture toward the more fundamental reality of the Aboriginal presence and the vexed problem of illegitimate occupation.

One can sometimes see American naval vessels on their way from Bremerton, the huge base near Seattle, passing through the Strait into the open Pacific. The Canadian navy, which is quite small, has one of its two bases in Esquimalt, a Victoria suburb. Most of the big vessels visible in the Strait are carrying cargo to and from China, Korea, and Japan: we are on the shipping route between East Asia and Vancouver and Seattle. The smaller vessels in the Strait are pleasure boats or whale-watching dinghies carrying tourists out to look at the orcas (killer whales) who live in the area. People hang-glide off the foreshore, and there always seem to be small aircraft or helijets going back and forth to Vancouver and Seattle. Closer to downtown is the dock where the big cruise ships come, stopping here on their way to Alaska. They look like floating apartment buildings. The day-trippers from Seattle go directly to the Inner Harbour by hydrofoil, and create a market for trinket sellers and buskers, which is very important during the summer. Otherwise, the downtown is dominated by offices of the provincial government – this is the province's oldest city and its capital – and increasingly by condominiums that serve a population of indeterminate origin (retirees from Eastern Canada? young office workers? Asian investors?). But, what seems to worry people there is the large number of homeless people, some of whom beg, some of whom are mentally ill, many of whom are dependent on alcohol or injection drugs, and some of whom are into petty crime and prostitution. People who invest downtown or operate businesses there are concerned, like their counterparts elsewhere in North America, about the flight to the suburbs, and want to create a business climate friendly to upper-middle class shoppers, tourists, and patrons of the art galleries, theatres, and concert venues downtown. The aspiration is to make the downtown into a classy place that suburbanites might like to patronize and that sophisticated and affluent urbanites might like to live in. This is a challenge because Victoria lacks the diversity that gives bigger places a buzz, and yet the presence of the homeless makes affluent people uneasy, if only because it makes them feel guilty. The climate here is milder than in the rest of Canada, and the urban legend is that people come here because it is easier to make a go of it sleeping rough in the winter than it is elsewhere. Whatever the truth, the presence of the homeless in downtown Victoria is palpable, and the subject of ongoing policy discussions and political controversies.

A key issue recently has been "the right to sleep" – that is the claim, partly vindicated by the courts, that a person has a right to sleep on public property (such as a park) if he or she wants to or has nowhere else to go (Young 2009). The "nowhere else to go" part of that claim is the one vindicated by the courts, which have thereby laid a responsibility on the relevant governments to provide shelter for those who do not have it. In most people's eyes, that responsibility is bound up with other ones: to help the mentally ill, the addicted, and the abused, and more generally to deal with the claims – and challenges – posed by people who have been marginalized and victimized, but who may push back in various ways. To the extent that it still exists, the welfare state guarantees everyone who qualifies some income and offers some public services as a matter of right, without cost. But, the qualifications are restrictive, the income supports inadequate, and the services spotty. Before the welfare state developed, there were many charitable agencies that responded – restrictively, inadequately, and spottily, to be sure – to the needs and demands of the poor and the dispossessed. These agencies have not gone away. In fact, they have multiplied, and not just because of the ostensible retreat of the welfare state. Social activism of one sort or another constantly produces new agencies, most of which provide services and engage in advocacy at the same time. The state or more specifically the federal, provincial, regional, and municipal governments are in constant interaction with such agencies. What arises is a kind of shared responsibility, characterized by government funding of particular projects or services provided by non-governmental organizations. Moreover, there are collaborative processes, whereby the various "stakeholders" (including users of the relevant services) are involved in efforts to identify problems, agree on a common direction, and share out responsibilities. However ineffectual such efforts often are, they are a standard form of government in Victoria, as elsewhere. It is with respect to "the community" dealing with homelessness issues that the "right to sleep" has been demanded: a right *not* to go into the shelter offered and instead to live large without restrictions normally involved in being a recipient of welfare or charity.

The idea of living large also comes up in a different way with respect to the claims of First Nations. In British Columbia, the treaty process was revived in the 1990s with the hope that it would somehow generate settlements with respect to Aboriginal claims. The results have been very limited so far, because of the perception on both sides that the point of a treaty is to get First Nations to relinquish their claims on lands other than the ones allotted to them by treaty. What First Nations actually want is something different: compensation to be sure, recognized rights with regard to their own territories, a privilege role in the government of those territories and access to the resources and revenues generated there, and the means to be self-governing generally. To be self-governing generally means being recognized as independent nations on a territory shared by other nations, including the one called Canada (Alfred 2005, 2008; Borrows 2002, 2010; Turner 2006). How the principles of sharing and the rights of self-government are to be understood when the various nations are conceived as living side-by-side, rather than in a relation in which one nation is deemed to have sovereignty over the others, is the unresolved issue (Tully 1995, Niezen 2003, Coulthard 2007, Shaw, K. 2008). First Nations want to occupy their own territories, but they also want to live large in a shared world, a world that has now become a city. The denial of these aspirations is at the heart of ongoing anxieties about the legitimacy of the Canadian state, Canadian society, and the Canadian economy. In Victoria, these anxieties are more obvious than they are in most other parts of Canada.

At the University of Victoria, where I work, the question of its relation to Aboriginal peoples is ever-present. The university has attempted to legitimize its own presence on the lands it occupies by commissioning totem poles and ceremonial regalia from Aboriginal artists. Recently, it put up a First Peoples House. There are programmes in Indigenous Governance, Indigenous Studies, and (now) Indigenous Law. There is an Office of Indigenous Affairs, an Indigenous Faculty Caucus, and various programmes oriented toward Indigenous students. Although there has been some encouragement from the federal and provincial governments for the university (and other universities in the country) to move in this direction, the main force of change is to be found in interactions between faculty and students, which generate pressures to respond in some fashion to the needs and demands of Indigenous students and Indigenous communities. One might describe this as "local self-government", something that arises at a site, between different authorities (the university, the professoriate, Indigenous nations, activist groups, etc.) in complex relations of contestation, cooperation, and negotiation. The state as such is at best a shadowy presence.

Back in the downtown, one sees similar things, especially around issues of injection drugs and homelessness. Vancouver has established North America's first legal supervised injection site, a kind of free zone where people can inject heroin or other "illegal" drugs without being hassled by the police, but with medical workers standing by to offer assistance. The federal government was never very keen about this, and the American government has been even more hostile. Nevertheless, Insite, as it is called, has strong support from the municipal government, the health authority, and even the police. There has been an effort to establish something similar in Victoria, but neighbourhood resistance to the first proposed site put paid to the original plan. Many of the same issues are now being played out with regard to encampments of the homeless downtown, generally with the homeless on one side, local businesses and apartment dwellers on the other, and the service-providing agencies caught in the middle. The details of recent controversies are not worth replaying here, but the pattern is generally familiar: homeless people and injection drug users insisting on their right to live in their own way, without interference; the authorities trying to pressure them in a different direction, towards "cleaning themselves up" and rejoining mainstream society; and various advocates, social workers, health workers, and others trying to generate a situation in which people are encouraged and enabled to live more "normal" lives without being forced to do so, and in which people who choose to live outside the mainstream still get some respect and support.[3] At one end of the spectrum, the emphasis is on freedom, at the other end on law and order, and in the middle a discourse of health and welfare (or shall we say "government"?).

There is much to say about the way homelessness has been produced as a discourse and as a phenomenon. There is equally much to say about injection drug use. (The heroin comes from elsewhere, of course, but BC Bud, marijuana grown up-Island and elsewhere in the province is a big cash crop. When California came close to legalizing the growth and sale of marijuana, there were great fears about the effect on the provincial economy. Marijuana is probably our most important export product. The drug gangs that war with one another for control of the trade also are involved in importing the other drugs. Victoria is an important distribution centre and its courts deal with more than their fair share of drug-related offences.) What I notice especially when I think about how the issues have been posed and by whom is that the politics, like the practices of government and self-government that are at stake, are at a site that cannot be understood in terms of the relationship between the state and society. There are many authorities involved: police forces, churches, health clinics, shelters, food banks, schools, friendship centres, business associations, charities, advocacy groups, and organizations of homeless people, injection drug users, and sex workers. That isn't a complete list. No one has complete control, and what the state – in any sense or in any locus – actually wants is only one issue among many. The federal government did not want Insite in Vancouver, but it got established anyway and is likely to continue in some form. What does that signify about the way politics works? If enough people of enough importance want something to happen, it may happen regardless of the attitude of the ostensibly sovereign authorities. In this case, a relevant coalition of professionals, advocates, reporters, and community workers emerged, with leaders within various authorities, and opposition that was just as widely dispersed. Elected politicians were involved, but they were not the only key figures, and one could scarcely have predicted the results by looking at organizational charts. What's at stake seems to be the *form* of local self-government. The struggle is over which people in which locale are to govern themselves and in which way and with what consequences for others. Given that we are all interconnected, self-government is always about governing others as well as one's self. How can such a practice be understood politically?

The traces of politics

Victoria has a municipal council. There are in fact thirteen municipalities in the area, and an overarching regional government, called the Capital Regional District (CRD). In so far as politics is contained within these agencies, it is limited, because both the municipalities and the CRD are subject to the authority of the provincial government. In any case, the powers of these local governments are quite restricted – they have no formal role in educational or health policy, for instance – and their "own source" revenue is mainly from property taxes and user fees. Income and sales taxes are controlled by the federal and provincial governments. So, much of the focus of these local authorities is on land use and local infrastructure, in relation to which their powers are significant. Planning processes, including "visioning exercises" that involve the wider public, are in a way the centrepiece of democratic politics in relation to these authorities. Such processes are supposed to be complementary to the electoral process, making citizen engagement more robust. Any reader familiar with local government in another country is liable to have a sense of how all this works. But, is municipal politics what is at issue when we look at politics through the city?

Another approach, less neighbourhood-focused, is to look at what people actually do. How do they engage politically? What do they do? On what scales and in which forms? When I think of some of the people I know, a range of activities comes to mind: assisting schools in East Africa, advising on the development of a new legal system in Vietnam, engaging with NGOs at the Climate Summit in Copenhagen or the World Social Forum in Porto Alegre, promoting alternative dispute resolution here in British Columbia, protesting against the WTO on the streets of Seattle, struggling with the tear gas outside the Summit of the Americas in Quebec, hanging from the trees to protest a new highway interchange outside Victoria, establishing hospices on southern Vancouver Island, working for the Land Conservancy, prosecuting or judging accused murderers, rapists, and smugglers, teaching children in remote Aboriginal communities, planting trees in logged-out areas, designing and building houses and gardens, finding land for young farmers, working for labour unions, making and selling jewellery, teaching people how to run safely and efficiently, providing various forms of health care, photographing the "wilderness", writing, playing, and conducting music, adjudicating the claims of people abused in public institutions, allocating compensation for expropriation, regulating the medical and legal professions, and designing software for cellphones.[4] This is a short and eclectic list. Each of these activities involves a political intervention of some sort, although it is not always conceived as such by the person concerned. Some of this activity comes under the heading of paid work or business. Some of it is within "the public sector". Some of it involves the authority of the state. But, if I abstract from questions about who pays for what, whether the activity is inside or outside the state, whether it is for or against capital or the powers-that-be, I begin to see remarkable patterns of activity that connect individual people to the world at large. Some people are focused on things hereabouts, but many are engaged, at least some of the time, in practices that connect them with distant places. In terms of what people do, there are many nodes that are part of wider networks.

But, to talk of "wider" networks is to beg the question once again. By virtue of what is a network wide or large? Take the Victoria Immigrant and Refugee Centre Society (VIRCS), for instance. (Yes, we have refugees here, and illegal migrants.) VIRCS has been part of the local scene since 1989, and in a sense it has its roots in struggles against military regimes in Central and South America. Like other such agencies elsewhere, it receives funding from the state, but also mobilizes immigrants, refugees, and their supporters to provide support for one another. A different face of Victoria – a face that is apparent if you look for it, even in Fairfield-Gonzales, where Filipino care-workers and nurses are ubiquitous in the care homes for the elderly and toddlers are wheeled about by Filipino nannies – is clearly present at VIRCS. How does that face relate to the one that appears in Esquimalt Harbour (not far from downtown), where a boatload of Tamil refugees from Sri Lanka is being held in custody and "processed" as I write this? Is the presence of these Tamil refugees a sign that we are a place of significance in the "real world" whereas before we were just an insignificant sort of place with local institutions like VIRCS? Or, we were already global in our presence thanks to VIRCS, in a way that we weren't by virtue of the Native Friendship Centre, which is somehow too local in its focus? Or, is the Native Friendship Centre somehow our ticket to the big time, because it is a reminder of the struggles of Indigenous peoples in the Andes, Central America, Amazonia, and the hills of India? What is it exactly about what we do here that brings our activities "up" to the global level, or opens them "out" to the world?

What I am meaning to suggest, of course, is that these ups and downs, ins and outs, globals and locals, theres and heres, nows and thens, futures and pasts all derive from almost incredibly crude representations of what we know (Walker 2010). As I have been arguing, we are induced to accept these crude representations because they are required by the statist ontology of the political, which suggests that there *must* be a hierarchy for things to be ordered at all. If we can't tell big from little, up from down, in from out, here from there, or any of those other things, where would be? Lost, for sure. And yet, we *are* lost, of course, because the order of things is not what we are required to imagine, but instead like the order of the city, which is always morphing, and in which questions of scale and hierarchy are difficult to address, to say the least.

As I have suggested elsewhere (Magnusson 2009), the scaling implicit in most accounts of the local and global is tied to the marker years of 1492, 1648, and 1789. There is an assumed story of a world that has become one by virtue of the European voyages of exploration, inter-state agreements, and the overarching liberal order. Captain Cook, one of the great figures of the Enlightenment, brought this area into the story in 1778, and by 1856 there was a colonial legislature to fit the white settlers into the state system on properly liberal terms. People here have been trying to live as they are supposed to do since then, although some of what they do is out of scale with what is expected. Some people try to retreat into the wilderness or hide in the cities and live in a way that prefigures the society that Marx foresaw. They may thus live large in unanticipated ways, connecting with their fellows through their own networks. Other people contest the order of things as they see it more directly, or simply establish their own ways of seeing and doing things without contestation, creating new rights of passage thereby. One benefit of living in Victoria and being reminded every day of Indigenous ways of life is that it is a little more difficult to take the standard story of liberal universalism for granted. Indigenous peoples have been unsettled by the settlers, but the settlers themselves are constantly displaced by the form of life to which they are committed. What can the city, either this particular one or the urban world of which it is part, actually be? What forms of life does it actually enable?

An obvious fact about the city is that it has no clear boundaries and no particular scale. It bleeds into the countryside and the next city or town. (Here we are connected especially to Vancouver, in relation to which Victoria is a sort of distant suburb, separated by water from the downtown.) More significantly, it opens out into the world through various networks and channels, so that the urban system of which it is part actually spans the world and colonizes every part of it. Although there are many different boundaries that appear to contain the city – boundaries of municipalities and states, but also physical boundaries like oceans and mountain ranges – none of them contain it completely, so that the urban world actually expands outward from neighbourhoods like mine to encompass the globe. Thus, the city is inherently multi-scalar. The activities it enables – or, more accurately, the activities that actually constitute the city as a form of life – occur on many scales simultaneously. More than that, the relevant scales relate to different sorts of spaces, for which we have varying names (cultural or economic, for instance) that reflect the fact that they do not cohere – are not even in the same registers, as I like to put it – even though they are all political. The bounds of people's activities are always expanding and contracting, shifting and changing, moving in and out of different registers. The city as city is a series of tracings and scalings, unmappable except from within. But, to a surprising extent we grasp this complexity and respond to it appropriately in our day-to-day lives. Where we have greater difficulty is in understanding what we do in political terms.

Dahl imagined that a city the size of Victoria would be (or could be) an optimal unit in terms of democracy: not so small that it would lack the capacity to deal with significant problems within its own territory, and not so large that its government would be remote from the people it governed. He recognized, as his image of Chinese boxes was meant to convey, that there would be other levels of government, but he wanted to suggest that a city of limited size, like Victoria, could be a particularly satisfying political unit, better in many respects than a large nation-state like his own. This is an appealing fantasy,[5] which harks back to the old concept of the Garden City (Howard 1902), but it would not persuade many people here in Victoria, whose experience of democracy, such as it is, can scarcely be related to any particular box, let alone this one. In geographic terms, Victoria is quite neatly contained, in that it is largely surrounded by the ocean, and has a range of hills at its back. Nevertheless, the local issues that mobilize people politically take them into various political spaces: the murder of a teenage girl by some of her classmates leads to national and international debates about bullying; police brutality toward a girl in custody revives a provincial and national controversy about proper civilian oversight; national and international pressures to change the sewage system resonate with local environmental groups, but bump up against local knowledge of ocean currents in the Strait; efforts to preserve particular sites from development generate a new organization that operates on a provincial scale; a form of political street theatre is developed locally and then is so widely mimicked elsewhere that it becomes stale. People are mobilized by many issues that seem to have little to do with Victoria as such, be it the earthquake in Haiti, the war in Afghanistan, oil sands development in Alberta, or drug wars in Vancouver. The relevant political spaces have no neat form, and they keep changing with the issues at hand.

If I were to follow the standard line of urban analysis, I might argue that there is a "regime" of sorts here, a set of understandings and practices that enable the relevant authorities to decide what is to be done with regard to the "development" of the region: where the big box stores are to go, how the downtown is to be maintained, where the offices and condos are to be built, where the main transportation corridors are to be, and so on. The regime seems rather ineffectual in terms of most conceptions of the public interest: development is driven by private developers, supported by public authorities who give them cover and deal with the problems generated. Such an analysis is accurate as far as it goes, but it conceals as much as it reveals. People here govern themselves and others in a multitude of ways that have little to do with urban development in this restricted sense: hence, what I can see in my own neighbourhood or downtown with respect to the homeless, or what I can observe in the glocal activities of my friends and acquaintances. The development regime responds to what is done otherwise, and to some extent determines what is done otherwise, but no account that I can imagine explains the overall pattern, which is not completely stable and is the effect of interactions that cannot be fully anticipated. This is a major source of frustration to planners and other would-be sovereigns. At its best, planning seems to be a mode of political engagement that enables people to call the powerful to account. It can be productive, not only of useful debate and discussion, but also of new modes of action. As radicals have pointed out, planning can be "insurgent" (Sandercock 1998). Even insurgent planning is likely to be haunted by the ghost of sovereignty, however, because it is inspired by the idea of imposing a rational order on the city. Democratization tends to subvert plans by bringing in new actors, demands, and ideas that rearticulate the complexity of the city, and make it less susceptible to an ordering generated through a single process. The city seems to spin out of control whatever we do.

In a curious way, this makes municipalities more relevant, not less. A municipality is not a sovereign authority, nor does it pretend to be. It is an authority amongst authorities that claims certain rights that may or may not be vindicated by the state. In so far as it makes good on its claim to exist, as a matter of right, it appears as an authority in a different register from the state. The state may claim authority over it, and demand that it accept its status as an agency of the state itself, and hence as a merely local authority (of the sort that Mill and the IULA had in mind). On the other hand, the municipality may, like an Indigenous Nation, claim authority in its own right, derived from the community it purports to embody. If the claimed authority is in a different register from the authority of the state – as is the authority claimed by professions, religious groups, and economic enterprises, for instance – then the issue as between the municipality and the state is not one that can be understood in terms of a hierarchical relationship. The municipality is no more or less of a "local authority" than the state is. It is simply an authority of a different kind.

What kind, one might well ask? It is difficult to say, for the reasons I have been explaining in this book. In a way, the municipality is just a memory of the past or a gesture toward certain possibilities, as are the town meetings of New England. On the other hand, the municipality is a constant reminder of the fact that we have so far failed to develop institutions that would enable "local self-government" in the forms we most need. The familiar structure of the modern state is an inadequate response to the problems and aspirations of the city as we live it locally and globally. We all know that. We all know that we govern ourselves otherwise, and that we govern others otherwise. None of us is outside the system. And yet, we struggle to see what we do politically. For me, the municipality is a tantalizing reminder of other ways of doing things, other ways of organizing ourselves politically.

There are traces of politics in everything that we do, because we have to govern ourselves to accomplish things and in accomplishing things we govern what others can be and do. The literatures to which I referred at the beginning of this book – the ones that invoked the possibility of politics

becoming otherwise – all seem to draw our attention to dangers and opportunities that are already present in our activities. Becoming political in a
fuller sense is at least partly a matter of achieving a certain consciousness,
becoming able to recognize what we do – and what others do to us – as
governmental, and hence subject to political contestation. We may be the
governed, but we are also governors. This is not just a matter of having
ostensibly democratic institutions. As becomes apparent when we examine
life in fine detail – in neighbourhoods, places of work, shopping plazas, transportation routes, or the camps of the dispossessed – most of the government
that occurs is inflected through other institutions and practices that can scarcely
be interpreted in terms of models of democracy. One of the insistent demands
in relation to all this is to localize: that is, to localize responsibility and call
it to account. When I think of things that are going on around me, I have
trouble working out what has to be exposed and called to account. Most of
the activities of people I know are ones that I approve of, more or less. I
could have made a list of things other people do that I disapprove of. It might
be a long list. But, the point, surely, is not whether I approve or disapprove.
The fact of the matter is that many people are doing things for good or
ill that involve government and self-government and in relation to which
political questions can and should be raised.

I suggested above that local self-government in its broadest sense is the
very principle of modern republicanism, and that what is at issue is usually
the form that local self-government should take: where should authority
be localized? what character should it have? how should it be called to account?
But, such issues do not arise in abstraction. They are bound up with the
activities, fears, and aspirations of the people concerned, none of which are
subject to simple description. If there is a virtue in talking about local
self-government as an ideal and a practice in which we are always already
engaged, it is that it calls attention to the complex matters that might
be subject to scrutiny, without invoking the state as the necessary mode of
resolution. The statist ontology of the political enables us to disavow our
political responsibilities by investing them in an imaginary sovereign. When
we think about local self-government as a practice in which we are already
engaged – as individuals and as members of various collectivities – we are
less inclined to disavow our responsibilities, and more inclined to ask why
authority is localized as it is. What goes under the sign of democracy is
a demand for redistribution of authority. For me, the municipality – a
non-sovereign authority with significant governmental powers – is a sign of
what that might entail.

To be sure, I would like everyone to be rationally self-governing, and to
govern others in a way that would enable them to be self-governing. I would
like the world to become a home for all of humanity, governed both by the
domestic virtues of economy and the larger rationality of ecology. Democratic
mutualism, not alien authority, would be the condition of possibility for our
existence, and everyone would be free somehow. If I think hard enough and

blot out what I do not want to see, I can bring the claims of both the homeless and Indigenous peoples under the big tent of my imagination, and allow everyone to live large, just as a benign sovereign would wish. Such flights of fancy are gratifying, at least to me if not to anyone else. Nonetheless, when I think of the homeless on the one hand and Indigenous peoples on the other, I am impelled to think of "the right to the city" in a different way, one that problematizes my own dream of the *polis*, as well as the complementary dreams of *oikos*, *nomos*, and *logos*. It is not up to me to decide who claims the right to the city or on what terms. It is not up to me to say what that right consists of. Whether it consorts with the rationalities of economy and ecology, conforms to the patterns of government and self-government that seem to generate benign urban order, or generates a productive politics, the right will be asserted in some fashion. People will assert that they have the right to live large in their own ways, to claim the city for their own, and to enact their own dreams, which may well be very different from my own. Such is politics.

Conclusion
Otherwise than sovereign

"Otherwise than Sovereign" was my original title for this book, and it took me some time to work out that my argument against a "sovereigntist" political imaginary was really an argument for seeing like a city. I should have twigged earlier, because my own experience of studying urban and local politics is one of puzzlement: sovereignty always seems like an imaginary presence, whereas practices of government and self-government are all around me. This does not mean that sovereignty does not exist or that it is unimportant. Quite the contrary: much of what people do is structured by the principle of sovereignty, and that principle is always part of people's political thinking. Nonetheless, there is another reality, the reality of a city and a wider urban order that emerges regardless, an order that is always otherwise than sovereign. That order is violent and unjust in many respects, but not necessarily *more* violent or *less* just than the order produced by plays of sovereignty – plays that are usually ineffectual anyway. To deal realistically with the world means coming to understand an order that takes its shape more by means *other* than plays of sovereignty and that offers political opportunities – and poses political dangers – that can scarcely be seen through the sovereigntist imaginary.

Let me end this book by saying a bit more about the place where I work, because I actually do see things from there, as much or more as from my own neighbourhood. The big issue at the University of Victoria is what to do about the bunnies. . . . Bunnies? . . . Well, yes: the bunnies seem to be taking over the campus, and we humans – many of us, anyway – are not too pleased about that. When I first starting teaching here, back in 1979, the most controversial animal was the skylark: like the bunny, an imported species. The skylarks had established a nesting area near the building where I then worked. That posed a difficult problem for the university authorities. On the one hand, they wanted the land for a new school of business. On the other hand, the skylark has iconic significance in Canada thanks to the poem, *In Flanders Fields* (McCrae 1919), which many of us had to memorize in school. It's still probably the most famous poem ever written by a Canadian, and it's the kind that many people like to hear on Remembrance Day – "Take up our quarrel with the foe: / To you with failing hands we throw / The torch;

be yours to hold it high." Less likely to be heard is Wilfred Owen's *Dulce et Decorum Est* (1920), and not just because it was written by an English and Welshman, rather than a Canadian: "If in some smothering dreams you too could pace / Behind the wagon we flung him in, / And watch the white eyes writhing in his face, / His hanging face, like a devil's sick of sin; / If you could hear, at every jolt, the blood / Come gargling from the froth-corrupted lungs, / Obscene as cancer, bitter as the cud / Of vile, incurable sores on innocent tongues, / My friend, you would not tell with such high zest / To children ardent for some desperate glory, / The Old Lie; *Dulce et decorum est / Pro patria mori.*" My father, who took part in the fire-bombing of Hamburg in 1943 and lost both his brothers and most of his friends during the fighting in Europe, used to say that there is no such thing as a "good war". That's what came to my mind when I saw the signs marking the sky-lark nesting area. As it happens, the skylarks went away for some reason, to the great relief of the university authorities. The authorities quickly implanted the school of business in the old nesting area, forestalling the sky-larks and driving us forward in the new spirit of enterprise that is supposed to have come upon us in the 1980s. It was about that time that the bunnies began to appear.

Rabbits are native to Vancouver Island, where the University of Victoria is, but native rabbits live out in the bush, not in the city. The University of Victoria was established in 1963, in a suburban area that had not yet been developed for housing. The Canadian Army had used the place for training during the Second World War, but it was now surplus to their requirements. The campus was planned and built-out on the standard North American model – the plans were from a firm of California architects – and it now sits in the midst of a typically sprawling mid-size city. No one knows where the bunnies came from exactly, but they are clearly released pets – bred to look pretty, rather than to blend into the background. Presumably, the bunnies are the descendants of little critters bought to please children caught up in the euphoria of Easter – which, as we know, is about bunnies delivering chocolate eggs, not about some man/god on a cross. The children get bored with the bunnies soon enough, and the bunnies get to run free on the university campus, where there is plenty to eat. The bunnies have become an attraction to potential undergraduates, who imagine themselves feeding carrots to these tame little animals, instead of running with the dog or cuddling the cat at home. For everyone else, however, the bunnies are a nuisance. They dig holes in playing fields, eat up all the nicely cultivated plants – at least, the ones the deer don't get to first: the deer do come in from the bush, but they are finding the city a nice place to live, thanks to all the people who grow succulent gardens – and leave their faeces where people can slip on them. Most of us – me, certainly – would like to get rid of the bunnies, or at least reduce their numbers drastically. But, of course, the university cannot murder a bunch of rabbits with impunity. Animal rights groups are well organized here, and they value the life of every single bunny, innocent creatures that they are. The university has been trying for years now to develop a bunny-removal strategy that will satisfy the animal-rights activists and bunny-loving students, but so far there hasn't been much success.[1]

In the midst of the bunny crisis, a loosely organized group of students launched their Food not Lawns campaign (Montgomery 2010). I suppose that in some parts of the world such a campaign would have involved massive bunny-roasts, but here it meant growing potatoes, carrots, radishes, and such, and trying to protect the plots from the bunnies with fences and other discouraging forms of human occupation. Bunnies were not the subject of the campaign, anyway. Instead, it was about urban agriculture: more specifically, the demand to turn all or part of the university's extensive lawns to a more useful purpose, namely growing food in the midst of the city. Actually, the whole question of the city was being posed in that campaign. The students were unhappy about our dependence on food jetted from distant parts of the world, and grown in neo-colonial plantations controlled by multinational agribusinesses. They wanted the university to play its part in teaching people how to grow at least some of their own food. Moreover, they wanted to encourage people to be locavores, who would purchase food grown or raised by local farmers and adjust their diet to the character of the food sources where they lived. At stake was a vision of a world in which people became much more attentive to the local communities and ecological regions within which they lived. People would not be so dependent on carbon-based fuels; they would produce more of what they needed for themselves, and buy mainly from small-scale local enterprises; they would be independent, but community-minded and environmentally sensitive; their "footprint" on the earth would be lighter, and they would not be so dependent on large bureaucracies or huge capitalist businesses; they would create an alternative, and live it, literally from the ground up. All these issues were raised in Facebook-mediated exchanges. There were no formal leaders of the campaign; nor did the participants have to subscribe to any particular set of actions or goals. When I was young, people might have called it a "happening", but this one had more serious political purposes.

The main action of the Food not Lawns campaign was to dig up a bit of lawn in front of the library and plant vegetables. Not much lawn was involved, and people not involved in the campaign took little notice of it. The university authorities didn't like it, however. They let the action continue for a day or two, and then sent in a team at night to level the garden and replant the grass. The campaigners responded by replanting the garden, but the university levelled it again. By that time, the university authorities were obviously getting worried, not least because they knew that the gardeners had their eyes on a much larger tract of land at the edge of the campus, a tract perfect for a big urban agriculture project, but very valuable to the university as "surplus" land to be sold off for residential development. For the university to succeed in its objective of being a centre of knowledge-based enterprise – something that the federal government, the province, and the business "community" very much want – it needs more revenue, and that means being entrepreneurial with its own lands. Urban agriculture of the sort that Food not Lawns wants – agriculture that goes against the grain of the globalized capitalist economy – doesn't fit well with such an agenda (M'Gonigle and Starke 2006). The university would have been prepared to deal with the gardeners by giving them a bit of land to do their own thing, but the gardeners were attentive to a larger vision that would have undermined what the university was trying to do. That larger vision entailed not only a different way of relating to the land, but a different configuration of local authority. How could what the university was doing be construed as "democratic"? On what basis was the university claiming the authority it said it had? What would a genuinely democratic way of doing things actually look like? There were no easy answers to such questions, but the gap between business as usual and the ideals that the gardeners invoked was quite obvious.

As far as I know, the gardeners have suspended their campaign. A number of them – chosen almost at random, it seems – received letters from the local John Howard Society (an international NGO that works with prisoners) saying that they could avoid prosecution by apologizing to the university and doing forty hours of community service. The university had evidently referred its complaint against the protesters – wilful damage in the amount of more than $10,000 – to the local police, who had in turn involved the John Howard Society, in a process designed to bypass both the Crown Prosecution Service and the courts. Apparently, the gardeners have chosen to comply, rather than incur the costs (and risks) involved in defending themselves against criminal charges. Some old radicals like me are disappointed about this – having had images of ourselves digging lawns and protecting our lettuces in defiance of the university, the bunnies, and the courts. What a noble cause!

Why do I mention all this? Isn't it trivial? People in other parts of the world are dealing with much more serious problems. What a place, where people are all fussed up about bunnies and skylarks, and think that serious political action means planting gardens in face of authorities who would be extremely reluctant to use any form of violence! If seeing like a city means imagining the world as a peaceful, orderly place where people have the luxury of "fighting" – figuratively, not literally – about things like this, then surely it has little to offer the serious analyst. Or, so a critic might suggest. I think otherwise, of course, and not because I suppose that life is as easy elsewhere as it is here for me and many other people. My claim, as I emphasized in Chapter 7, is that the urban world is ubiquitous, and that we can start just about anywhere in trying to figure out the patterns of government and politics with which we have to engage. I have no problem starting from my neighbourhood in Victoria or from the campus where I work. It is a matter of seeing what is there and following the connections that a state-centric view of things tends to obscure.

Take imperialism, for instance. Is it here in my community? Was it manifest during the gardeners' protest? Of course. One of the immediate issues that they confronted arose from Native claims – or, rather, from the widespread recognition among the gardeners themselves that they were claiming a right as against the university to grow vegetables on land that had been dedicated as lawn, but that Native people, the Lekwungen, had a prior right not just to the lawn but to the whole campus and the wider region within which Victoria and its suburbs had developed. So, questions of imperialism and colonialism were raised by the carrots (and also by the bunnies, which were eating up native species and interfering with efforts to restore the former meadows and woodlands). Moreover, the question of local food production was bound up with other issues of economy and ecology. As already noted, Victoria has a large and highly visible homeless population, mostly concentrated in the downtown area, some distance from the campus. The gardeners are very conscious of this, and some of them have been involved with the Coalition to End Homelessness and the Food not Bombs campaigns. Urban gardening connects with activities like food-sharing, sheltering, and alternative modes of social action that challenge the established hierarchies of urban life. The gardeners are mostly the sort of people who try to relate to the homeless as equals, rather than as objects of charity or subjects of discipline. So, what's being enacted in and through the gardening initiative – and others like it, here and elsewhere – is a different view of what the city can and should be. The intent is to enact a different form of urban life, one that is sensitive to the needs of the poor and the dispossessed, that challenges centuries of colonialism and imperialism, and that involves a form of democracy that transcends the claims of the state and the market. These are no small things.

How realistic is all of this, however? Can such action lead anywhere? I am reminded of walking down a street in Samarkand, Uzbekistan, in the summer of 2001, a couple of months before the 9/11 attack on the World Trade Center. I had been invited by an ex-student to teach at a summer school for "politology" instructors at colleges and universities in Kazakhstan, Kyrgyzstan, and Uzbekistan. I probably wasn't of much use to them, but I learned a lot, and got to see Samarkand and Bokhara, two of the great trading cities on the ancient Silk Road between China and the West. One evening, we were all walking in a large group toward a restaurant. There were no sidewalks and few cars, and so we were spread out across much of the street. I almost fell into a hole, however. Someone had dug up the street, but hadn't bothered to put up any barriers or warning lights in front of the diggings. I assumed, rather innocently, that there weren't any holes in the street big enough to swallow up a grown man. One of the wiser people with me put out an arm and stopped me from falling in. As my Canadian host observed, "The problem here is that the state really doesn't exist." There was and is a dictator, of course, but partly because of that, "the state" as an institution is woefully underdeveloped. People know that any rule can be ignored if the proper bribe is paid. So, a kind of anarchy prevails in which people dig up streets without notice or proper authority and pay little heed to the needs of their neighbours or passers-by. How is this different from digging up lawns at the University of Victoria, some might ask? Doesn't the gardeners' action subvert the conditions of possibility for the sort of world the gardeners want, undermining the authority of the state and authorizing actions that are not as benign and large-spirited as their own? Isn't the state what we actually need for human betterment? The state in this sense is an ethical order, and (as liberal democrats are supposed to know) it is dependent on a certain balance of resistance and respect for authority. It cannot be conjured into existence by calling a dictator a president and his thugs the police, and so its presence in a place like Uzbekistan is doubtful. A more benign order, like the one the gardeners seek, has to evolve out of the activity of people who are prepared to stand up for their own rights while demanding as much and as good for others. One of the inspirations for the gardeners came from the seventeenth-century English "Diggers", who claimed a similar right in face of the lords and gentlemen who were usurping the common land in a perverse movement that helped generate the modern capitalist economy. *Pace* Hayek, one can work peacefully, rationally, cooperatively, and lawfully for a better world, and that does not necessarily mean submitting to the authorities that be, even if they can point to the state as the ultimate authorizer of their authority.

To be realistic, I think, is to bring the diggings in Samarkand and Victoria into relation to one another, and that means "seeing like a city" rather than "seeing like a state". One can see that unauthorized diggings can have very different rationales and effects, and that close analysis of such diggings can reveal much about political conditions in various places. One also can ask, in a normative mood, about the conditions of possibility for the sort of benign activity in which the gardeners are engaged. Is it true, as some people claim, that obedience to the state is the condition of possibility for benign activity? Or, does benign activity emerge otherwise, out of the complicated practices of government and self-government that characterize urbanism as a way of life? Do people learn to respect one another when they have to find solutions to everyday problems that arise when strangers live side by side? These are difficult questions, for which there are no simple answers. If, by the state, we mean the carefully elaborated system of rules and procedures with which people in the West have become familiar over the last couple of hundred years, we are indeed talking about something important, something as beneficial as it is frightening and vexing. It is in and through the state that supreme leaders of one sort or another claim the right to round up "terrorists", then put them in jail and torture them. This is something that the President of Uzbekistan does quite regularly – with implicit support since 9/11 from the Western powers. On the other hand, it is also in and through the state that the actions of supreme leaders are challenged: through the courts, through committees and commissions of inquiry, and through the actions of civil servants, journalists, and political activists who claim for themselves the right to uphold the principles embodied in the state as against leaders who would corrupt those principles. In this sense, the state is always in and against itself, in so far as it embodies a set of principles that involve the rule of law, human rights, procedural justice, democratic equality, and respect for competing claims. If there is a state in the proper sense, as my friend suggested, people do not dig up streets without proper permission, and if they get such permission they make sure they do their work in a way that causes the least inconvenience to others and avoids harms to them as much as possible. I would add this: if there is a state in the proper sense, people who dig up university lawns to make a point do so very carefully and with much attention to the possible harm they might cause; moreover, the authorities react with similar restraint; matters are resolved, or not, in peaceful ways. But, what happens politically or governmentally is never neatly confined within the boundaries of the state, either as an ideal or as an ensemble of practices.

Let me take two more examples, from Mexico and Kenya. As we all know, Mexico is beset by criminal gangs struggling for control of the trade in drugs to the United States. Or, that's one way of looking at it. Another way of looking at it is that the Mexican state has failed so completely in parts of the country that its authority has been usurped by drug cartels. The state's efforts to re-establish its authority have yet to bring the promised benefits.

> According to Medina [a politician opposed to the current Mexican government], it [President Calderón's war on drug traffickers] has ruined the economy in Tierra Caliente and shattered the community's social peace. La Familia [the dominant drug cartel in the area] had provided employment, insured public security, and helped the poor. "If you were sick and had no money, they'd take you to the hospital and pay for medicine. If you couldn't afford tortillas, they'd buy some for you." The heavy deployment of troops and federal police in the area had forced La Familia to lie low. So who would look after the poor now? The *government*? Medina gave me an arch look, daring me to answer the question. No, it would not. La Familia had even been obliged to close a group of rehabilitation centers it ran for alcoholics and drug addicts. Local police were poorly paid and, therefore, incompetent and corrupt. When La Familia was in charge, nobody stepped out of line. You didn't even need to lock your door at night. "If they find you drunk in public, they'll take you off, pull down your pants, and beat you with a long stick with holes in it."
>
> (Finnegan 2010, p. 42)

Of course, if you got further out of line and challenged La Familia's authority or interfered with its business, you would probably be killed and your mutilated body would be put on display as a warning to others. Machiavelli described similar practices in Renaissance Italy, and spelled out their logic. People in Tierra Caliente and elsewhere in Mexico are evidently caught between rival authorities, some of which are exceptionally brutal, others exceptionally corrupt, and all incapable of delivering the dream of order we associate with "the state".

It wouldn't be hard to find examples of this sort in other parts of the world. But, consider this story as well:

> In the ashes of a looted market in one of Africa's biggest slums, gang leader Bernard Njira stood with a machete in his hand, trying to decide whether to kill the man who had approached him. It was 2008, in the depths of Kenya's post-election bloodshed, and his gang of young thugs had just destroyed one of the biggest markets in the Kibera slum. Now came a man who wanted them to rebuild it. Mr. Njira had been a criminal for 10 years: a thief, a mugger, a drug dealer and killer. The man who approached him was from Jamii Bora, a microfinance lender that supported many of the market's impoverished vendors. The gang assumed he was a police investigator. "I almost killed him," Mr. Njira recalls. "I removed one of my machetes." The man refused to back down. Amazed by his courage and persistence, the gang leaders began talking to him. A few weeks later, they rebuilt the market – and gave up their life of crime. They joined the microfinance group and became its most visible supporters, creating a metal workshop and a soccer team to bring hope to the slum.
>
> (York 2010)

That makes it sound simple, as obviously it is not (and as the rest of York's story reveals). Nevertheless, stories like these are a reminder of the fact that "bad guys" are not simply bad guys, and that a more benign order can be developed through the sort of practices that Jamii Bora and the gardeners in Victoria advocate. What are the conditions of possibility for successes of the sort York describes? Is it a matter of the presence or absence of the state, or is the presence of a relatively benign state the *effect* of proliferating practices of government and self-government of the sort highlighted here?

I don't find it hard to see how people can be crushed and how a perverse order can be imposed. More difficult to discern is what enables people to live better lives without killing, despoiling, or subjugating those who are weaker or less fortunate. To the extent that I understand this, it is not through my meditations on the state – which are frequent enough – but through my observations of the way people do things peacefully without harming others. Perhaps I would understand things better if I lived in Kibera, Tierra Caliente, or Samarkand, but I have to begin where I am. One thing I know is that places of extreme violence are the exception rather than the rule. The Western media like to focus on the exception, however: "If it bleeds, it leads", according to a common rule of journalism. Academic writers are not much different. We get feverish commentary from the left and the right about the ills of places ravaged by criminal gangs, marauding armies, racist mobs, religious fanatics, and unscrupulous businesses. We learn about the destructive effects of capitalist development, imperialist rivalry, and neo-liberal governmentality. And, we get periodic calls to arms, in which young men – and women now, too – are encouraged to take up the torch, hunt down the bad guys, and . . . well, this is where things get murky. Are we to kill the bad guys or offer them microcredit? How would we know? *Ex hypothesi*, the situation is such that benign order is practically unimaginable. And yet, such order does emerge in places. How? If, by a benign order, we simply mean a place where people can go to market without worrying about being confronted by men with machetes, such an order already exists in most places. Terrorist cells that plant bombs are more of a threat, to be sure, and robbers with guns are a common enough presence. But, life goes on, and people work out ways of dealing with such threats, whether or not the police and the army are effective. The practices of government and self-government that enable urban life work well in some places and well enough in most places to allow people to live without paralysing anxiety. How is this possible? We will not learn much about that if we focus only on the situations that lead us to despair. After all, desperate men and women are the ones most likely to resort to violence and simply destroy whatever frightens or puzzles them.

I began this book by noting some of the things that I could see when I allowed myself to see like a city. In particular, I noted:

(1) Both particular cities and the "global city" are self-organizing.
(2) A multiplicity of political authorities in different registers and at different scales is characteristic of urban life.
(3) Practices of self-government enable civilized order and produce public benefits both in the presence of sovereign authority and in its absence.
(4) Order is always temporary and local.
(5) Transformations are non-linear and hence inherently unpredictable.

To say that particular cities and the global city are self-organizing is not to say that any particular city or the global city is *well* organized. It is simply to say that both are organized in some fashion, and that the mode of organization is not well understood in terms of the presence or absence of the state, however conceived. To say that there is a multiplicity of political authorities in different registers and at different scales is to call attention to the presence of authorities that pass themselves off as cultural, religious, economic, or social, but that are no less political (or powerful) for that. Again, the ordering amongst these authorities is not well understood in terms of the presence or absence of the state. To say that practices of self-government enable civilized order and produce public benefits both in the presence of sovereign authority and in its absence is to draw attention to the practices whereby tolerable orders are produced, sustained, improved, or transformed, either with the state, against the state, or without the state. To say that order is always temporary and local, and is subject to change and transformation, is to state the obvious. To say that transformations are non-linear and hence inherently unpredictable is also to state the obvious, but it is to draw attention to a fact that would-be rulers of the world or the city tend to forget. And, of course, we are all would-be rulers.

When I see like a city, I do *not* see the world as a place without violence and injustice: quite the contrary. To see like a city is to put the state under erasure, and reveal what it obscures. The picture is not pretty in most parts of the world: not only violence and injustice, but environmental degradation, impoverishment, and misplaced hatred. On the other hand, people are trying to better their lives in Samarkand and Tierra Caliente, as much as in Kibera and Victoria. What they are doing and why, what they hope to achieve and what they have already achieved only becomes clear when we examine their activities *as political*. If we assume, as the dominant political ontology suggests, that what is significant politically is always already determined by the nature of the state and the structure of the state system, we are bound to miss much, if not most of what is important. I cannot judge what is important with any confidence. Nor can anyone else. On the other hand, I can see that certain practices, like the ones of Jamii Bora in Nairobi and the gardeners in Victoria, model a world that would be better to live in than the one I know. . . . Is their idealism sufficient? Certainly not. . . . Have they discerned what most needs to be done? I doubt it. . . . Is what they do full of contradictions. Of course. . . . Where I am led is not to a particular political programme, but to a variety of practices that warrant investigation. To pursue that investigation, one would have to be equally attentive, if not more attentive, to the practices that forestall people's hopes and sustain the violence, injustice, and other ills at issue. But, the questions one needs to ask become clearer if we see that we are dealing with a city-like political order. Oppressors and activists are urban in their frames of reference and modes of engagement. So are we as analysts. We will learn more if we put the state under erasure and investigate what people do politically and how they are governed as denizens of particular cities within the global city.

Notes

Introduction: re-imagining the political

1 For exemplary works from different periods, see Cook and Morgan 1971, Benello and Roussopoulos 1971, Boggs 1986, Cohen and Arato 1992, Hardt and Negri 2000, and Conway 2004. On the concept of everyday life, see De Certeau (1984) and Lefebvre (2008). I use the term in a loose sense.

2 Anxieties about the state are of course especially apparent in work that focuses on the camp and the border zone (*e.g.* Agamben 1998), but even in these instances, there are gestures towards a politics that occupies a different space.

3 I am thinking not only of the usual suspects like Foucault, Derrida, and Deleuze, but also of Althusser and Lefebvre in the earlier generation, and people like Nancy (1991, 2007), Rancière (1995, 1998) and Badiou (2005, 2006) more recently.

4 One thinks not only of Gandhi, Mandela, and Havel, but also of Martin Luther King. Eurocentric thinkers on the left have difficulty admitting that they owe anything other than their musical tastes to the American experience.

5 Although some theorists now insist on a distinction between politics and the political (*e.g.* Nancy 1991), that is not a distinction that I find useful – for reasons that will become apparent in the course of this book.

6 By "modern republicanism" I mean something more general than what is now described as "civic republicanism". I take it that the liberal-democratic nation-state is the standard model of sovereignty, and that it presupposes both the sovereign individual (the bearer of human rights) and the sovereign order of states. That the three forms of sovereignty at stake – of the individual, the state, and the state system – are in tension with one another is obvious, and the "realist" resolution is to privilege the state as the locale for serious politics (Hinsley 1986, Walker 1993). When I refer to modern republicanism, I am thinking of the whole tradition of thought that posits "the state" as both the problem and the solution to the dilemmas of sovereignty. The state is the problem because it has sovereignty, and it is the solution because it can be ordered constitutionally as a *rechtstaat* or republic (Stankiewicz 1969, Skinner 1978, Vincent 1987, Bartelson 1995, 2001). On the other hand, as I suggest in Chapters 6 and 7, an idea or ideal of self-government is also implicit in modern republicanism, and that idea has other implications that I explore here.

7 The idea that sovereignty is essentially a principle of international relations is one of the many delusions of IR theory (Walker 1993, 2010). As any reading of early modern political theory – say from Bodin (1992) to Rousseau (1983) – soon makes clear, the problem of sovereignty was originally posed in terms of relations within what would now be called the "domestic" realm, as between kings on the one hand and barons, bishops, and burgesses on the other, or more generally between the highest rulers and their subjects. Absolute monarchy was the

original model of sovereignty. That there was an outside to the realm – and hence an issue of relations with savages, barbarians, or rulers of other realms – was normally acknowledged, but treated as a different matter under the heading of war or military preparedness. So-called state sovereignty is a particular form of a more general principle that poses the problem of order in terms of a choice between anarchy and submission.

 8 It is worth noting that so-called criminal gangs are amongst the relevant political authorities. Like multinational corporations, they often claim to have purely economic purposes. This allows them to differentiate themselves from other authorities, including ones that claim sovereignty. So-called terrorist groups are different, in that they are usually caught up in sovereignty-aspirations.

 9 This is one of the themes of my previous work. See especially Magnusson 1996, 1997, and 2000a.

 10 "The media have been keen to report that 'half the world's population now lives in cities,' but we are overlooking the main event: half the world has become a City" (Brugmann 2009, 10). I would go further: in an important sense, the whole of the world has become a city. Compare Kingwell 2008.

 11 Although I follow Foucault (and others: especially Burchell *et al.* 1991, Dean 1999, and Rose 1999) in using the term "governmentality", the analysis here is not an "application" of Foucault's thought. What interests me about his work is his willingness to examine things that others have ignored, try different angles of approach, invent new analytical categories, and resist the pressure to reify his own thought. I make the connection between governmentality and self-government not only because it was a connection that he himself saw, but also because it emphasizes the crucial link – I would say symbiosis – between government and self-government. Although others want to insist on the connection between govern-mentality and the state, I want to point out that governmentality has other origins and other dynamics, some of which Foucault discussed, but many of which he did not. He gestures toward the city, although he does not analyse it in detail.

 12 As a result, I say less about "the literature" or "the debates in the literature" than many people would like. I will leave those tasks to PhD students writing their dissertations. Personally, I find many of the debates uninteresting, because they rehearse old issues, turn on small points of difference, and descend into arguments about terminology. I try to advance my arguments in terms that are reasonably accessible, and that do not depend on knowledge of particular writers.

 13 There are many exceptions of course: in fact, I invoke one of these exceptions in my Conclusion.

 14 The next seven paragraphs are taken, with some alteration, from Magnusson 2010.

 15 See Webb and Webb (1906–29) for an analysis of the way English institutions developed. Compare Teaford (1975, 1984) for the American case.

 16 I take the concept of the "shock city" from Asa Briggs (1968), who put Manchester of the 1840s and Chicago of the 1890s in that category. His point was that what shocks us is the latest urban form, which is at odds with what just preceded it. One of the problems with an analysis that begins from the latest shock city is that it is coloured from the beginning with a kind of anxiety or panic – just the sort of anxiety or panic that leads to dreams of resolution through sovereign authority. Arguably, that is one of the problems with the Chicago School sociology that I discuss in Chapter 3.

 17 See Brugmann 2009 for an analysis that takes up some themes similar to the ones I develop here, and that does encompass the Global South. Compare Appadurai 1996, Ong 1999, and Smith, M. 2001. One notices in the literature a curious blend of dystopianism (Davis 2006) and utopianism (De Soto 2000, Brugmann 2009) that is fed by debates in the Global North about the nature of the present crisis (or crises: there are always many, and they are always present in some form or

another), the threats associated with that crisis (which always seem to involve the four horsemen of the apocalypse), and the role of the state and/or capitalism on the one hand and new forms of enterprise or political action on the other. People who only *visit* the Global South (but claim to have some knowledge of it) like to invoke it as an image of what is to be avoided or as a ground from which they can make claims about what the Global North should be and do. I prefer to work from my own experience and let others judge how well the analysis applies more generally.

18 "The Urban, the Governmental and the Political," Second International Workshop on Politics and Governmentality, Keele University, England, 19 June 2002.

19 "Ontologies of the Political: *The Death and Life of Great American Cities*," Jane Jacobs Symposium on *Form, Place, and Power*, University of Toronto, Toronto ON, 18 October 1997; "Toward a Political Ontology of Urbanism as a Way of Life," Urban Affairs Association Annual Meeting, Los Angeles CA, 6 May 2000; "Seeing Like a City: How to Urbanize Political Science," Urban Affairs Association Annual Meeting, Baltimore MD, 24 April 2008; and "The Symbiosis of the Urban and the Political," American Association of Geographers Annual Meeting, Las Vegas NV, 25 March 2009.

20 "A Foucault for Political Scientists," Pacific Northwest Political Science Association Annual Meeting, Victoria BC, 17 October 2009.

21 "Seeing Like a City, Seeing Like a State," Canadian Political Science Association Annual Meeting, Vancouver BC, 3 June 2008.

22 "Ecology, Governmentality and Freedom" (with Sébastien Malette), Western Political Science Association Annual Meeting, Vancouver BC, 19 March 2009.

23 "Scaling Government to Politics," Conference on the Political Economy of Scale, York University, Toronto ON, 5 February 2005.

24 "The Principle of Local Self-Government," Conference for the Study of Political Thought, Toronto ON, 28 November 2003.

25 See especially Magnusson 1996, 2000a, 2000b, 2002, 2005b, and 2006.

1 Urbanism as governmentality

1 See, for instance, Arendt 1958 and 1961, Wolin 2004, Crick 2005, Dahl 1970, Rawls 1971, Held 1995 and 1996, Habermas 1996, Pettit 1997, Honohan 2002, and Viroli 2002.

2 On this point, see especially Arendt 1958 and Crick 2005. Compare Rawls 1971, Habermas 1996, and Tully 2008.

3 Among the more influential accounts are Park *et al.* 1925, Mumford 1938, and Lefebvre 2003. See Smith, M. 1979, Chorney 1990, and Parker 2004 for commentary.

4 I discuss Weber's work on the city at greater length in Chapter 3.

5 I explore this further in Chapter 4.

6 I explore this theme in the Canadian context in Magnusson 2005a.

7 Isin 2007 describes this in terms of a "scalar logic". For earlier versions of my own argument about this matter, see Walker and Mendlovitz 1990 and Magnusson 2006. Compare Agnew and Corbridge 1995.

8 On governmentality, see Burchell *et al.* 1991, Rose 1999, Dean 1999, Foucault 2003, 2007, and 2008, and Miller and Rose 2008.

9 Of course, the options available to the world's poor are of a different character, but they may nonetheless involve long-distance connections between workers in cities and their families in remote villages, often in other countries. M. Smith (2001) speaks aptly of "transnational urbanism" in this context. Compare Appadurai 1996 and Brugmann 2009.

10 Apparently, farmers and traders in the Global South increasingly use cellphones to track market conditions and work out their sales and wholesale orders. This is another indicator of the way that the rural is being absorbed into the urban.

11 For many people, perhaps most, the conditions of incorporation are about as bad as one can imagine, as Davis 2006 explains.

12 "Established cities can succeed for some decades to deny growing migrant populations access to economic and political rights. But short of mass relocation and murder, as in Pol Pot's dystopian anti-urban regime, there is an inevitable democracy in the Urban Revolution that continues to revolutionize world politics. Centralized, inegalitarian governments, initially empowered by their control of rural territories and populations, have steadily lost their exclusive grip over economic resources and international relations as their countries urbanize. Once settled in cities, even the most marginalized populations, under the most totalitarian regimes, can leverage urban density, scale, association, and extension to build their own economies, wealth, power, and political alliances. Their rebellions on every continent have continuously taken modern regimes and the mass media by surprise because they have not understood the nature of urban advantage. Urban advantage is a classic form of public good. The potential offered by a city's density, scale, association, and extension infrastructure is accessible to all who determine to use and shape it, regardless of the impediments put in their way" (Brugmann 2009, 55–56). This is an optimistic vision, but one that we should bear in mind, given the dystopianism of many accounts of the city, a dystopianism that has a long history in Western thought (Parker 2004) and that has fed into the idea that the city must be controlled by the state if it is to be a good city: that is, a properly civilized city.

13 I take up this issue in a different way in Chapter 6, as well as in Magnusson 2009.

14 That is my interpretation of his overall analysis: compare Magnusson 2002 and 2005a. I return to Foucault in Chapter 4.

15 This growing together is very evident now in rapidly urbanizing areas of Asia, Africa, and Latin America. Although most of the megacities are contained within the bounds of a single state, some – like the greater Singapore region – extend across more than one international boundary.

16 My thanks to David Wolfe for this anecdote.

17 The award of the Nobel Prize in Economics to Elinor Ostrom – an urbanist and political scientist – is a belated acknowledgement of this influence, and a sign that many are looking for "neo-liberalism with a human face" (if I may adapt a term from an earlier era, when the possibilities of socialism were still a live issue). See Ostrom 1990.

18 Compare Walker and Mendlovitz 1990 and Walker 1993.

2 Ontologies of the political

1 Useful discussions of this subject include: Der Derian and Shapiro 1989, Walker and Mendlovitz 1990, Walker 1993, 2010, Campbell and Dillon 1993, Bartelson 1995, 2001, Agamben 1998, Hardt and Negri 2000, Patomäki 2002, and Isin 2002.

2 The next two paragraphs are taken from Magnusson 2010.

3 Conley 2002 is a partial exception.

4 See Foster 1997, chapter 2, for a careful review of the American debates.

3 Politics of urbanism as a way of life

1 For recent trends in urban analysis, see especially Davies and Imbroscio (2008, 2010) and compare it with Judge *et al.* (1995). As I hope is apparent, my rereading of earlier theorists here is not meant to discount familiar criticisms, which are generally apt.

2 I have practically nothing to say about their later work: to deal with it adequately would take me too far afield. I find Sennett (1977) and Jacobs (1984) particularly interesting in terms of the themes I develop here. See also Sennett 1994.

3 Significantly, Wirth was one of the translators of Karl Mannheim's (1936) *Ideology and Utopia*, a book that had great influence on Western socialist thinking.

4 Obviously, Wirth had an idealist standard of self-government. In Chapter 7, I comment at greater length on the concept of local self-government, which seems especially pertinent to the issues I am considering here, but it is worth noting immediately that people can be self-governing to quite a great extent, and nonetheless be governed or manipulated from without.

5 This is an old idea: see Rousseau 1983, 36–38 and Mill 1991, 269–84.

6 See Kataoka 2009 and Zukin 2010 for two recent critiques of what has been done in Jacobs's name. Jacobs abstracted too much from the political economy of urban development, and idealized street-level relations in dense urban neighbourhoods, but she nonetheless had a useful appreciation of the way cities work at their best – which is one of the reasons why her work continues to influence planners and resonate with many urbanites.

7 See Florida 2002, 2005, 2008 for a popular version of this line of thinking. For more judicious analyses see Castells 1996, Scott, A. 2001, Sassen 2002, Brenner 2004, Brenner and Keil 2006, and Keil and Mahon 2009.

4 The art of government

1 Americans should certainly appreciate this remark, in light of recent debates about health insurance in the USA.

2 In France, it was a matter of the relation between the Franks, the Romans, and the Gauls, there having been at least two conquests.

3 "The Symbiosis of the Urban and the Political," Annual Meeting of the American Association of Geographers, Las Vegas, Nevada, 25 March 2009, p. 20.

5 Seeing like a state, seeing like a city

1 For much more thorough and nuanced analyses of the development of the American discipline see Gunnell 1993 and 2004.

2 Scott's concerns are different from mine, but the contrast he makes between "state simplifications" and "métis" or "knowledge embedded in local experience" (Scott, J. 1998, 311) is pertinent to my analysis. He notes that "processes as disparate as the creation of permanent last names, the standardization of weights and measures, the establishment of cadastral surveys and population registers, the invention of freehold tenure, the standardization of language and legal discourse, the design of cities, and the organization of transportation" can be understood in terms of the state's efforts to "get a handle on its subjects and their environment" (Scott, J. 1998, 2). As Scott argues, this is not just a matter of enhancing the state's under-standing to enable more effective rule. Its subjects and the land they inhabit have to be reshaped to fit the state's purposes. The results are often disastrous. My point is that political theory too has been shaped to fit the project of the state.

3 This is one way of interpreting international relations theory, in its various guises.

6 *Oikos, nomos, logos*

1 The "eco" in economy and ecology derives from the Greek, *oikos*. As I hope is apparent, my purpose in this chapter is not to engage in any detail with economics, ecology, or ecological economics as bodies of thought, but to get at the implications

of thinking of the *logos* or *nomos* – what ideally is to govern us – through the *oikos* rather than the *polis*. See Latour 2004, 131–36, for a different approach. Compare Haraway 1991, 1997, Cronon 1996, and Luke 1997.

2 Ecological thought comes in many variants, of course. See Goodin 1992, Worster 1994, Torgerson 1999, Meyer 2001, Eckersley 2004, Dobson and Eckersley 2006.

3 For a more sceptical view, see Krech 1999. Compare Cronon 1983 and Brody 2001.

4 Notions of transcendence suggest the absent presence of God in understandings of ecological order.

7 From local self-government to politics

1 One of the long-standing hopes of the settlers in North American was that Native spaces would become irrelevant. That has not happened, and one of the effects is that political claims are articulated in a different register – with respect to different spatialities and temporalities – than the one to which Dahl alludes. The one cannot be mapped onto the other without distortion.

2 See Lutz (2008, 49–117), for a historical analysis of Aboriginal–White relations in the Victoria area. Clayton (2000) offers an account of the "imperial fashioning" of Vancouver Island as a whole, and Harris (2002) explains how the Reserve system was established throughout the province.

3 Mark Willson offers a much more incisive analysis in his forthcoming University of Victoria PhD dissertation, tentatively entitled, "The Construction of Homelessness: Advanced Liberal Ethics and the Unfreedom of the Poor".

4 Obviously, I don't know very many people in business. Is that a problem?

5 At least to the settler population: I don't think it has much appeal to Indigenous people.

Conclusion: otherwise than sovereign

1 With respect to the bunnies, I seem to have spoken too soon. An effective bunny removal programme was implemented after I submitted the manuscript: see http://communications.uvic.ca/rabbits/ There's scarcely a bunny to be seen. The students suspect murder, although the university denies it.

References

Agamben, G. (1998) *Homo Sacer: Sovereign Power and Bare Life*, Stanford CA: Stanford University Press.

Agnew, J., and S. Corbridge (1995) *Mastering Space: Hegemony, Territory and International Political Economy*, London: Routledge.

Alfred (2005) *Wasáse: Indigenous Pathways of Action and Freedom*, Peterborough ON: Broadview.

—— (2008) *Peace, Power, Righteousness: An Indigenous Manifesto*, 2nd edn, Toronto: Oxford University Press.

Althusser, L. (1969) *For Marx*, London: Allen Lane.

Amin, A., and N. Thrift (2002) *Cities: Reimagining the Urban*, Cambridge: Polity.

Appadurai, A. (1996) *Modernity at Large: Cultural Dimensions of Globalization*, Minneapolis: University of Minnesota Press.

Archibugi, D., and D. Held (eds) (1995) *Cosmopolitan Democracy: An Agenda for a New World Order*, Cambridge: Polity.

Arendt, H. (1958) *The Human Condition*, Chicago: University of Chicago Press.

—— (1961) *Between Past and Future*, London: Faber.

Aristotle (1996) *The Politics* and *The Constitution of Athens*, Cambridge: Cambridge University Press.

Atleo, R. (2004) *Tsawalk: A Nuu-chah-nulth Worldview*, Vancouver: UBC Press.

Badiou, A. (2005) *Metapolitics*, London: Verso.

—— (2006) *Theoretical Writings*, London: Continuum.

Bartelson, J. (1995) *A Genealogy of Sovereignty*, Cambridge: Cambridge University Press.

—— (2001) *The Critique of the State*, Cambridge: Cambridge University Press.

Beauregard, R., and S. Body-Gendrot (eds) (1999) *The Urban Moment: Cosmopolitan Essays on the Late-20th Century City*, Urban Affairs Annual Reviews, vol. 49, Thousand Oaks CA: Sage.

Beck, U. (1999) *World Risk Society*, Cambridge: Polity.

Benello, C., and D. Roussopoulos (eds) (1971) *The Case for Participatory Democracy: Some Prospects for a Radical Society*, New York: Viking.

Bercovitch, S. (1980) *American Jeremiad*, Madison: University of Wisconsin Press.

Berman, M. (1982) *All That is Solid Melts into Air: The Experience of Modernity*, New York: Simon and Schuster.

Bish, R., and V. Ostrom (1973) *Understanding Urban Government: Metropolitan Reform Reconsidered*, Washington DC: American Enterprise Institute.

Bodin, J. (1992) *On Sovereignty*, ed. J. Franklin, Cambridge: Cambridge University Press.

Boggs, C. (1986) *Social Movements and Political Power: Emerging Forms of Radicalism in the West*, Philadelphia: Temple University Press.

Bookchin, M. (1987) *The Rise of Urbanization and the Decline of Citizenship*, San Francisco: Sierra Club Books.

—— (1991) *The Ecology of Freedom: The Emergence and Dissolution of Hierarchy*, Montreal: Black Rose Books.

Borrows, J. (2002) *Recovering Canada: The Resurgence of Indigenous Law*, Toronto: University of Toronto Press.

—— (2010) *Canada's Indigenous Constitution*, Toronto: University of Toronto Press.

Braudel, F. (1981–84) *Civilization and Capitalism, 15th–18th century*, 3 vols., London: Collins.

Brenner, N. (2004) *New State Spaces: Urban Governance and the Rescaling of Statehood*, Oxford: Oxford University Press.

Brenner, N., and R. Keil (2006) *The Global Cities Reader*, Abingdon OX: Routledge.

Briggs, A. (1968) *Victorian Cities*, London: Penguin.

Brody, H. (2001) *The Other Side of Eden: Hunters, Farmers and the Shaping of the World*, Vancouver: Douglas & McIntyre.

Brugmann, J. (2009) *Welcome to the Urban Revolution: How Cities are Changing the World*, Toronto: Penguin Canada.

Bryce, J. (1893) *The American Commonwealth*, 3rd edn rev., London: Macmillan.

Burchell, G., C. Gordon and P. Miller (eds) (1991) *The Foucault Effect: Studies in Governmentality*, Chicago: University of Chicago Press.

Campbell, D., and M. Dillon (eds) (1993) *The Political Subject of Violence*, Manchester: Manchester University Press.

Castells, M. (1977) *The Urban Question: A Marxist Approach*, London: Edward Arnold.

—— (1983) *The City and the Grassroots: A Cross-cultural Theory of Urban Social Movements*, Berkeley: University of California Press.

—— (1996) *The Rise of the Network Society*, Oxford: Blackwell.

Chorney, H. (1990) *City of Dreams: Social Theory and the Urban Experience*, Toronto: Nelson.

Cicero (1991) *On Duties*, Cambridge: Cambridge University Press.

Clarke, S. *et al.* (2002) "Urban Scholarship after September 11, 2001", *Urban Affairs Review* 37(3), 460–67.

Clayton, D. (2000) *Islands of Truth: The Imperial Fashioning of Vancouver Island*, Vancouver: UBC Press.

Cohen, J., and A. Arato (1992) *Civil Society and Political Theory*, Cambridge MA: MIT Press.

Commission on Global Governance (1995) *Our Global Neighbourhood*, Oxford: Oxford University Press.

Conley, V. (2002) "Chaosmopolis", *Theory, Culture & Society* 19, 127–38.

Conway, J. (2004) *Identity, Place, Knowledge: Social Movements Contesting Globalization*, Toronto: Fernwood.

Cook, T., and P. Morgan (eds) (1971) *Participatory Democracy*, San Francisco: Caulfield Press.

Coulthard, G. (2007) "Subjects of Empire: Indigenous Peoples and the 'Politics of Recognition' in Canada", *Contemporary Political Theory* 6(4), 437–60.

Council of Europe (1985) "European Charter of Local Self-Government", ETS No. 122. Online. Available <http://conventions.coe.int/treaty/en/Treaties/Word/122.doc> (accessed 15 December 2004).

Crick, B. (2005) *In Defence of Politics*, 5th edn, London: Continuum.

Cronon, W. (1983) *Changes in the Land: Indians, Colonists, and the Ecology of New England*, New York: Hill and Wang.

—— (ed.) (1996) *Uncommon Ground: Rethinking the Human Place in Nature*, New York: Norton.

Dahl, R. (1967) "The City in the Future of Democracy", *American Political Science Review* 61(4), 953–70.

—— (1970) *After the Revolution?* New Haven: Yale University Press.

Davies, J., and D. Imbroscio (eds) (2008) *Theories of Urban Politics*, 2nd edn, Thousand Oaks CA: Sage.

Davies, J., and D. Imbroscio (2010) *Critical Urban Studies: New Directions*, Albany NY: State University of New York Press.

Davis, M. (2000) *Ecology of Fear: Los Angeles and the Imagination of Disaster*, London: Picador.

—— (2006) *Planet of Slums*, London: Verso.

Day, R. (2005) *Gramsci is Dead: Anarchist Currents in the Newest Social Movements*, Toronto: Between the Lines.

De Certeau, M. (1984) *The Practice of Everyday Life*, Berkeley: University of California Press.

De Landa, M. (2000) *A Thousand Years of Nonlinear History*, New York: Swerve Editions.

Deleuze, G., and F. Guattari (2004) *Capitalism and Schizophrenia*, 2 vols., London: Continuum.

De Soto, H. (2000) *The Mystery of Capital: Why Capitalism Triumphs in the West and Fails Everywhere Else*, New York: Basic Books.

Dean, M. (1999) *Governmentality: Power and Rule in Modern Society*, London: Sage.

—— (2007) *Governing Societies: Political Perspectives on Domestic and International Rule*, Milton Keynes: Open University Press.

Der Derian, J., and M. Shapiro (eds) (1989) *International/Intertextual Relations: Postmodern Readings of World Politics*, Lexington MA: Lexington Books.

Dobson, A., and R. Eckersley (2006) *Political Theory and the Ecological Challenge*, Cambridge: Cambridge University Press.

Eckersley, R. (2004) *The Green State: Rethinking Democracy and Sovereignty*, Cambridge MA: MIT Press.

Ferguson, A. (1995) *An Essay on the History of Civil Society*, ed. F. Oz-Salzberger, Cambridge: Cambridge University Press.

Finnegan, W. (2005) "The Terrorist Beat: How is the N.Y.P.D. Defending the City?" *The New Yorker*, 25 July.

—— (2010) "Letter from Mexico: Silver or Lead: The Drug Cartel La Familia Gives Local Officials a Choice: Take a Bribe or a Bullet", *The New Yorker*, 31 May.

Florida, R. (2002) *The Rise of the Creative Class*, New York: Basic Books.

—— (2005) *The Flight of the Creative Class*, New York: Harper Collins.

—— (2008) *Whose Your City?* New York: Basic Books.

Foster, K.A. (1997) *The Political Economy of Special-Purpose Government*, Washington DC: Georgetown University Press.

Foucault, M. (1997) "What is Enlightenment?" in *Ethics, Subjectivity and Truth*, ed. Paul Rabinow, New York: The New Press.

—— (2003) *"Society Must be Defended": Lectures at the College de France, 1975–1976*, New York: Picador.

—— (2007) *Security, Territory, Population: Lectures at the College de France, 1977–1978*, New York: Palgrave Macmillan.

—— (2008) *The Birth of Biopolitics: Lectures at the College de France, 1978–1979*, New York: Palgrave Macmillan.

Friedmann, J., and G. Wolff (1982) "World City Formation: An Agenda for Research and Action", *International Journal of Urban and Regional Research* 6, 309–44.

Frug, G. (1980) "The City as a Legal Concept", *Harvard Law Review* 93(6), 1053–154.

—— (1999) *City-Making: Building Cities without Building Walls*, Princeton: Princeton University Press.

Gellner, E. (1983) *Nations and Nationalism*, Oxford: Basil Blackwell.

Gertler, M., and D. Wolfe (eds) (2002) *Innovation and Social Learning: Institutional Adaptation in an Era of Technological Change*, Basingstoke: Palgrave Macmillan.

Gierke, O. (1900) *Political Theories of the Middle Age*, Cambridge: Cambridge University Press.

Goodin, R. (1992) *Green Political Theory*, Cambridge: Polity.

Gunnell, J. (1993) *The Descent of Political Theory: The Genealogy of an American Vocation*, Chicago: University of Chicago Press.

—— (2004) *Imagining the American Polity: Political Science and the Discourse of Democracy*, University Park PA: Penn State University Press.

Habermas, J. (1996) *Between Facts and Norms*, Cambridge MA: MIT Press.

Haraway, D. (1991) *Simians, Cyborgs, and Women: The Reinvention of Nature*, New York: Chapman and Hall.

—— (1997) *Modest_Witness@Second_Millennium.FemaleMan©_Meets_OncoMouse™: Feminism and Technoscience*, New York: Routledge.

Hardt, M., and A. Negri (2000) *Empire*, Cambridge MA: Harvard University Press.

Hardt, M., and A. Negri (2004) *Multitude: War and Democracy in the Age of Empire*, New York: Penguin.

Harris, R. (2002) *Making Native Space: Colonialism, Resistance, and Reserves in British Columbia*, Vancouver: UBC Press.

Harvey, D. (1973) *Social Justice and the City*, Baltimore: Johns Hopkins University Press.

—— (1982) *The Limits to Capital*, Oxford: Basil Blackwell.

—— (1985) *The Urbanization of Capital*, Baltimore: Johns Hopkins University Press.

—— (1989) *The Condition of Postmodernity: An Inquiry into the Origins of Cultural Change*, Oxford: Blackwell.

—— (2003) *Paris, Capital of Modernity*, New York: Routledge.

—— (2005) *A Brief History of Neoliberalism*, Oxford: Oxford University Press.

Hawley, A. (1950) *Human Ecology: A Theory of Community Structure*, New York: Ronald Press.

—— (ed.) (1968) *Roderick D. McKenzie on Human Ecology: Selected Writings*, Chicago: University of Chicago Press.

Hayek, F. (1944) *The Road to Serfdom*, London: Routledge.

—— (1960) *The Constitution of Liberty*, Chicago: University of Chicago Press.

—— (1973–79) *Law, Legislation and Liberty*, 3 vols., Chicago: University of Chicago Press.

—— (1982) *Law, Legislation and Liberty: A New Statement of the Liberal Principles of Justice and Political Economy*, vols. 1–3 in 1 vol., London: Routledge and Kegan Paul.

Hegel, G. (1965) *Philosophy of Right*, Oxford: Oxford University Press.

Held, D. (1995) *Democracy and the Global Order: From the Modern State to Cosmopolitan Governance*, Cambridge: Polity.

—— (1996) *Models of Democracy*, Cambridge: Polity.

Hewson, M., and T. Sinclair (eds) (1999) *Approaches to Global Governance Theory*, Albany NY: State University of New York Press.

Hinsley, F. (1986) *Sovereignty*, 2nd edn, Cambridge: Cambridge University Press.

Hobbes, T. (1968) *Leviathan*, London: Pelican.

Holsti, K. (1995) *International Politics: A Framework for Analysis*, 7th edn, Englewood Cliffs NJ: Prentice-Hall.

—— (2004) *Taming the Sovereigns: Institutional Change in International Politics*, Cambridge: Cambridge University Press.

Honohan, I. (2002) *Civic Republicanism*, London: Routledge.

Howard, E. (1902) *Garden Cities of Tomorrow*, London: S. Sonnenschein.

Hume, D. (1987) *Essays: Moral, Political and Literary*, Indianapolis: Liberty Fund.

International Union of Local Authorities (IULA) (1993) "World Wide Declaration of Local Self Government". Available <http://www.iula-int.org/iula/upload/template/templatedocs/iulaworldwidedeclarationoflocalselfgovernment.htm> (accessed 11 September 2003).

Isin, E. (ed.) (2000) *Democracy, Citizenship, and the Global City*, London: Routledge.

—— (2002) *Being Political: Genealogies of Citizenship*, Minneapolis: University of Minnesota Press.

—— (2007) "City.State: Critique of Scalar Thought", *Citizenship Studies* 11(2), 211–28.

Jacobs, J. (1961) *The Death and Life of Great American Cities*, New York: Random House.

—— (1969) *The Economy of Cities*, New York: Random House.

—— (1984) *Cities and the Wealth of Nations*, New York: Random House.

—— (1992) *Systems of Survival: A Dialogue on the Moral Foundations of Commerce and Politics*, New York: Random House.

Jameson, F. (1991) *Postmodernism, or, The Cultural Logic of Late Capitalism*, Durham NC: Duke University Press.

Judge, D., G. Stoker and H. Wolman (eds) (1995) *Theories of Urban Politics*, London: Sage.

Kaldor, M. (2003) *Global Civil Society: An Answer to War*, Cambridge: Polity Press.

Kant, I. (1991) *Political Writings*, ed. H.S. Reiss, Cambridge: Cambridge University Press.

Kataoka, S. (2009) "Vancouverism: Actualizing the Livable City Paradox", *Berkeley Planning Journal* 22, 42–56.

Keane, J. (2003) *Global Civil Society?* Cambridge: Cambridge University Press.

Keil, R. and R. Mahon (eds) (2009) *Leviathan Undone? Towards a Political Economy of Scale*, Vancouver: UBC Press.

Kingwell, M. (2008) *Concrete Reveries: Consciousness and the City*, Toronto: Penguin Canada.

Knobloch, F. (1996) *The Culture of Wilderness: Agriculture as Colonization in the American West*, Chapel Hill: University of North Carolina Press.

Knox, P., and P. Taylor (eds) (1995) *World Cities in a World-System*, Cambridge: Cambridge University Press.

Krech III, S. (1999) *The Ecological Indian: Myth and History*, New York: W.W. Norton.

Kropotkin, P. (2006) *Mutual Aid. A Factor of Evolution*, New York: Dover Publications.

Latour, B. (2004) *Politics of Nature: How to Bring the Sciences into Democracy*, Cambridge MA: Harvard University Press.

Lefebvre, H. (1991) [1974] *The Production of Space*, Oxford: Basil Blackwell.

—— (1996) *Writings on Cities*, Oxford: Basil Blackwell.

—— (2003) [1970] *The Urban Revolution*, Minneapolis: University of Minnesota Press.

—— (2008) *Critique of Everyday Life*, 3 vols., London: Verso.

—— (2009) *State, Space, World*, ed. N. Brenner and S. Elden, Minneapolis: University of Minnesota Press.

Lipschutz, R. (2009) *The Constitution of Imperium*, Boulder CO: Paradigm.

Locke, J. (1963) *Two Treatises of Government*, Cambridge: Cambridge University Press.

Logan, J., and H. Molotch (1987) *Urban Fortunes: The Political Economy of Place*, Berkeley and Los Angeles: University of California Press.

Luke, T. (1997) *Ecocritique: Contesting the Politics of Nature, Economy, and Culture*, Minneapolis: University of Minnesota Press.

Lutz, J.S. (2008) *Makúk: A New History of Aboriginal–White Relations*, Vancouver: UBC Press.

McCrae, J. (1919) *In Flanders Fields and Other Poems*, New York: Putnam's.

Machiavelli, N. (1995) *Discourses on Livy*, Chicago: University of Chicago Press.

McLuhan, M. (1964) *Understanding Media: The Extensions of Man*, New York: Signet.

Magnusson, W. (1996) *The Search for Political Space: Globalization, Social Movements and the Urban Political Experience*, Toronto: University of Toronto Press.

—— (1997) "Globalization, Movements, and the Decentred State", in W. Carroll (ed.) *Organizing Dissent: Contemporary Social Movements in Theory and Practice*, 2nd edn, Toronto: Garamond Press, 94–113.

—— (2000a) "Hyperspace: A Political Ontology of the Global City", in R. Ericson and N. Stehr (eds) *Governing Modern Societies*, Toronto: University of Toronto Press, 80–104.

—— (2000b) "Politicizing the Global City", in E. Isin (ed.) *Democracy, Citizenship, and the Global City*, London: Routledge, 289–306.

—— (2002) "The City as the Hope of Democracy", in C. Andrew, K. Graham, and S. Phillips (eds) *Urban Affairs: Back on the Policy Agenda*, Montreal and Kingston: McGill-Queen's University Press, 331–44.

—— (2005a) "Are Municipalities Creatures of the Provinces?" *Journal of Canadian Studies* 39(2), 5–29.

—— (2005b) "Protecting the Right of Local Self-Government", *Canadian Journal of Political Science* 38(4), 1–26.

—— (2005c) "Urbanism, Cities and Local Self-Government", *Canadian Public Administration* 48(1), 96–123.

—— (2006) "The City of God and the Global City", *CTheory.net* td043–10/5/2006.

—— (2009) "Scaling Government to Politics", in R. Keil and R. Mahon (eds) *Leviathan Undone? Towards a Political Economy of Scale*, Vancouver: UBC Press.

—— (2010) "Seeing Like a City: How to Urbanize Political Science", in J. Davies and D. Imbroscio (eds) *Critical Urban Studies: New Directions*, Albany NY: State University of New York Press.

Magnusson, W., and K. Shaw (eds) (2003) *A Political Space: Reading the Global through Clayoquot Sound*, Minneapolis: University of Minnesota Press.

Mannheim, K. (1936) *Ideology and Utopia*, London: Routledge.

Marx, K. (1977) *Selected Writings*, ed. David McLellan, Oxford: Oxford University Press.

Massey, D. (2005) *For Space*, Los Angeles: Sage Publications.

Meyer, J. (2001) *Political Nature: Environmentalism and the Interpretation of Western Thought*, Cambridge MA: MIT Press.

M'Gonigle, M., and J. Starke (2006) *Planet U: Sustaining the World, Reinventing the University*, Gabriola Island BC: New Society Publishers.

Mill, J. (1991) *On Liberty and Other Essays*, Oxford: Oxford University Press.

Miller, P. and N. Rose (2008) *Governing the Present*, Cambridge: Polity.

Molotch, H. (1976) "The City as a Growth Machine: Toward a Political Economy of Place", *American Journal of Sociology* 82(2), 309–32.

—— (ed.) (2003) "Symposium on Urban Terror", *International Journal of Urban and Regional Research* 27(3), 649–98.

Montgomery, N. (2010) "Molarization and Singularization: Social Movements, Transformation and Hegemony", unpublished MA thesis, University of Victoria.

Mumford, L. (1938) *The Culture of Cities*, San Diego: Harcourt Brace.

Nancy, J.-L. (1991) *The Inoperative Community*, Minneapolis: University of Minnesota Press.

—— (2007) *The Creation of the World, or Globalization*, Albany NY: State University of New York Press.

Nicolaidis, K., and R. Howse (eds) (2001) *The Federal Vision: Legitimacy and Levels of Governance in the United States and the European Union*, Oxford: Oxford University Press.

Niezen, R. (2003) *The Origins of Indigenism: Human Rights and the Politics of Identity*, Berkeley: University of California Press.

Oakeshott, M. (1962) *Rationalism in Politics and Other Essays*, Indianapolis: Liberty Fund.

Ong, A. (1999) *Flexible Citizenship: The Cultural Logics of Transnationality*, Durham NC: Duke University Press.

Ostrom, E. (1990) *Governing the Commons: The Evolution of Institutions for Collective Action*, Cambridge: Cambridge University Press.

Ostrom, V., R. Bish, and E. Ostrom (1988) *Local Government in the United States*, San Francisco: ICS Press.

Ostrom, V., C. Tiebout, and R. Warren (1961) "The Organization of Government in Metropolitan Areas", *American Political Science Review* 55, 831–42.

Owen, W. (1920) *Poems by Wilfred Owen*, London: Chatto and Windus.

Park, R., E. Burgess, and R. McKenzie (1925) *The City*, Chicago: University of Chicago Press.

Parker, S. (2004) *Urban Theory and the Urban Experience: Encountering the City*, London: Routledge.

Patomäki, H. (2002) *After International Relations: Critical Realism and the (Re)construction of World Politics*, London: Routledge.

Pettit, P. (1997) *Republicanism: A Theory of Freedom and Government*, Oxford: Oxford University Press.

Pierre, J. (ed.) (2000) *Debating Governance*, Oxford: Oxford University Press.

Pirenne, H. (1925) *Medieval Cities*, Princeton: Princeton University Press.

Plato (1991) *The Republic of Plato*, trans. Allan Bloom, 2nd edn, New York: Basic Books.

Pocock, J. (2003) *The Machiavellian Moment*, 2nd edn, Princeton: Princeton University Press.

Polanyi, K. (1944) *The Great Transformation*, New York: Rinehart.

Polanyi, M. (1951) *The Logic of Liberty*, Chicago: University of Chicago Press.

Rancière, J. (1995) *On the Shores of Politics*, London: Verso.

——— (1998) *Disagreement: Politics and Philosophy*, Minneapolis: University of Minnesota Press.

Rawls, J. (1971) *A Theory of Justice*, Cambridge MA: Harvard University Press.

Reynolds, S. (1997) *Kingdoms and Communities in Western Europe, 900–1300*, 2nd edn, Oxford: Clarendon Press.

Rose, N. (1999) *Powers of Freedom: Reframing Political Thought*, Cambridge: Cambridge University Press.

Rosenau, J. (1990) *Turbulence in World Politics: A Theory of Change and Continuity*, Princeton: Princeton University Press.

Rosenberg, J. (1994) *The Empire of Civil Society: A Critique of the Realist Theory of International Relations*, London: Verso.

Rousseau, J. (1983) *On the Social Contract, Discourse on the Origin of Inequality, Discourse on Political Economy*, Indianapolis: Hackett.

Sandercock, L. (ed.) (1998) *Making the Invisible Visible: A Multicultural Planning History*, Berkeley: University of California Press.

Sassen, S. (1991) *The Global City: New York, London, Tokyo*, Princeton: Princeton University Press.

——— (1996) *Losing Control? Sovereignty in an Age of Globalization*, New York: Columbia University Press.

——— (ed.) (2002) *Global Networks, Linked Cities*, New York: Routledge.

——— (2006) *Territory, Authority, Rights*, Princeton: Princeton University Press.

Saunders, P. (1986) *Social Theory and the Urban Question*, 2nd edn, London: Hutchinson.

Savitch, H. (2003) "Does 9–11 Portend a New Paradigm for Cities?" *Urban Affairs Review* 39(1), 103–27.

——— (2008) *Cities in a Time of Terror: Space, Territory, and Local Resilience*, London: M.E. Sharpe.

Schmitt, C. (2006) *Political Theology: Four Chapters on the Concept of Sovereignty*, Chicago: University of Chicago Press.

——— (2008) *Constitutional Theory*, Durham NC: Duke University Press.

Scott, A. (ed.) (2001) *Global City Regions*, New York: Oxford University Press.

Scott, A., and E. Soja (eds) (1996) *The City: Los Angeles and Urban Theory at the End of the Twentieth Century*, Berkeley: University of California Press.

Scott, J. (1998) *Seeing Like a State: How Certain Schemes to Improve the Human Condition Have Failed*, New Haven: Yale University Press.

Sennett, R. (1970) *The Uses of Disorder: Personal Identity and City Life*, New York: Vintage.

—— (1977) *The Fall of Public Man: On the Social Psychology of Capitalism*, New York: A.A. Knopf.

—— (1994) *Flesh and Stone: The Body and the City in Western Civilization*, New York: W.W. Norton.

Shaw, K. (2008) *Indigeneity and Political Theory: Sovereignty and the Limits of the Political*, London: Routledge.

Shaw, M. (2000) *Theory of the Global State: Globality as Unfinished Revolution*, Cambridge: Cambridge University Press.

Simmel, G. (1971) *On Individuality and Social Forms*, Chicago: University of Chicago Press.

Sinclair, T. (ed.) (2004) *Global Governance*, 4 vols., London: Routledge.

Skinner, Q. (1978) *The Foundations of Modern Political Thought*, 2 vols., Cambridge: Cambridge University Press.

—— (1998) *Liberty before Liberalism*, Cambridge: Cambridge University Press.

Skinner, Q. and B. Stråth (eds) (2003) *States and Citizens: History, Theory, Prospects*, Cambridge: Cambridge University Press.

Smith, A. (1993) *An Inquiry into the Nature and Causes of the Wealth of Nations*, Oxford: Oxford University Press.

Smith, M. (1979) *The City and Social Theory*, New York: St Martin's Press.

—— (2001) *Transnational Urbanism*, Oxford: Blackwell.

Smith, N. (1991) *Uneven Development: Nature, Capitalism and the Production of Space*, Oxford: Blackwell.

Soja, E. (1996) *Thirdspace: Journeys to Los Angeles and Other Real-Imagined Places*, Oxford: Basil Blackwell.

Sorkin, M., and S. Zukin (eds) (2002) *After the World Trade Center: Rethinking New York City*, New York: Routledge.

Stankiewicz, W. (ed.) (1969) *In Defense of Sovereignty*, New York: Oxford University Press.

Stone, C. (1989) *Regime Politics: Governing Atlanta, 1946–1988*, Lawrence: University Press of Kansas.

—— (2005) "Looking Back to Look Forward: Reflections on Urban Regime Analysis", *Urban Affairs Review* 40(3), 309–41.

Swanstrom, T. (2002) "Are Fear and Violence at War?" *Urban Affairs Review* 38(1), 135–40.

Teaford, J. (1975) *The Municipal Revolution in America: Origins of Modern Urban Government, 1650–1825*, Chicago: University of Chicago Press.

—— (1984) *The Unheralded Triumph: City Government in America, 1870–1900*, Baltimore: Johns Hopkins University Press.

Teschke, B. (2003) *The Myth of 1648: Class, Geopolitics and the Making of International Relations*, London: Verso.

Tiebout, C. (1956) "A Pure Theory of Local Expenditures", *Journal of Political Economy* 64, 416–24.

Tocqueville, A. de (1945) *Democracy in America*, New York: Vintage Books.

Torgerson, D. (1999) *The Promise of Green Politics: Environmentalism and the Public Sphere*, Durham NC: Duke University Press.

Tully, J. (1995) *Strange Multiplicity: Constitutionalism in the Age of Diversity*, Cambridge: Cambridge University Press.

—— (2008) *Public Philosophy in a New Key*, 2 vols., Cambridge: Cambridge University Press.

Turner, D. (2006) *This is Not a Peace Pipe: Towards a Critical Indigenous Philosophy*, Toronto: University of Toronto Press.

Vincent, A. (1987) *Theories of the State*, Oxford: Basil Blackwell.

Virilio, P. (2005) *City of Panic*, Oxford: Berg.

Viroli, M. (2002) *Republicanism*, New York: Hill and Wang.

Walker, R. (1993) *Inside/Outside: International Relations as Political Theory*, Cambridge: Cambridge University Press.

—— (2010) *After the Globe, Before the World*, London: Routledge.

Walker, R. and S. Mendlovitz (eds) (1990) *Contending Sovereignties: Redefining Political Community*, Boulder CO: Lynne Rienner.

Wallerstein, I. (1974–89) *The Modern World System*, 3 vols., New York and San Diego: Academic Press.

Webb, S. and B. Webb (1906–29) *English Local Government*, 11 vols., London: Longmans, Green.

Weber, M. (1958) *The City*, New York: Free Press.

—— (1978) *Economy and Society*, 2 vols., Berkeley: University of California Press.

—— (2004) *The Vocation Lectures*, ed. David Owen and Tracy B. Strong, Indianapolis: Hackett.

Wirth, L. (1938) "Urbanism as a Way of Life", *American Journal of Sociology* 44(1), 1–24, reprinted in Wirth, *On Cities and Social Life*.

—— (1964) *On Cities and Social Life*, ed. Albert J. Reiss Jr., Chicago: University of Chicago Press.

Wolin, S. (2004) *Politics and Vision*, 2nd edn, Princeton: Princeton University Press.

Worster, D. (1994) *Nature's Economy: A History of Ecological Ideas*, Cambridge: Cambridge University Press.

York, G. (2010) "Africa's Outcasts Follow a New Path Out of Poverty", *Globe and Mail*, September 4, A8.

Young, M. (2009) "Rights, the Homeless, and Social Change: Reflections on Victoria (City) *v.* Adams (BCSC) (2009)", *BC Studies* 164, 103–13.

Zolo, D. (1997) *Cosmopolis: Prospects for World Government*, Cambridge: Polity Press.

Zukin, S. (1991) *Landscapes of Power: From Detroit to Disneyworld*, Berkeley: University of California Press.

—— (1995) *The Cultures of Cities*, Oxford: Blackwell.

—— (2010) *Naked City: The Death and Life of Authentic Urban Places*, New York: Oxford University Press.

Index

QM LIBRARY
(MILE END)

WITHDRAWN
FROM STOCK
QMUL LIBRARY